# Management
# Economics

**Dr. William G. Forgang** is Professor of Business and Economics and Chairman of the Department of Business, Accounting, and Economics at Mount Saint Mary's University. He is the author of two previous books: *Competitive Strategy and Leadership* (Rowman and Littlefield, 2001) and *Strategy-specific Decision Making* (M.E. Sharpe, 2004).

**Dr. Karl William Einolf** is an Associate Professor of Economics at Mount Saint Mary's University. He received his Ph.D. from Lehigh University in 1999. Dr. Einolf has published papers in numerous business and economics journals and has presented his work at many national and international conferences.

# Management Economics

An Accelerated Approach

**William G. Forgang and Karl W. Einolf**

*M.E.Sharpe*
Armonk, New York
London, England

**Library of Congress Cataloging-in-Publication Data**

Forgang, William G., 1946–
   Management economics : an accelerated approach / William G. Forgang, Karl W. Einolf.
      p. cm.
   Includes index.
   ISBN-10: 0-7656-1778-1 (cloth : alk. paper); ISBN-13: 978-0-7656-1778-1 (cloth : alk paper)
   1. Managerial economics.  I. Einolf, Karl W., 1967–  II. Title.

HD30.22.F67 2006
330.024'65—dc22                                                        2006003847

Printed in the United States of America

The paper used in this publication meets the minimum requirements of
American National Standard for Information Sciences
Permanence of Paper for Printed Library Materials,
ANSI Z 39.48-1984.

BM (c)   10    9    8    7    6    5    4    3    2    1

# Brief Contents

# Detailed Contents

# Tables and Figures

**Figures**

# Acknowledgments

We enjoy at Mount Saint Mary's University many benefits of a collegial work setting and an environment conducive to completing lengthy and stressful projects. The productivity of the faculty in the Department of Business, Accounting, and Economics is a source of inspiration and support. Special thanks are extended to Dr. Michael Barry, Assistant Professor of Economics, who advised us on an early draft, and to Donald Butt, MBA, CPA, CMA, who contributed two case studies. Sandy Kauffman, Administrative Assistant, provided valued help, and her colleague Lisa Rynkiewicz kept the office running.

The M.E. Sharpe team was delightful and helpful. Lynn Taylor and Nicole Cirino made our work easier. Thanks!

Through the project, our wives and families provided important support, and their patience is greatly appreciated. Nancy Forgang's remarkable faith and spirit are an inspiration. Maria Einolf's love and patience are also an inspiration. Her willingness to take over the management of two young sons during this project was tremendous. A special thanks to Nicholas and Thomas for hanging candy canes off Karl's laptop to keep him properly grounded.

# A Note to Students and Instructors

This book is designed for adult learners in a one-semester accelerated or online course in management economics at the MBA level or a two-semester accelerated or online sequence in macro- and microeconomics at the baccalaureate level. Responding to adult learners' interest in education that is immediately relevant to their daily lives, the book presents macro- and microeconomics as environments within which we live, work, and make decisions. This environmental approach has two learning objectives. First, by understanding how the macro- and microeconomic environments affect the outcomes of business and household decisions, the successful reader is able to offer sound advice and make appropriate choices. Second, readers who understand the macro- and microeconomic environments contribute effectively to discussions of contemporary business and economic issues and earn respect in the workplace.

Accelerated and online teaching and learning formats impose challenges that differ from those of traditional-length semesters. In accelerated formats, there are limited learner-instructor contact hours, extended-length class periods, and week-long gaps between classes. One three- or four-hour class session per week requires instructors to vary instructional methods, and the span between classes requires materials that support independent learning. These challenges and the need for effective independent learning materials are intensified in online formats, where there are no traditional classroom hours.

Accelerated and online courses create obstacles to the development of learning communities. In accelerated and online formats face-to-face discussion is limited or may not occur, but a continuous dialogue is an important teaching and learning tool.[1] Therefore, this book includes exercises, cases, and assignments to foster electronic communications to build a learning community. Also, accelerated and online formats serve students with diverse skills, experiences, and interests. In response, exercises and examples touch on a variety of topics and allow learners to apply tools of economic analysis to their own personal and professional circumstances.

## Pedagogical Features

To meet the needs of accelerated and online formats, this book includes several important pedagogical features.

- Macro- and microeconomics are broad areas of study, and topics are selected judiciously. This text focuses on general themes and concepts and on the application of economic ideas to professional and personal experiences and problems.
- Each chapter includes exercises that apply

text materials to recurring managerial and personal circumstances. In accelerated classes, the exercises promote discussion and enrich longer class sessions. In an online course, the exercises promote chat room discussions. Some of the exercises direct learners through Internet research; others require data analysis or the use of a spreadsheet program, or apply economic analysis to issues in management, finance, marketing, and competitive strategy.

- Discussion questions appear at the end of each chapter for learners to self-test their command of topics. Instructors can use the practice problems as written assignments or to guide discussion.

- A case study is offered at the end of each chapter. The case studies present unstructured management problems for which the application of tools of economic analysis guides problem solving and leads to a recommendation. The case studies sharpen learners' abilities to organize data and arguments and to make decisions. The case studies can be written assignments or used to promote class or chat room discussions.

- Each chapter begins with a statement of the learning objectives. At the end of each chapter, there is a list of review terms.

- Application boxes appear throughout the book. Application boxes (1) provide examples of the use of economics concepts in recurring management and personal problems, (2) display the application of economic ideas in marketing, finance, management, and strategic management to bridge disciplines and to integrate the business curriculum, (3) raise topics of related interest and offer instructors the opportunity to broaden discussions, and (4) present contemporary economic data to link concepts to real-world data.

- Many of the activities require quantitative analysis, and this approach reflects the discipline of economics. However, emphasis is placed on methods of business problem solving. After learners identify the issues and build an orderly approach to the analysis, only arithmetic skills are needed to find a solution.

## The Approach to Economics

Three themes recur throughout this book. First, micro- and macroeconomies are environments within which we live, work, and make decisions. The successful learner understands how these economic environments affect the outcomes of decisions. Better choices result from aligning decisions with the realities of the economic environment. Second, economic analysis helps problem solvers organize data and arguments, develop critical thinking skills, and make more effective decisions. Third, economics is a rich discipline that extends into many other courses in a business curriculum, including marketing, management, finance, law, and strategy. By linking the applications of economics to other disciplines, this text integrates the business curriculum.

## Learning Objectives

Adult learners in an accelerated or online program seek an academic degree delivered in a manner consistent with the pressing demands on their lives. However, a degree is useful only if it represents significant learning. Therefore, economics is presented to help adult learners (1) make decisions consistent with economic realities, (2) discuss contemporary business, economic, and public policy issues to earn credibility in professional and social situations and to be informed citizens, (3) earn the respect and confidence of co-workers by displaying an understanding of the economic environment within which decisions are made and by demonstrating an orderly approach to problem solving, and (d) recognize economic concepts in other business courses.

## To Instructors

The title of this book purposely refers to management economics and not to managerial economics. Managerial economics is an established discipline that applies statistical and mathematical techniques to a wide range of managerial decision-making situations. Many contemporary managerial economics texts require extensive prior study in micro- and macroeconomics, statistics, and mathematics. In contrast, this book does not assume prior command of these subjects, and general themes of economic analysis and problem solving replace advanced quantitative methods.

Many accelerated courses consist of seven class sessions, and this book has seven chapters. In an MBA course, one chapter per week may be assigned and discussed. For those instructors offering a two-course sequence in economics, Chapters 1 through 3 cover macroeconomic topics and Chapters 4 through 7 examine microeconomic issues. Two chapter appendices provide supplemental learning opportunities. Appended to the first chapter are materials on regression analysis to support discussions of forecasting and demand estimation. Appended to Chapter 4 are materials on currency valuations to permit extended discussion of international trade and finance. In an undergraduate two-semester sequence in micro- and macroeconomics, instructors have additional time to develop and discuss, extend discussions, work exercises in class, and integrate contemporary business and economic events into their courses.

This book offers considerable instructional flexibility. Assignments can proceed at a pace commensurate with the length of the semester. Written assignments and in-class or chat room assignments can be selected based on the length of the semester and the backgrounds of learners. Topic selection and emphasis can be matched with the interests of the learners and the orientation of the instructor. The activities provide opportunities to vary the pace and instructional methodologies in class, to prompt dialogue, and to build a learning community.

## To Learners

This book raises many topics, and learners will not master all of them. Don't get frustrated. See the big issues and focus on the application of economic ideas to your professional and personal circumstance. Recognize that the goal is not to memorize a few ideas but to develop a way of thinking and an approach to problem solving. At the end of each chapter, review the lists of terms. Complete as many of the activities as possible; use the discussion questions as self-tests.

The potential rewards from the careful reading of this book are enormous. Your professional credibility and worth within your organization grow with your ability to (1) demonstrate sound methodological approaches to problem solving, (2) offer recommendations within the context of macro- and microeconomic realities, and (3) discuss contemporary business and financial issues and events. The journey is not simple. Prepare for the challenge. Enjoy the opportunity to learn how the economy affects your daily professional and personal lives, and grow into a more effective advisor and decision maker.

## Note

1. Rena M. Paloff and Keith Pratt, *Lessons from the Cyberspace Classroom: The Realities of Online Teaching* (San Francisco: Jossey-Bass, 2001), p. 5.

# Management
# Economics

# 1

# The Macro- and Microeconomic Environments

This introductory chapter defines the economic problem, discusses its societal, managerial, and personal implications, and presents the macro- and microeconomies as environments within which we live, work, and make decisions. The macro- and microeconomic environments are complex and dynamic, external to firms and individuals, and beyond the control of decision makers. However, these economic environments affect the outcome of business and personal choices. Understanding how the economic environments influence the outcomes of decisions makes better choices possible.

---

**Learning Objectives**

The successful reader:

- Understands the economic problem, recognizes opportunity costs, and applies cost-benefit and marginal analysis to allocate scarce resources among competing uses
- Is aware of the nature of a free market economic system
- Realizes how the macroeconomic (aggregate output, employment, and income) and microeconomic (competitive conditions) environments affect the outcome of business and personal decisions
- Grasps how to align decisions with macro- and microeconomic realities

---

## The Economic Problem

### Scarcity and Decision Making

Economics is frequently defined as the science of scarcity.[1] Scarcity is the result of two conditions: (1) our infinite desire to consume goods and services and (2) finite productive resources that constrain our ability to produce. The first condition involves more than desires for consumer products. Contributing to unlimited wants are aspirations for quality education, health care, environmental protection, financially secure retirements, a contemporary infrastructure that provides clean water, abundant energy supplies, safe transportation systems, and support for basic research, exploration, and the arts. The second condition recognizes that the endowments of land, labor, capital, and entrepreneurial resources are limited and prevent fulfillment of our unlimited material wants.

With scarcity pervasive, choosing among competing and desirable alternative uses of scarce resources is a fact of life. At the societal level, finite productive resources are allocated among defense, roads and sewers, food, consumer products, health care, and education. In turn, the scarce goods are distributed among members of the community. Within a firm, scarce resources necessitate choosing among equipment, maintenance, personnel, compensation, research and development, and marketing. Further, in a firm's marketing department finite personnel are allocated among inside sales, outside sales, and the production of new marketing materials. In a household, scarce time is allocated among family, work, school, and civic obligations. Similarly, scarce financial resources are allocated among different goods and services and savings. *Given scarcity, finite resources are allocated among attractive alternative uses with the end goal of maximizing well-being.*

### Scarcity and Macro- and Microeconomics

Given scarcity, society's material well-being is maximized by achieving two conditions over a fixed period of time: (1) producing as much as possible and (2) producing the most desired mix of goods. The first part of the response to scarcity analyzes an economy's total production, and *macroeconomics* examines aggregate output and the utilization of resources. *Macroeconomic policy* refers to deliberate governmental actions to achieve full employment with stable prices. *Fiscal policy* refers to governmental decisions to alter spending on goods and services or to change tax rates in order to affect output, employment, households' disposable income, and businesses' profits. Macroeconomic policy also includes the Federal Reserve System's *monetary policy*—deliberate changes in interest rates with the intention of affecting output, employment, and income.

The second part of the response to scarcity recognizes that material well-being is enhanced by fulfilling wants in priority order. In *microeconomics*, the study units are individual firms, industries, and households, and microeconomics examines what determines the mix of goods produced. Microeconomic topics include how firms and households make decisions and interact, the competitiveness of markets, supply and demand,

wage determination, costs of production, pricing, production, and the consuming behavior of households. *Microeconomic policy* refers to governmental actions designed to affect the output of individual industries, including taxes on selected goods (alcohol), subsidies for others (some agricultural products), regulations (legal drugs, worker safety, environmental protection, and food products), the outright ban of products (some drugs), tariffs that limit imports, antitrust actions, and government provision of selected goods and services such as defense, police and fire protection, and public education.

### Production Possibilities and the Constrained Maximum

The economic problem of scarcity is displayed numerically in Table 1.1. The table refers to a hypothetical economy that produces books and food. If this economy dedicates all of its resources to the production of food, a maximum of 80 units is produced (point A) over a fixed time period and no books are produced. If all of the resources produce books, the maximum production over the period is 60 units (point E). Points B, C, and D represent different maximum combinations of books and food this economy is able to produce over a fixed time span, given its resource endowment and technology.

The data in Table 1.1 are transformed into a graph, and Figure 1.1 is the economy's *production possibilities curve*.

The production possibilities curve shows the maximum combinations of the two goods this economy is able to produce over a fixed time period. The following points are noted:

- Production inside the production possibilities curve (point L) occurs when labor, equipment, or natural resources are not fully utilized or

*Table 1.1*
**Production Possibilities Data**

|                | Point A | Point B | Point C | Point D | Point E |
|----------------|---------|---------|---------|---------|---------|
| Units of food  | 80      | 60      | 40      | 20      | 0       |
| Units of books | 0       | 19      | 35      | 48      | 60      |

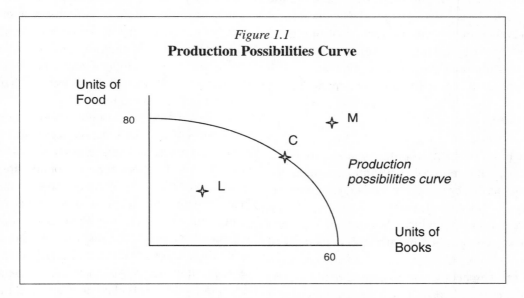

*Figure 1.1*
**Production Possibilities Curve**

utilized inefficiently. Society's material well-being is not maximized. At point L more of both goods can be produced.

- Production outside the boundary of the curve (point M) is not feasible given the economy's endowment of resources, labor skills, and technology. There are not enough workers, equipment, or resources to produce at this rate.
- Production at points along the production possibilities curve corresponds to full employment and the efficient use of resources. Every worker has a job, every piece of equipment is used, and the economy is producing in the most efficient ways.
- With an economy operating on the production possibility curve, more of one product is produced only by producing fewer units of the other product. The *opportunity cost* of more units of food is fewer units of books.
- Point C is arbitrarily selected to show the *constrained maximum*. Relative to point C, no other feasible combination of food and books improves well-being. The constrained maximum has three components: full employment, efficient production, and the production of the most desired combination of goods.
- The constrained maximum is found through *marginal analysis*. To find point C, the issue is not whether food is preferred over books. The constrained maximum is found by assessing the gain in well-being from one more book relative to the loss of well-being from one unit less of food.

- Over time, an economy's production possibilities curve changes shape and location. The curve shifts outward if the labor force grows in size or becomes more skillful, technology improves, or new natural resources are discovered. The shape of the production possibilities curve changes if a technological advance favors the production of one good over the other. The curve shifts inward if the labor force shrinks, skills decline, equipment depreciates, or resources are depleted.

### Opportunity Costs

The scarcity problem imposes *opportunity costs*. Given scarcity, more of one product is obtained only by sacrificing units of the other. For example, begin at point A in Table 1.1, where the hypothetical economy produces 80 units of food and no books. The production of the first 19 units of books has an opportunity cost of 20 units of food. From the perspective of economic analysis, the cost of additional books is not defined in terms of dollars; rather, the cost is expressed in terms of fewer units of food.

### Application Box 1.1

Most businesses require budget requests for the following period to be submitted at the same time. This bureaucratic necessity allows decision makers to examine competing requests to weigh the opportunity costs. Decision makers who do not identify and evaluate opportunity costs are destined to spend too much in one area and not enough in another. The misallocation of resources prevents any society, business, or household from maximizing its material well-being.

From a societal perspective, issues of opportunity costs include the following: (1) Allocating scarce resources to produce consumer products limits the economy's ability to produce new machines, education, and research. This choice limits the society's ability to produce in the future. (2) Allocating scarce resources to produce consumer products necessitates fewer parks, less-effective defense, and weaker public health programs. (3) Allocating scarce resources to produce luxury products limits the society's ability to meet the basic needs of every member of the community.

Business units and households also face opportunity costs. For a professional services firm, financial resources are scarce. Management chooses between competing and important needs for additional personnel and technology improvements. To make the best decision, management assesses the relevant opportunity cost. Do the benefits of additional personnel outweigh the inability to improve the technology? Households are similarly challenged by opportunity costs. A decision to pursue an academic degree prevents alternative uses of the money, including savings, home repair, or a vacation. Time is also scarce, and an opportunity cost of the pursuit of a degree is lost time with family and friends.

### Application Box 1.2

Consider a commercial printing firm. At 65 percent capacity use of its presses, there is no scarcity of production capability. A new job can be completed without displacing another project. A new job is accepted if the expected revenues exceed the incremental costs of production.

At 100 percent capacity use of its presses, a new job displaces another. Decision makers must examine the revenues and costs of any new job and also its opportunity cost.

Given scarcity, opportunity costs cannot be avoided, and understanding opportunity costs is crucial for effective decision making. No proposed use of a finite resource can be evaluated as good or bad in the absence of the assessment of the alternatives. No decisions regarding the use of a scarce resource should be made without careful assessment of the opportunity costs.

The concept of opportunity costs can be rephrased to identify *trade-offs*. A trade-off occurs when one action precludes another. For example, a company policy to promote from within offers incentives and opportunities for advancement. The trade-off is the lost opportunity to recruit talent from the widest possible pool of potential workers. A company that offers an across-the-board pay raise on the grounds of equity loses the ability to reward meritorious work. A decision to produce the industry's most technologically advanced product leads to higher research and materials costs; the firm trades off the ability to compete on the basis of a lower price. Decision makers who recognize and evaluate trade-offs make more effective choices.

### Cost-Benefit Analysis

Opportunity costs are evaluated through *cost-benefit analysis*, which measures the gains in well-being associated with more of one product relative to the loss of well-being associated with less of the other product. Refer to Table 1.1 and begin at point A, where the society produces 80 units of food and no books. To determine if this combination of food and books corresponds to the constrained maximum, ask the following question: is societal well-being higher at point A or point B? The cost-benefit calculations require the assessment of the gain in well-being from the addition of 19 units of books and the loss of well-being associated with 20 fewer units of food. If the gain exceeds the loss, society is better off at point B and resources should be reallocated.

## Application Box 1.3

Cost-benefit analysis indicates that maximizing decisions are made "on the margin." Marginal analysis examines the effects of incremental changes.

Economists have helped dairy farmers make better decisions during periods of low prices using marginal analysis. Participants in the 2002 Illinois Farm Business Management Forum stated that their average cost per one hundred pounds of milk production (cwt) was $13.90. However, the price of milk varies and has been as low as $11 per cwt and higher than $15 per cwt.

Suppose the current price of milk is $12.50 per cwt. Producing milk is not profitable and farmers search for ways to cut costs. Often they consider cutting production. However, increasing production may be a better alternative.

Most cows are milked twice a day. If farmers increase milking to three times per day, they gain an additional eight pounds of milk per cow per day. Why produce more milk that will sell at less than the average cost? The marginal cost of additional milk production is $8.61 per cwt, which is much less than the market price. Therefore, the additional milk makes a profit of $3.89 per cwt, which may help the farmer turn a profit (or at least reduce losses) during periods of low milk prices. Marginal analysis improves decision making.

*Source:* Geoffrey E. Dahl, Dale H. Lattz, and Gary Schnitkey, "Marginal Cost Versus Marginal Revenue: Why Cutting Costs Is Not Always the Answer," March 13, 2002, Illini DairyNet Online Paper at the University of Illinois, www.traill.uiuc.edu/dairynet/paperdisplay.cfm?contentID=349.

The next step in the cost-benefit analysis asks: is material well-being further improved by moving from point B to point C? The same question is repeated until no further reallocation of resources improves well-being. This combination is the constrained maximum, which is defined by the full and efficient use of resources and the production of the most desired mix of goods.

Cost-benefit analysis helps businesses and households allocate scarce resources. For example, a marketing manager has a staff of ten people. To increase the level of service to existing accounts, the manager considers redirecting staff time from soliciting new accounts. The manager estimates the gains associated with the incrementally higher levels of service and customer retention against the losses attributable to securing fewer new accounts. For the marketing manager the decision is not whether to seek new accounts or to service existing customers. Rather, the management challenge is to find the most effective allocation of resources between seeking new accounts and servicing existing ones.

### Are Opportunity Costs Constant?

To analyze incremental costs and benefits, it is necessary to ask if opportunity costs are constant. Is the opportunity cost (in terms of food) of producing the first book equal to the opportunity cost of producing the fiftieth book? To begin the analysis, start at point A in Table 1.1. Examining the movement from point A to point B shows that the first 19 books require a sacrifice of 20 units of food. Successive sacrifices of 20 units of food yield increasingly smaller numbers of books.

Accordingly, larger amounts of books must be surrendered to increase food production. Opportunity costs are not constant. They increase because productive resources are not equally adaptable to making food and books. The first 19 units of books

---

**Application Box 1.4**

Managers must consider the suitability of resources to different tasks. A very competent technical worker may, for example, be ineffective when promoted to a managerial role. Work space and machinery suitable for one product may be less suited for the production of something else. Because resources tend to be at least somewhat specialized, opportunity costs increase.

---

are made by resources skillful at these tasks and less skillful at making food. As more books are produced, resources working in the food industry shift to the book industry. These resources are less suitable for making books and more suitable for making food. The first books produced do not cost as many units of food as the last books produced.

### Are Incremental Benefits Constant?

In cost-benefit analysis incremental gains in well-being diminish as the number of units of one product consumed rises. Successive increases in the quantities of a particular good within a fixed time period yield *diminishing returns*. The gain in well-being from the first unit of books is very large, but incremental units of books yield successively smaller benefits. Furthermore, as additional food is sacrificed to increase the number of books, the marginal benefits of those additional books decline, and the losses in well-being associated with incrementally less food rise. Ultimately, a combination of food and books is found where the gain in well-being from one more unit of a product equals the loss of well-being from the other. No reallocation of scarce resources improves well-being. This outcome describes the constrained maximum.

## Application Box 1.5

Diminishing returns occur in many settings. Consider a firm that increases its advertising budget to boost sales. The initial increase has a larger impact on sales than successive increases. Further, more spending on advertising necessitates less spending on something else, perhaps the number of outside sales personnel. Successive reductions in the size of the sales force lead to increasingly larger reductions in sales. The challenge for management is to find the most effective allocation of scarce resources between advertising and sales personnel.

Increasing returns are also recognized. The first advertisement of a product adds little to sales; successive advertisements have increasing returns. Ultimately, even more advertising has a diminishing effect on sales.

## Application Box 1.6

Resource misallocations are often a hidden cost. A centrally planned economy such as the former Soviet Union is often guilty of resource misallocations. By having a government bureaucracy choose the combination of goods produced and ignoring the market mechanism, centrally planned economies often produce goods people do not want and have shortages of products people do want.

A household misallocates resources by purchasing low-priority items, perhaps the result of ill-advised impulse purchases. The household is solvent and lives comfortably but does not have the funds to replace a leaky roof. The household could have been better off by properly allocating its scarce resources.

### The Constrained Maximum

The assessment of the costs and benefits at the margin leads to the ideal allocation of the scarce resources and achieves the constrained maximum. The constrained maximum is the combination of goods that maximizes well-being such that no reallocation of resources can improve it. The failure to achieve the constrained maximum means resources are misallocated among competing uses and well-being is not maximized.

Society, businesses, and individuals often misallocate resources. For society, a misallocation of resources occurs if the gain in well-being from additional consumer products is smaller than the loss of well-being from the sacrifice of public education. A business manager misallocates resources if personnel time or budgets are used for low-priority tasks. A household misallocates resources if scarce time or money is allocated to less-important items.

Any misallocation of resources is detrimental to material well-being. Society as a whole, a business, or a household achieves greater material well-being by effectively allocating scarce resources among competing uses. Further, resource allocation issues are often controversial, and misallocations occur because (1) alternative uses of resources are not clearly identified, (2) analysis of the costs or benefits is incomplete, or (3) different values are applied to the assessment of the opportunity costs. Though it is difficult to measure the consequences of resource misallocations, the losses in well-being are real and detrimental to societal, business, or individual well-being.

### How Are Opportunity Costs Assessed?

At the societal level, the process of assessing opportunity costs and allocating scarce resources is complex. How is it decided if the marginal gain from more books exceeds the marginal cost from fewer units of food? In a market economy, many resource allocation decisions result from the interplay between buyers and sellers, both of whom are motivated by self-interest. Households express preferences through their purchasing patterns, and businesses produce goods that satisfy households' material wants and generate profits. Both buyer and seller actions affect prices, and both react to price changes. The price of a good or service is the signal through which buyers and sellers communicate.

In a free market economy, the mix of goods produced is affected by disparities in purchasing power. Scarce resources are directed through profit signals, and the pursuit of profit leads to the production of expensive yachts, mansion-like homes, and other luxuries while some members of society lack sufficient food, clothing, and shelter. Even in a market economy, some resource allocation decisions are made through the voting booth and the political process. For example, votes express the citizenry's preferences in terms of defense, health care, education, and tax rates. These expressions of importance are clouded because one vote covers many issues, and one vote cannot reflect the intensity of preferences for individual items. Further, our votes lead to one societal decision, and all must abide by that even if their individual preferences differ.

Businesses develop complex systems to allocate scarce resources among competing uses. Many organizations establish strategic planning committees to identify priority uses of scarce resources. Most businesses require requests for capital purchases to be submitted at a certain time to allow decision makers to evaluate the alternatives and assess the opportunity cost. Similarly, organizations establish a *hurdle rate* to evaluate capital spending proposals. The hurdle rate is the firm's opportunity cost of the use of capital (the

---

### Exercise 1.1

Identify a business or personal choice made in an environment of scarcity.

(a) What is the scarce resource?
(b) Describe the opportunity cost and identify the benefits associated with more of one and the costs of less of the other.
(c) What is meant by the constrained maximum?
(d) Describe the consequences of failing to meet the constrained maximum.
(e) For your organization, provide examples of the misallocation of resources and the consequences. Do all of your colleagues agree with your assessment of the allocation of resources? Explain any differences of opinion.

---

### Exercise 1.2

Discuss the following opportunity costs:

(a) The trade-off between responding to collective needs and personal freedom
(b) The trade-off between efficiency and greater economic equality

---

rate of return a firm forgoes by choosing one proposal over another) to ensure the most effective use of its scarce resources.

To effectively apply cost-benefit analysis, decision makers must identify the relevant costs and benefits and measure them with a common denominator. The assessment of opportunity costs is further complicated by the risks of uncertain outcomes and by the need to evaluate costs and benefits that occur in different time periods.

## Identification of the Costs and Benefits

It is sometimes difficult to identify all of the costs and benefits of a resource allocation decision. One problem is caused by sequential and complex cause-effect relationships. For example, the long-term costs of a decision that has environmental consequences are difficult to identify. Drilling for oil offshore can provide many benefits, including the greater availability and lower price of energy. Some costs are associated with the possibility of an oil spill. However, the consequences of a spill are difficult to assess. They occur over time and depend upon complex cause-effect relationships with weather patterns, migration paths, and food chains. The inability to identify accurately all of the costs and benefits of a resource allocation decision creates opportunities for contentious debate and partisan politics.

## Measuring the Costs and Benefits

To evaluate the costs and benefits of a resource allocation decision, all of the relevant costs and benefits must be measured in dollar terms. For example, a municipality estimates the cost of a new park. To make a decision, all of the benefits must be evaluated, including the gains in well-being from the open spaces. The aesthetic benefits are real but difficult to express in dollar terms. Further, consider a business decision that adversely affects long-term employees and the community within which the firm is located. How are loyalty, social responsibility, and ethical behavior translated into dollars? Disagreements over the importance and valuation of these subjective concerns create conflict over resource allocation decisions.

## Risk

Cost-benefit analyses often include uncertainty. Consider a firm analyzing expansion into a new

**Application Box 1.7**

Adult students often pursue an advanced degree hoping to increase their income. At the point of enrollment, there is no certainty of earning the degree or higher pay. An abundance of data links education to earnings. However, an individual's pursuit of a degree is made under conditions of uncertainty.

market. The firm is not known in the new territory, and expansion requires resources to develop effective distribution channels. The financial benefits of the expansion are attractive but uncertain. An alternative use of the resources is the purchase of a new piece of production equipment. Engineering estimates and experiences of other users of the equipment lead to a confident estimate of reduced costs. The assessment of the opportunity cost of the allocation of resources is clouded by uncertainty.

One approach to a risk-laden resource allocation decision is to calculate the *expected value* of the options. Table 1.2 assumes two alternative projects, A and B. Each project costs $1 and has three possible outcomes. For project A, there is a 25 percent probability of losing $2. There is a 25 percent chance of earning $20, and a 50 percent chance of gaining $10. The expected value of this project is $9.50 = (0.25 × -$2) + (0.50 × $10) + (0.25 × $20). For project B, the expected value is $6.30 = (0.10 × $12) + (0.80 × $5) + (0.10 × $11). Each project has an expected value that exceeds the initial cost. Project A has a higher expected value, but project B involves less risk. For project B, each outcome promises a return greater than the cost of the project.

The selection of project A or B is complicated in three ways. First, the assigned probabilities are not the result of repetitive trials akin to rolling dice or picking cards from a deck. The subjective nature

*Table 1.2*
**Expected Value**

| Project A | | | | Project B | | | |
|---|---|---|---|---|---|---|---|
| Outcome | Probability | Gain | Gain × Probability | Outcome | Probability | Gain | Gain × Probability |
| 1 | 0.25 | –$2 | $–0.50 | 1 | 0.10 | $12 | $1.20 |
| 2 | 0.50 | $10 | $5 | 2 | 0.80 | $5 | $4.00 |
| 3 | 0.25 | $20 | $5 | 3 | 0.10 | $11 | $1.10 |
| Expected value project A = $9.50 | | | | Expected value project B = $6.30 | | | |

of the probabilities means that different analysts are likely to disagree. Second, when multiple trials of an experiment occur, the outcome approaches the expected value. However, choosing between projects A and B is a one-time choice, and the decision maker cannot anticipate the expected value outcome of repetitive trials. Third, project A has the higher expected value, but project B carries less risk. With project B, there is no chance of losing money. Each outcome returns more than the $1 cost of the project. Is the higher expected value for option A worth the risk? The answer depends on the decision maker's aversion to risk. The higher the degree of aversion to risk, the more attractive project B becomes.

A decision maker's aversion to risk grows with the consequences of losing. The adverse results of a bad decision include loss of money, reputation, and job security. Disagreements over the allocation of resources often emerge because individuals tolerate and assess risks differently. Understanding differences in risk tolerances helps to clarify disagreements over the allocation of scarce resources.

*Present Value*

The assessment of opportunity costs is also complicated when benefits or costs occur over time. For example, a business faces two options. The first is a promotional campaign expected to yield an immediate boost to sales and profit. The opportunity cost is not investing in the research

and development of a new product that promises profitable returns in the future. How are comparisons made if costs and benefits are realized in different time periods?

To make a comparison, sums spent or revenues earned are expressed in a common time period and compared using *present value analysis*. For example, at 5 percent interest, $1 today grows to $1.05 (= $1 × 1.05) in one year. At 5 percent interest, the present value of $1.05 in one year is $1 (= $1.05 ÷ 1.05). Similarly, the present value of $1 in one year (at 5 percent) interest is $0.952 (= $1 ÷ 1.05). This statement means that $0.952 today

**Application Box 1.8**

At 7 percent interest, $2 in one year has a present value equivalent of $1.87. The calculation identifies the sum needed today, at 7 percent, to accumulate $2 in one year. The present value (PV) of $2 in one year at 7 percent is:

$$PV = \$2 \div 1.07 = \$1.87$$

The present value factor of $1 in one year at 7 percent is 0.9346 (= 1 ÷ 1.07). See the present value tables at the end of the book.

The present value factor of $1 in two years at 7 percent is 0.873 (=1 ÷ (1.07 × 1.07)).

*Table 1.3*
## Investment Options

| Project | Profit Year 1 | Profit Year 2 | Profit Year 3 | Profit Year 4 | Profit Total |
|---------|--------------|--------------|--------------|--------------|--------------|
| A | $50 | $40 | $30 | $0 | $120 |
| B | $0 | $20 | $30 | $75 | $125 |

grows to $1 in one year at 5 percent interest. There is a present value equivalent between $1 today and $1.05 in one year at 5 percent interest.

The present value of $1 two years from now at 5 percent is $0.907 (= [$1 ÷ 1.05] ÷ 1.05). The present value of $1 two years in the future is lower than the present value of $1 in one year because interest earnings compound for two years. The present value of a fixed sum declines as the time period to receive or expend the amount increases.

The present value of a sum paid or received in the future is also affected by the interest rate. At 5 percent interest the present value of $1 in one year is $0.952. At 10 percent, the present value of $1 in one year is $0.909 (= $1 ÷ 1.10). The higher the interest rate, the lower the present value of a future amount.

### Application Box 1.9

The present value of $1 in three years at 7 percent is:

$$\$1 \div (1.07 \times 1.07 \times 1.07) = \$0.8163$$

The present value factor is 0.816.

At the same interest rate, the present value of $1 in five years is lower: $0.7130.

At 9 percent the present value of $1 in five years is $0.650.

The present value factor is 0.650.

The application of present value analysis is highlighted through the following example. Consider the two investment projects in Table 1.3. Both projects require an up-front outlay of $100 and offer returns over four years. There is no salvage value at the end of the period for either investment option. For simplicity, the tax consequences of the income are ignored. Both projects offer returns in excess of other uses of the resources.

Project B offers a larger total profit over the four years. Project B returns $125, whereas A offers only $120. However, the profits from project A are earned faster. To compare the profits earned in different time periods, Table 1.4 calculates the present value of each option at 5 percent interest.

Table 1.4 indicates the following: (1) The present value of the returns from projects A and B exceeds the initial investment outlay in each case. (2) The present value of the return on project A is higher even though project B offers a greater total dollar return, because the return from project B is realized further in the future. In present-value terms, project A is more attractive.

Decision makers are also challenged by their *rate of time preference*. The rate of time preference reflects the decision maker's preference for immediate gratification. Consider a politician who seeks reelection. This individual has a high rate of time preference, preferring projects that offer a quick return. Similarly, a CEO compensated on the basis of the upcoming quarter's stock price seeks immediate returns. The politician and the CEO apply a very high rate of time preference to their decision. Disagreements over the proper

Table 1.4
**Present Value of Investment Options**

| Option A | Year 1 | Year 2 | Year 3 | Year 4 |
|---|---|---|---|---|
| Profit | $50 | $40 | $30 | $0 |
| Present value factor at 5% | 0.952 | 0.907 | 0.864 | 0.823 |
| Present value | $47.62 | $36.28 | $25.91 | $0 |
| Present value of option A at 5 percent = $109.28 | | | | |
| Option B | Year 1 | Year 2 | Year 3 | Year 4 |
| Profit | $0 | $20 | $30 | $75 |
| Present value Factor at 5% | 0.952 | 0.907 | 0.864 | 0.823 |
| Present value | $0 | $18.14 | $25.91 | $61.70 |
| Present value of option B at 5 percent = $105.75 | | | | |

allocation of resources occur whenever there are differences in the valuation of current versus future benefits.

## Application Box 1.10

Present value analysis has many applications in business and finance, including capital budget analysis and bond valuation.

*Capital budget:* Consider the purchase of a new machine. It requires a current outlay. Revenues and labor, materials, and utilities costs accrue in different time periods. Capital budget analysis poses the following question: is the present value of the expected stream of earnings greater than the up-front cost?

*Valuation of a bond:* The sale of a bond involves a promised stream of interest payments over time and the repayment of principal at a predetermined time. The future payments are expressed in present value terms to determine what the buyer is willing to pay. The present value of the stream of interest payments plus the return of the face value of the bond is the price of the bond.

### Exercise 1.3

(a) Provide examples of opportunity costs from your professional and personal experiences. How did you assess the opportunity cost, given the uncertainty of one of the outcomes? How did you assess the benefits (or costs) that accrue in different time periods?

(b) Do people in your organization have different tolerances for risk? How do these differences affect their assessment of opportunity costs?

(c) Do individuals in your organization have different rates of time preference? How do these differences affect their assessment of opportunity costs?

### Opportunity Costs and International Trade

To examine the implications of opportunity costs on international trade, Figure 1.2 displays the production possibilities curve for two countries.

To simplify the analysis, four assumptions are made: (1) Both countries produce only food and

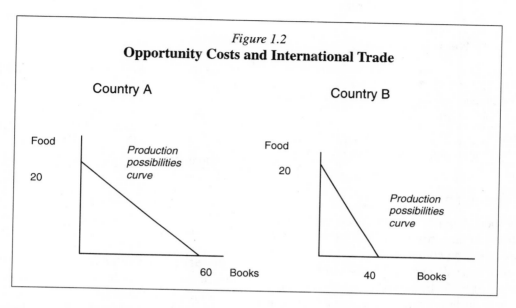

*Figure 1.2*
**Opportunity Costs and International Trade**

Country A

Country B

books. (2) Both countries produce at full employment. (3) Opportunity costs are constant in each country. In country A, the opportunity cost of 1 unit of food is 3 units of books. In country B, the opportunity cost of 1 unit of food is 2 units of books. (4) In the absence of trade, country A produces and consumes 10 units of food and 30 units of books; country B produces and consumes 10 units of food and 20 units of books.

In country B, food is cheaper in terms of books. The opportunity cost of 1 unit of food is 2 units of books. In country A, to obtain 1 unit of food the necessary sacrifice is 3 units of books. In contrast, books are cheaper in country A. One unit of books requires the sacrifice of 0.33 units of food, whereas the cost of a unit of books in country B is 0.5 units of food. Country A has a relative cost advantage producing books, and country B has an advantage producing food. Country A's *comparative advantage* leads to specialization in the production of books. Country B's comparative advantage leads to specialization in the production of food.

Table 1.5 compares world output before and after specialization. Before specialization, country A produces and consumes 10 units of food and 30 units of books; country B produces and consumes 10 units of food and 20 units of books. World output is 20 units of food and 50 units of books.

With specialization, country A produces all of the world's books, 60 units. Country B produces all of the world's 20 units of food. Specialization increases world output by 10 units of books.

---

### Exercise 1.4

(a)  How much would you pay for a promissory note that offers $100 at the end of each of the next five years and $1,000 at the end of the fifth year, assuming a 7 percent interest rate?

(b)  Assume the financial outlook for this firm weakens. To compensate for the greater risk, investors require a 10 percent return. Calculate the price of the bond. How does the greater risk affect the firm's ability to raise capital from the bond market?

*Table 1.5*
**Gains from Trade**

| Good | Country A | Country B | Totals |
|------|-----------|-----------|--------|
| Output by Product and Country Before Specialization | | | |
| Food | 10 | 10 | 20 |
| Books | 30 | 20 | 50 |
| Output by Product and Country After Specialization | | | |
| Food | 0 | 20 | 20 |
| Books | 60 | 0 | 60 |

After specialization country A has only books and country B has only food, thereby necessitating trade. Assume countries A and B agree upon a price of 1 unit of food for 2.5 units of books. In the absence of trade, however, the countries would have to rely on their own production; because of opportunity costs, country A would have to surrender 3 units of books for 1 unit of food, and country B would get only 2 units of books for 1 unit of food. After trade, each country is materially better off, each gaining 5 units of books.

The analysis shows the advantage of free trade between nations. However, there are significant caveats. (1) The analysis ignores the upheavals in country A as it abandons the production of

**Exercise 1.5**

Using the following production possibilities data:

| | Point A | Point B | Point C |
|---|---------|---------|---------|
| Apples | 200 | 100 | 0 |
| Televisions | 0 | 200 | 300 |

| | Point A | Point B | Point C |
|---|---------|---------|---------|
| Apples | 450 | 225 | 0 |
| Televisions | 0 | 75 | 150 |

(a) State the opportunity cost in each country. Identify the country in which the opportunity cost of apples is lower and the country in which the opportunity cost of televisions is lower.

(b) Which country should specialize in the production of apples? Which should specialize in televisions?

(c) Each country produces at point B prior to trade. Calculate the gain in world output from specialization.

(d) State a mutually acceptable trade rate between apples and televisions.

**Application Box 1.11**

Despite the theoretical benefits of free trade between nations, intense debates and political challenges abound. For example, textile production in Asian countries has displaced many U.S. workers. Those in the United States who favor tariffs or import quotas contend that the competition in the textile industry is unfair because the trading rivals have lower costs due to sweatshop manufacturing facilities and no child labor laws.

food. Businesses close; employees lose their jobs and endure a difficult transition. Similar transitions occur in country B. (2) Both countries become dependent upon the other's production, and this dependency is uncomfortable when a country surrenders the production of a good or service fundamental to its security or national interest. (3) Opportunity costs in a country are not constant over time, as industries mature and surmount learning hurdles. Specializing based on current opportunity costs can be shortsighted. (4) The benefits of free trade depend upon both countries operating under similar rules. For example, one country has stricter environmental, worker safety, and child labor restrictions. Its production costs are higher because of different rules and not because of an inherent production advantage. Producers of these goods often request protection from the imports of other nations.

## Fundamental Questions and Economic Systems

The scarcity problem raises five questions that must be addressed by all economies: (1) What to produce? (2) For whom to produce? (3) How to produce? (4) How much to produce? (5) How to accommodate change in the mix of goods produced or the methods of production? Each society develops institutions and practices to address these five questions, finding a balance among reliance upon tradition, free markets and self-interested behavior, and centralized command.[2]

### Application Box 1.12

Individual firms, even within a free market economy, reflect characteristics of different types of economies. Some economies and firms operate by tradition: "This is how we have always done things." Others operate by command: "I am in charge, and this is what you will do." Others follow market principles, in which self-interest is a factor. These firms and economies are open and creative and encourage risk taking and innovation.

Firms managed by market principles need leaders who trust that rewarding skill, effort, and innovation lead to a more dynamic and successful business.

### What to Produce?

Given that no society produces unlimited quantities of goods and services, production choices must be made. These choices include the mix of consumer products, machines to increase future production capability, and public products such as defense, education, courts of law, and community health.

In a *traditional economic system,* individuals engage in the tasks and processes determined by their ancestors. The mix of goods produced is a result of the history and traditions of the community. In a *command-oriented system,* a centralized authority determines the mix of goods produced. Command systems do not rely upon profit motives to determine the mix of goods produced. In a *free market economy*, profit-seeking entrepreneurs assume risks of production, and voluntary purchases by households validate the production decisions of businesses.

### For Whom to Produce?

This delicate question involves the distribution of the output among individuals. Simply, who gets how much? In a traditional economic system, the distribution of scarce goods is determined by a caste or hierarchical system. Command systems establish income distribution criteria based on need or an alliance with the centralized authority. In a free market economy, an individual's compensation reflects his or her contribution to the production process. Businesses hire and pay up to the worker's dollar contribution to the production process.

This distribution of income raises an interesting trade-off between efficiency and equity.[3] Work incentives are maximized when financial rewards are determined by one's contributions to the production of goods salable for profit. Furthermore, this merit-based compensation system encourages individuals to acquire skills valued in the market-

## Application Box 1.13

### Mean Income Received by U.S. Households in Quintiles, 2001

| Quintile | Current Dollars |
|---|---|
| Lowest 20% | $10,136 |
| Second 20% | $25,468 |
| Third 20% | $42,629 |
| Fourth 20% | $66,839 |
| Fifth 20% | $145,970 |
| Top 5% | $260,464 |

*Source:* U.S. Bureau of the Census, www.census.gov/hhes/www/income/histinc/h03.html.

place. In contrast, communism emphasizes equal benefits for all, but this means weaker incentives to be productive. Capitalism's merit-based compensation system leads to an unequal distribution of income. Public policy efforts to achieve greater income equality achieve equity objectives at the cost of reduced work effort.

### How to Produce?

In any economy, the methods of production include the choice of technology and the balance between labor and machinery. A traditional economy relies upon ancestral procedures. In command economies, resources and technologies are assigned by the central authority. In a market economy, profit-seeking entrepreneurs employ the lowest-cost methods of production to maximize their profits.

### How to Accommodate Change?

The question of accommodating change recognizes that the array of goods produced shifts over time, as do production technologies. For example, contemporary business offices use technologies today that were unavailable a few short years ago. How is it decided that new products are offered in the marketplace and that new technologies are put to use? Traditional economies are inherently slow to produce new goods and adopt new processes. In command economies, new goods and processes are introduced upon the direction of a centralized authority. Market economies enjoy the responsiveness of risk-taking, self-interested entrepreneurs who have profit incentives to introduce new goods and production methods. The profit motive sparks ingenuity and innovation, and market economies are quick to adopt new technologies and to respond to changing resource prices.

### How Much to Produce?

Given scarcity, this question appears easy to answer: as much as possible! However, societies make several decisions that constrain their ability to produce. For example, a society exempts young children and the elderly from work even though they have abilities to produce. Further, a society chooses not to exploit certain natural resources because the extraction threatens wilderness areas. Both choices constrain the ability to produce. Some values supersede the production of as much as possible.

The five fundamental questions drive political debates. Politicians debate what to produce. Sometimes the specific issue is the size of the defense budget. For whom to produce is debated when considering the distribution of the tax burden, the appropriate disparities between rich and poor, and the magnitude of social welfare programs. How to produce is at issue when policy debates examine tax and environmental policies that affect production technologies and the number of jobs. How much to produce is often the underlying theme

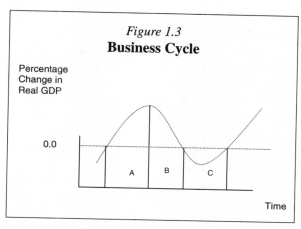

*Figure 1.3*
**Business Cycle**

Percentage Change in Real GDP

0.0

A    B    C

Time

---

## Exercise 1.6

(a) Examine a recent or current political campaign and discuss platform proposals in terms of the five fundamental questions.

(b) How do liberals and conservatives differ in their answers to the five fundamental questions? Express your own political opinion.

(c) Examine the decision-making process and management style in your firm. Do they resemble command or market systems? Make recommendations to the senior leadership in your firm.

---

of environmental issues and retirement policies. How to accommodate change arises whenever the policy debate involves issues that affect innovation and risk taking.

## The Economic Environments

Macro- and microeconomics examine society's response to the scarcity problem, and one of the important themes of this book is that macro- and microeconomics are environments within which we live, work, and make professional and personal decisions. By understanding how these environments influence the outcomes of our decisions, more effective choices can be made.

### Macroeconomics and the Business Cycle

Macroeconomics examines the economy's aggregate rate of production, employment, and income. Within this macro environment decisions are made about production schedules, procurement, employment, compensation, plant expansion, cash management, and debt management, among other things. For example, manufacturers of durable consumer products such as automobiles and appliances align production schedules with households' willingness and ability to make purchases. Similarly, household decisions such as purchasing a home, choosing among alternative financial investments, incurring debt, and retirement planning must also be aligned with the realities of the business cycle.

The U.S. economy has experienced periodic swings in the level of economic activity over time, and the recurring upswings and downswings define the *business cycle*. Figure 1.3 shows the percentage change in a nation's real gross domestic product (output after inflation) over time. Three stages of the business cycle are identified: (1) segment A is an expansionary period, (2) segment B is a period of real output rising at a decreasing rate, and (3) segment C is a recession period, where recession is defined as two or more consecutive quarters of decline in real GDP.

Figure 1.3 displays the three stages of the business cycle, but business cycles are not of equal duration or intensity. Though individual business cycles are unique, recurring data patterns exist. An abundance of macroeconomic data is available through the popular press and the Internet, and Chapters 2 and 3 examine the forces that drive and measure macroeconomic performance.

**Application Box 1.14**

A firm's stock price is sensitive to its current and expected earnings. Some stocks, referred to as cyclical, are particularly sensitive to macroeconomic fluctuations. Wise investors purchase cyclical stocks in advance of an expansion of the macroeconomy and sell before business conditions weaken.

Variations in cyclical stock prices reflect changes in investor expectations of the future macroeconomic conditions. Investor expectations may be wrong. But changes in the price of cyclical stocks often anticipate periods of expansion or decline.

**Application Box 1.15**

Many decisions, such as hiring, production, pricing, procurement, compensation, and plant expansion decisions, are made differently at different stages of the business cycle. Personal investment choices, major purchases, accruing debt, and changing one's job are decisions sensitive to the business cycle.

Individual firms and industries are differently sensitive to macroeconomic fluctuations. For example, a household's consumption of bread is relatively unaffected by variations in employment and income. Bread makers and those firms that provide inputs are insensitive to the business cycle. In contrast, households' willingness to purchase airline tickets for vacation travel or to buy new homes, cars, furniture, or appliances is affected by macroeconomic fluctuations. Producers of these business-cycle-sensitive products and their suppliers keenly observe economic trends to align production decisions with the macroeconomy.

Generalizations about an industry's sensitivity to the business cycle are hazardous. Within an industry, firms can be differently sensitive to changing business conditions. For example, routine purchases of bread are unaffected by the business cycle; however, sales of luxury baked goods may be sensitive to macroeconomic fluctuations. Further, bakers of low-priced cookies may find their sales are inversely related to the strength of the macroeconomy. In periods of economic weakness households may shift from ice cream desserts and pies to inexpensive cookies. Similarly, businesses engaged in mortgage defaults, sales of repossessed property, and bankruptcies realize variations counter to the business cycle. It is important, therefore, for each firm to examine its historical performance relative to the business cycle, to continuously monitor economic indicators, and to align decisions with the realities of the macroeconomy.

*The Macroeconomy as a Selling Environment and Macroeconomic Forecasting*

Macroeconomic conditions are important aspects of the environment within which firms hire, purchase inputs, produce, price, sell, and manage their finances. When output, employment, and income are rising, finding buyers is generally easier. When output, employment, and income are rising slowly or declining, finding and keeping customers is more difficult. The fortunes of many firms rise and fall with the strength of the macroeconomy. In turn, the fortunes of employees, suppliers, and stockholders similarly rise and fall with the macroeconomy.

Decisions in which outcomes are affected by the business cycle are complicated by lags. For example, a retail shop owner orders merchandise several months in advance of the selling season. It is insufficient to monitor the current macroeconomy.

## Application Box 1.16

Some business and economic data are reported monthly, while other data are reported quarterly. To facilitate comparisons of percentage changes from one period to the next, it is customary to express the percentage change as an annual rate. Assume that GDP rose from $100 to $102 from the first to the second quarter of the year. If the same 2 percent per quarter rate of growth for the quarter continues for the year, what is the annualized rate (AR) of change?

To express a 2 percent increase in the GDP at an annual rate, the effects of compounding must be considered. A 2 percent quarter-to-quarter increase is an 8.2 percent annual rate of growth. The formula for the percentage change at an annual rate (AR) is:

$$AR = [(\$102 \div \$100)^4 - 1] \times 100 = 8.2 \text{ percent}$$

*Table 1.6*

**Percentage Change in Sales and Percentage Change in National Income**

| Period | Percentage Change in Sales | Percentage Change in National Income |
|---|---|---|
| 1 | 3.48 | 1.96 |
| 2 | 10.65 | 5.9 |
| 3 | 9.75 | 4.8 |
| 4 | 7.25 | 4.5 |
| 5 | 7.07 | 2.9 |
| 6 | 0.92 | 1.5 |
| 7 | −0.61 | 0.21 |
| 8 | −2.65 | −1.39 |
| 9 | 0.2 | 0.0 |
| 10 | 1.2 | 0.77 |
| 11 | 4.36 | 1.7 |
| 12 | 8.34 | 3.7 |
| 13 | 2.4 | 1.82 |
| 14 | 8.96 | 4.1 |
| 15 | 9.34 | 5.1 |
| 16 | 3.5 | 1.89 |
| 17 | 9.24 | 4.29 |
| 18 | 4.5 | 2.56 |
| 19 | 7.3 | 4.1 |
| 20 | 6.45 | 3.2 |

Managers try to anticipate conditions in the macroeconomy at the time the selling season begins and over the duration of the selling period. Managers forecast the macroeconomy in order to align decisions with the realities of the macroeconomy over the time period the decision is in effect.

For a hypothetical manufacturing firm, Table 1.6 presents historical data of the percentage change in sales by quarter and the corresponding percentage change in national income. National income is the sum of incomes earned across the economy over a fixed period of time. The hypothesis is that the firm's sales grow more rapidly as the economy expands more rapidly.

Simple visual inspection of the data in Table 1.6 indicates that (1) the percentage change in the firm's sales has been volatile, with sales growing rapidly at some times, growing slowly at others, and declining in certain periods, and (2) sales tends to change by a larger percentage than the associated percentage change in national income.

To capture a more sophisticated look at the data, Figure 1.4 is a scatter plot displaying how the percentage change in sales varies with the percentage change in national income. The percentage change in sales is plotted vertically and is the *dependent variable*. The percentage change in the national income is plotted on the horizontal axis and is the *independent variable*. The hypothesis is that percentage change in sales is determined by the percentage change in national income.

Inspection of the scatter diagram reveals the following: (1) The general pattern of data points falls upward and to the right, indicating that the percentage increase in the firm's sales is greater as the economy grows more rapidly. (2) The steep upward slope of the pattern of the data points indicates that this firm's sales grow and shrink more rapidly than

*Figure 1.4*
**Scatter Plot**

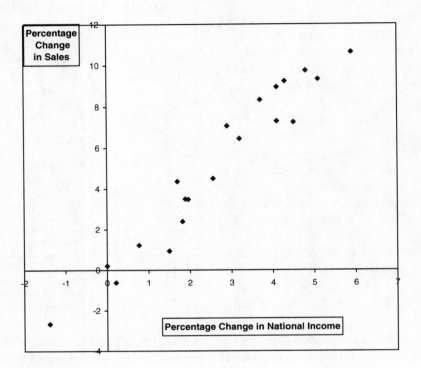

the economy. This defines a firm that is relatively sensitive to the business cycle. (3) The percentage change in national income does not explain all of the variation in sales. The data points do not fall in a precise pattern. Therefore, factors other than the percentage change in national income affect the percentage change in sales, perhaps including changes in the pricing or marketing of competitors' products.

A firm's sensitivity to the business cycle influences many managerial decisions. (1) Business-cycle-sensitive firms minimize fixed costs. Fixed costs do not go up or down with the level of production and include loan payments, rent, property tax, and long-term contractual agreements. High fixed costs make profits volatile in a business-cycle-sensitive

firm. Profits rise quickly during periods of expanding sales because costs rise more slowly than sales; profits decline more rapidly than the economy, as sales revenues fall more rapidly than costs. (2) Such firms prefer equity financing because debt requires periodic interest payments, and interest costs are a fixed cost. (3) Companies sensitive to the business cycle avoid long-term fixed-payment contracts and see advantages to leasing property and equipment in lieu of purchases. (4) They seek flexible operating systems that allow production to accelerate or slow down in response to changing business conditions. (5) They see advantages to just-in-time inventory systems that minimize the risk of accumulating unsold goods. (6) Business-cycle-sensitive companies carefully observe the economy, engage in macroeconomic forecasting, and make decisions in alignment with the realities of their selling environment.

Individuals who work in business-cycle-sensitive firms share the concerns of their employer. Pay increases and the risk of layoff are related to the strength of the economy. As business-cycle-sensitive employers avoid fixed costs, it is dangerous for their employees to establish personal spending patterns and fixed obligations based on income levels in strong economic times. Similarly, investors purchase business-cycle-sensitive stocks in anticipation of an economic expansion and sell them when they think a business downturn is imminent. Further, business-cycle-sensitive firms transmit their volatility across the economy through variations in their demand for resource inputs, employment, and payment of wages.

*Sales Forecasting and the Macroeconomy*

Figure 1.4 plots the period-to-period percentage change in sales for a firm over twenty consecutive periods relative to the percentage changes in national income. The source of the data is Table 1.6. The firm's sales are sensitive to the business cycle. Therefore, if the firm overproduces, inventories rise. Cash and profit problems develop, constraining the firm's ability to continuously upgrade products to meet rising buyer expectations. However, if the firm underproduces, inventories are depleted. The firm does not meet customer demand. Potential sales and profits are lost in the current period. Also, potential customers develop relationships with rival sellers, and the adverse effect on profits continues over multiple time periods. Precise forecasts of sales are important to a firm's long-term financial health.

The scatter plot in Figure 1.4 is transformed into a forecasting tool in Figure 1.5, which includes a straight line that describes the general pattern of the data points. The line generalizes the relationship be-

---

*Table 1.7*
### Forecasting Equation

Percentage Change in Sales = −.232 + 1.983
(Percentage Change in National Income)

---

*Table 1.8*
### Sales Forecast

| Forecast Period | Percentage Change in National Income | Percentage Change in Sales |
|---|---|---|
| 1 | 2.4 | 4.52 |
| 2 | 4.8 | 9.27 |
| 3 | 1.7 | 3.13 |
| 4 | −0.8 | −1.82 |

---

tween the percentage change in sales and the percentage change in national income. The line imposed on the scatter plot minimizes the vertical deviations from individual data points to the straight line. This line is hand-sketched by eyeballing the data or calculated by regression and correlation techniques.

Figure 1.5 yields an equation to forecast the percentage change in sales based on the percentage change in national income. Recognize that all straight lines are defined by two values: the intercept of the vertical axis and the slope. Table 1.7 shows the forecasting equation. The exact coefficients in Table 1.7 are calculated through the regression analysis feature in Excel (see Appendix 1.1).

Table 1.8 shows the percentage change in national income for the following four periods. The percentage change in sales is calculated by inserting the percentage change in national income into the equation.

The calculation for the first forecast quarter is based on the expectation that national income changes by 2.4 percent. The percentage change in sales is projected to be 4.52 percent (= −0.232 + (1.98 × 2.4)).

The forecast of sales in Table 1.8 involves two risks. First, the percentage change in national

*Figure 1.5*
**Scatter Plot**

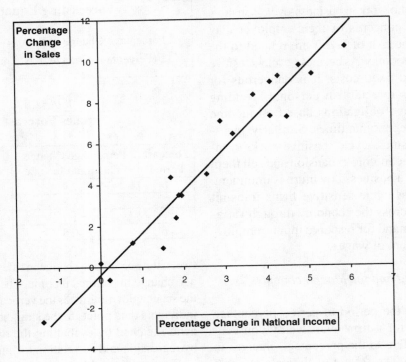

income over the next four quarters cannot be currently observed. These values are themselves forecasts. If the forecasts of the percentage change in national income are in error, the forecasts of the percentage change in sales are in error. Second, if any other factor besides change in national income affects sales changes, the forecast is in error, and in fact the scatter plot (see Figure 1.4) suggests that other factors do have an impact.

Despite these forecast risks, progress is made when the firm understands the relationship between its sales and the macroeconomy, as it can then make informed decisions regarding production schedules, procurement of resource inputs, cash management, and personnel needs. It is useful to note that many firms are more sensitive to their regional, state, or municipal economy than to the national economy. These firms monitor local economic indicators such as employment, payroll, and sales.

*Forecasting with a Lag*

As noted in the example above, if the forecast of the percentage change in national income is in error, the forecast of the percentage change in sales is in error. To avoid this type of forecasting error, it is helpful to find an independent variable that anticipates the changes in the dependent variable. Consider a restaurant chain whose monthly sales are affected by advertising outlays in the prior month. In this example, sales are the dependent variable and lag the independent variable (advertising) by one month. The forecaster observes

## Application Box 1.17

To develop a forecasting equation, plot the data onto a graph and hand-sketch the line that best describes the pattern of points. The straight line minimizes the vertical deviations from the points to the line. Then extend the line to the left until it crosses the vertical axis, where the independent variable is 0. This is the intercept. Estimate the slope of the line. Select any pair of points on the line and calculate the ratio of the rise divided by the run (see below).

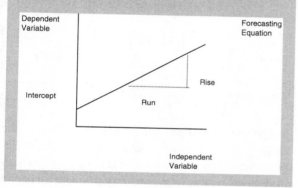

the level of advertising in the current month and forecasts sales for the next month.

The equation in Table 1.9 displays a *lagged relationship*. The hypothesis is that the dependent variable (sales) is affected by the independent variable, denoted as variable $X$ (advertising), in the prior period ($_{t-1}$). Sales are a lagged dependent variable.

An equation with a lag allows the forecaster to observe the independent variable before forecasting. However, other forecasting problems remain: (1) It is necessary to find an independent variable that accurately forecasts the dependent variable with a lag. (2) Often it takes time to collect and report data, and this delay negates the opportunity to use the forecasting equation. For example, retail

## Exercise 1.7

Use the data in the table below. Plot the relation between this firm's percentage change in sales and the percentage change in the gross domestic product. Estimate the straight line. Describe the relationship and comment upon the type of product this firm sells.

| Sales and the Economy | | | | | |
|---|---|---|---|---|---|
| Period | % Change Sales | % Change Real GDP | Period | % Change Sales | % Change Real GDP |
| 1 | 3.5 | 4.3 | 11 | 1.0 | −1.5 |
| 2 | 3.3 | 4.9 | 12 | 1.2 | 1.5 |
| 3 | 2.9 | 5.1 | 13 | 1.6 | 1.7 |
| 4 | 4.1 | 5.3 | 14 | 2.2 | 6.2 |
| 5 | 3.1 | 4.2 | 15 | 3.1 | 6.5 |
| 6 | 2.6 | 3.9 | 16 | 3.1 | 5.7 |
| 7 | 2.0 | 1.6 | 17 | 3.3 | 4.5 |
| 8 | 1.8 | 0.5 | 18 | 2.7 | 3.2 |
| 9 | 1.4 | −2.3 | 19 | 1.6 | 3.5 |
| 10 | 1.3 | −3.5 | 20 | 1.9 | 2.6 |

(a) Draw the scatter plot freehand and estimate the straight line that best describes the scatter plot.

(b) Identify the expansionary and contractionary stages of the business cycle, and comment on the business cycle sensitivity of this firm.

(c) Assume the next four quarter percentage changes in real GDP are 1.0 percent, 4.5 percent, 3.0 percent, and −1.2 percent. Calculate the expected percentage changes in sales.

sales lag the Consumer Confidence Index, but the time needed to gather and report consumer confidence data limits retailers' abilities to forecast next month's sales. (3) Forecasters who are interested in their firm's sales next year are challenged to find a variable observable today that affects sales next year. (4) Forecasts with a lag always require the assumption that all else is equal. For example, the relationship between car sales and interest rates

*Table 1.9*
**Forecasting with a Lag**

$$Sales_t = a + b(X_{t-1})$$

where:
$Sales_t$ = sales in the current period
$a$ = intercept
$b$ = slope
$X_{t-1}$ = advertising in the prior period

*Table 1.10*
**Gross Domestic Product**

| Good | Units | Market Price | Units × Prices |
|---|---|---|---|
| Food | 50 | $6 | $300 |
| Books | 15 | $5 | $75 |
| Gross domestic product = $375 | | | |

**Exercise 1.8**

(a) Provide examples from your workplace where a lagged relationship may exist.
(b) Use the data in Table 1.6 and estimate, by hand or through Excel, the forecasting equation with a one-period lag.

may be affected by drastic changes in the price of gasoline.

Building a lag into a forecasting equation is a simple task. Referring to Table 1.9, a one-period lag between the percentage change in national income and the percentage change in sales is achieved by dropping the first percentage change in sales observation and the last percentage change in national income, then aligning the first data point for national income with the second data point for sales.

*Macroeconomic Measurements*

The primary measurement of the macroeconomy is *gross domestic product* (GDP). GDP is the market value of all currently produced final goods and services within the borders of the country. To sum the production of diverse goods and services, the market price in dollars serves as a common denominator. Because goods sold in one period may have been produced in a prior period and placed in inventory, the GDP measures current production rather than current sales. Only final goods and services are measured, to avoid double counting. For example, a spark plug used in a new motor vehicle is not separately part of the GDP; it is included in the market value of the new automobile.

Table 1.10 displays a simplified calculation of the GDP for an economy that produces only books and food. The GDP, $375, is the summation of the number of units produced of each good multiplied by the good's market price. The $375 figure is referred to as the *nominal GDP* because goods are valued at their current prices.

Given the definition of the GDP, several points follow. (1) Goods that do not pass through formal markets are excluded from the GDP, including those produced and consumed at home, bartered

*Table 1.11*

**Change in Gross Domestic Product**

| Good | Units Year 1 | Price Year 1 | Dollars Year 1 | Units Year 2 | Price Year 2 | Dollars Year 1 |
|------|------|------|------|------|------|------|
| Food | 50 | $6 | $300 | 52 | $6.10 | $317.20 |
| Books | 15 | $5 | $75 | 17 | $5.15 | $87.55 |
| | | GDP (year 1) = $375 | | | GDP (year 2) = $404.75 | |

*Table 1.12*

**Real Gross Domestic Product**

| Good | Year 2 Output | Year 1 Prices | Dollars |
|------|------|------|------|
| Food | 52 | $6 | $312 |
| Books | 17 | $5 | $85 |
| | | Real GDP (year 2) = $397 | |

items, and illegal activities. (2) Changes in the quality of the goods are not included. (3) The distribution of the output among individuals is not considered. (4) Over time, the GDP is affected by changes in output and also by changes in prices.

The effect of price changes is shown in Table 1.11. The economy's nominal GDP is calculated for two consecutive years. In Table 1.11 the amounts of food and books produced increase in year two and the prices of both products increase. How much of the increase in GDP is attributable to more goods and how much to higher prices?

The data in Table 1.11 indicate that this economy's nominal GDP grew from $375 in year one to $404.75 in year two, a 7.9 percent rate of growth. To calculate the change in real output, it is necessary to remove the effect of rising prices. The *real gross domestic product* is calculated in Table 1.12 by valuing the production in year two at year one prices, yielding a figure of $397.

*Table 1.13*

**Price Deflator**

$$\text{Price Deflator (Year 2)} = \frac{\text{Nominal GDP}}{\text{Real GDP}}$$

$$= \frac{\$404.75}{397}$$

$$= 1.02$$

Real GDP differs from nominal GDP by excluding the effects of rising prices. Over time, real GDP provides a more accurate indicator of the change in the nation's output. In the example, real GDP grew over the period from $375 to $397, a 5.9 percent rate of real economic growth.

By comparing nominal GDP to real GDP, the price deflator is calculated; see Table 1.13.

Table 1.13 shows that prices rose 2 percent from year one to year two. Of the 7.9 percent nominal GDP growth, 5.9 percentage points are attributable to increases in output and 2 percentage points of the growth are the result of higher prices.

Figure 1.6 shows the annualized percentage change in real GDP since 1980. The historical data reveal that the U.S. economy has experienced periods of rapidly rising real output and periods of recession, the latter denoted by the shaded vertical bars.

The changes in real GDP raise important questions. What is rapid growth, what is slow growth, and what growth rate can be sustained over time? Real growth over time comes from two sources: growth of the size of the labor force and productivity gains. Many economists believe the combination of growth in the labor force and growth in productivity permits 3.5 to 4 percent real growth in output per year. An actual real growth rate of 3.5 to 4 percent per year leaves the unemployment rate unchanged. Therefore: (1) growth faster than 3.5 percent to 4 percent is needed to reduce the rate of unemployment, (2) following

*Figure 1.6*
**Quarterly Growth in Real U.S. GDP at Annual Rates, percent**

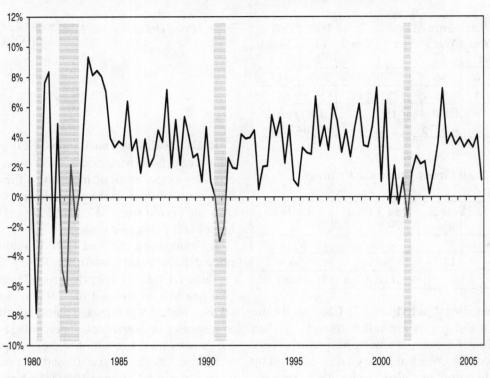

*Source:* St. Louis Federal Reserve.

periods of recession, real growth often exceeds 3.5 to 4 percent as unemployed workers rejoin the workforce, (3) economic growth in excess of 3.5 to 4 percent for a prolonged period threatens price inflation as production rates strain existing capacity, and (4) some economists suggest that an accelerated pace of technological advance boosts productivity and that more rapid economic growth can be sustained without inflation.[4]

Swings in the percentage growth in real gross domestic product reflect the business cycle. When real GDP is growing rapidly, business conditions are favorable. Firms find customers are plentiful and profits rise. When real GDP grows slowly or falls, businesses have trouble finding buyers;

sales and profits tumble. As seen in Figure 1.6, the business cycle does not follow a regular pattern, and short-term fluctuations are difficult to predict. However, effective decision makers are aware of the effects of short-term economic fluctuations on their organization and are regular observers of contemporary economic data and economic conditions.

The Consumer Price Index (CPI) is an often-cited and important measure of inflation. The CPI is calculated and reported monthly. The calculation process is cumbersome, though the concept is simple. A fixed market basket of goods and services, descriptive of a typical consumer's buying pattern, is determined. The basket of items is

---

**Exercise 1.9**

Using www.economagic.com, plot since 1980 the following data series:

(a)  Percentage change in real gross domestic product
(b)  The unemployment rate
(c)  Personal income

Do the following:

(a)  Identify the recession periods.
(b)  Comment on the relationships between the data series.
(c)  Approximate the average rate of real GDP growth.

Instructions:

(a)  Log on to www.economagic.com.
(b)  Click on "Most Requested Series."
(c)  Select the series.
(d)  Select GIF chart.
(e)  Display the recession periods.
(f)  Print.

---

priced in a base year, and the same basket of goods and services is repriced in ensuing periods. The percentage change in the cost of the fixed basket of goods and services is the rate of inflation.

The CPI has several flaws. (1) The fixed market basket of goods does not account for changes in the quality of products. For example, health care costs have risen rapidly, but it is difficult to separate higher-quality care from price inflation. Better care is more costly, but quality-related price increases are not inflation. (2) A fixed basket of goods and services does not account for shifts in buying habits in response to price changes. For example, if the price of apples rises, consumers shift to eating pears. The fixed market basket of goods is more costly, but the substitution of goods allows buyers to evade some of the effects of inflation. (3) Increases in the cost of the fixed market basket of goods mask changes in the price of individual products. This is important because the prices of some products, including energy and food, are volatile. Spikes in these prices, while other prices remain relatively constant, distort changes in consumer prices. Hence, it is often useful to examine the core rate of inflation, which excludes volatile food and energy prices.

Figure 1.7 shows the percentage change in the Consumer Price Index since 1980.

Whereas the societal effects of unemployment are quite clear, the effects of inflation need some discussion.

- Rising prices, all else equal, reduce the purchasing power of a paycheck. If all paychecks rise by the same rate, buyers sustain their real purchasing power. However, some groups are better able to protect the purchasing power of their wages than others, and inflation redistributes purchasing power.
- Volatile price changes reduce the willingness of buyers and sellers to engage in long-term contracts. This reluctance reduces investment in capital goods needed for economic growth.
- Some firms adjust their prices in accord with inflation based on their dominance of a market or their production of a good or service that is essential for buyers. Firms that operate in highly competitive and price-sensitive environments are less able to raise their prices. This phenomenon redistributes profits and redistributes firms' abilities to adjust wages and dividends.
- Rising prices distort choices, including the preference for savings relative to current

*Figure 1.7*
**The Consumer Price Index**

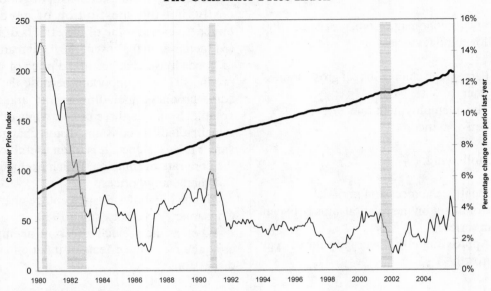

*Source:* St. Louis Federal Reserve

consumption. For example, given an outlook for rising prices, an immediate purchase in advance of the price increase encourages current consumption over savings for the future.

Although the U.S. economy has not experienced a prolonged period of falling prices since the 1930s, deflation can cause profits to fall and employees to be laid off. The effects of deflation include the following:

- Businesses and individuals are reluctant to borrow to build new factories and homes because the fixed principal and interest rate obligations become more costly in the future in real terms.
- During periods of falling prices, firms may be unable to afford to pay off debts or meet other fixed obligations, necessitating further wage cutting and layoffs.

Several points are noted:

- Inflation slows during periods of recession and immediately thereafter.
- Prices tend to rise in periods that precede recessions.
- Inflation rates have been generally lower since 1990 than through the 1970s and 1980s.

In Chapter 2, a model is developed that explains the sources of macroeconomic fluctuations, and macroeconomic measurements are extended to provide decision makers with tools to monitor the economy.

### The Microeconomy

The scarcity problem calls for a two-pronged response. The macroeconomic response to scarcity involves producing as much as possible, and the strength of the macroeconomy is reflected in output, employment, and income statistics. The microeconomic response to scarcity involves producing the most desired mix of goods. In microeconomics, the study units are individual consumers, households, industries, and firms. Microeconomics analyzes buyers and sellers and individual markets within the economy.

The detailed study of microeconomic concepts occurs in Chapters 4 through 7. The remaining pages of this chapter establish the microeconomic environment within which decisions are made and which affects the outcomes of business and household decisions.

*The Production Cost Chain*

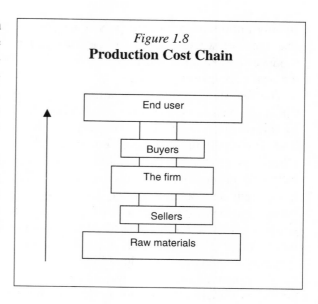

*Figure 1.8*
**Production Cost Chain**

One main theme in microeconomics is the firm's competitive environment, and the *production cost chain* is a useful organizing tool. The production cost chain (see Figure 1.8) shows the multiple stages of production of a good or service from the raw material stage to the final product in the hands of the end user.

Figure 1.8 refers to a firm that manufactures coated paperboard shipping containers. The suppliers of inputs (primarily corrugated paper and chemicals) are denoted in the figure as sellers and include large paper manufacturers and chemical processors. These sellers, in turn, purchase inputs from other suppliers, eventually tracing back to raw materials. The firm coats the corrugated paperboard with wax and other chemicals and molds it into shipping containers for sale to agricultural producers of meats, fruits, and vegetables. These buyers need containers that can withstand weight, moisture, and refrigeration during the shipment of their products to markets. The end users of the shipping containers are the purchasers of the agricultural products.

Figure 1.8 displays the sequence of interme-

diate stages of production from raw materials (inputs to the paper-making process and chemicals) through sellers (paper makers and chemical producers) to the manufacturer of the shipping containers, which are sold to buyers (agribusinesses) for transport to grocery stores. Intermediate stages of production pass through established markets. The production cost chain identifies dependencies between firms and industries and highlights the zones in which *the five forces of competition* operate. This facilitates the analysis of a firm's competitive environment and leads to recommendations compatible with a firm's microeconomic environment.

*The Five Forces of Competition*

The five forces of competition describe a firm's microeconomic environment and include (1) direct rivals, (2) sellers of substitute products, (3) the threat of entry of new competitors, (4) buyer power, and (5) seller power.[5] All markets are characterized by these five forces, though each force is not equally important in all industries. Each force is described below with reference to the coated paper producer and summarized into a unified view of the firm's competitive setting.

The first competitive force is *direct rivals*. A firm's competitive environment is partially defined by its most direct competitors. The manufacturer of coated paper shipping containers competes against others who produce and sell similar products. The following observations are important: (1) Given the weight and bulk of coated paper shipping containers, the geographic scope of a seller's market is limited. (2) Once a coated paper container meets shippers' specifications, a better container (perhaps defined by greater durability or weight or temperature tolerance) does not make the product more attractive to customers. For producers whose products meet the technical requirements, the competition between rivals is based primarily on price. (3) In this industry, fledgling efforts are under way to develop a recyclable coated shipping container. If successfully developed, this differentiated product gains two important competitive advantages: it reduces the buyer's disposal costs, thus lowering the total cost of the containers to the buyer, and it may attract buyers interested in a recyclable shipping container that reduces waste and protects the environment.

A second competitive force refers to *substitute products*. Plastic shipping containers serve similar needs as coated paper products and are a substitute. After use, plastic containers are stored by the buyer and eventually returned to the seller, who cleans and reuses or disposes of the container. Plastic products intensify the competition in the coated paper shipping container industry.

The *threat of entry* of new competitors is a third competitive force. All firms compete against the threat of entry of new rivals into their industry. In capitalist economic systems, entrepreneurs seek opportunities and markets that offer financial promise. Barriers to entry define the ease or difficulty of a new rival entering an industry. Entry barriers are high where capital costs discourage potential new firms, where patents protect existing processes, where special skills and knowledge are needed, and where license requirements restrict new firms. Low barriers to entry facilitate the mobility of resources and allow scarce productive resources to flow to industries to meet demand. Low exit barriers allow entrepreneurs to readily abandon the production of a product in favor of another. Where exit barriers are high, perhaps because of large fixed investments, firms aggressively protect their existing customers.

The entry of new firms and the migration of scarce resources into a profitable industry are advantageous for society. Resources flow to the production of those goods most desired by buyers. One negative effect is that easy entry erodes the profitability of firms already in the industry. Therefore, firms already in the industry try to build barriers to entry to discourage new competitors and protect their profitability.

In the coated paper container industry, the threat of entry of new firms is low. The market is saturated: excess productive capacity exists, and profit margins are low. Market conditions are not attractive to the entry of new firms. However, integrated paper companies are a threat to extend their product reach into coated papers, though they lack the knowledge and experience to work with wax and chemical coatings. Also, firms already in the coated paper industry but serving other geographic territories are a threat to extend their geographic reach. Extending into new territories allows a firm to increase its asset utilization rate, lower its average cost of production, and raise profitability.

*Buyer power* is also a competitive force. All market transactions involve a buyer and a seller. Buyers and sellers come to the marketplace with differences in negotiating power. The concept of buyer power is examined by looking up the production cost chain to the immediate buyers of a firm's product. Consider a small producer who provides an intermediate-stage product to a large manufacturer. Assuming other producers meet the large manufacturer's needs, the market power resides in the hands of the buyer, and the buyer negotiates favorable prices. In the case of the coated shipping container industry, the buyers are agribusinesses who need the containers to ship produce to market. There are several regional sellers of coated shipping containers and only a few large buyers. The negotiating power resides in the hands of the buyers of the containers, and this diminishes the profit margins of the coated paper sellers.

*Seller power* is the fifth competitive force. This analysis of market power looks backward in the production chain from the firm to the suppliers of inputs. Bargaining power relationships differ by market. For the coated paper makers, the principal suppliers are the large integrated paper makers. However, there is a small number of paper makers and there are many potential suppliers of unsophisticated chemicals. The market power resides with the paper makers. The manufacturers of the coated paper containers are at a disadvantage, which places additional pressure on their profit margins.

This brief review of the coated shipping container market suggests several negative forces: (1) slow growth in the demand for the product, (2) many direct rivals, (3) viable substitutes, (4) price pressures from buyers, and (5) price pressures from suppliers. In sum, the competitive analysis leads to two options. First, coated paper producers seek to be the most successful price competitor by having the lowest costs. Production efficiency is achieved by process innovation, better use of by-products, or improved inventory management. The development of a recyclable shipping container is part of a low-price strategy if it reduces buyers' disposal costs. Second, coated paper producers try to dif-

ferentiate their product in a manner valued by their customers in order to improve profit margins. For example, a recyclable product is an option if buyers are concerned about the natural environment.

The production cost chain facilitates analysis of competitive options by considering the firm's *horizontal and vertical reach.*

With reference to Figure 1.8, a firm expands its horizontal reach by extending its mix of products into related items or markets. A coated paper manufacturer extends its horizontal reach by producing waxed paper trays or plates for sale to the fast-food industry or coated papers for outdoor display boards. A broader horizontal reach extends coated paper products to packages for processed food, freezer products, and microwave containers. Extending the horizontal reach is diversification. It redeploys assets into a more favorable industry and can increase asset use rates, lead to cost reductions in manufacturing, marketing and distribution, or extend a brand name to related products.

Extending the firm's vertical reach involves completing more of the activities in the production cost chain. *Integrating backward* involves performing some of the functions provided by input sup-

---

**Application Box 1.19**

The 2005 merger of Procter and Gamble (P&G) and Gillette highlights the importance of buyer and seller power.

With the acquisition of Gillette, P&G became a market leader in razors and blades. As P&G grows even bigger, it has more clout to negotiate for shelf space and prices with leading retailers, including Wal-Mart and grocery store chains.

*Source:* Jenn Abelson, "How Well Will Gillette Fit into the P&G Lineup?" *Boston Globe,* June 12, 2005.

---

### Exercise 1.10

(a) For the fast-food hamburger industry, describe each of the five forces of competition.

(b) Discuss the implications for the firm with respect to pricing, product development, expected profitability, and innovation.

(c) What are the opportunities to extend the vertical and horizontal reach of a firm in this industry?

---

pliers. A coated paper manufacturer who produces its own chemical coatings engages in backward vertical integration. *Integrating forward* involves completing tasks currently performed by buyers of the product. A paper manufacturer engages in forward vertical integration by applying chemical coatings to its paper products and selling its containers to agribusinesses.

### Market Characteristics

Individual firms operate in industries that have many different characteristics. Marketplace characteristics drive decision making within the firm and affect the outcomes of decisions. The following items provide examples (though not exhaustive ones) of marketplace conditions.

Some industries are characterized by products whose features are almost identical, thereby making it difficult for buyers to distinguish one firm's products from another's. Many such markets exist, including agricultural products, long-distance phone service, and Internet services. Industrial commodities such as crude oil, copper, and aluminum fall into this category. Where it is difficult or unimportant to buyers to distinguish between individual sellers, price is the most important competitive variable.

Firms in a commodity-like industry recognize that advertising is not productive because buyers are unable to distinguish between sellers. In commodity industries, promotions are industry-wide because single firms cannot distinguish themselves from rivals. Trade association promotions include "Got milk?" and "Beef: it's what's for dinner."

Firms who sell products in these markets concentrate on lowering their costs of production. While no firm willingly incurs unnecessary costs, the price competition in commodity-like markets drives sellers to find the highest possible level of production efficiency. To be the low-cost producer, decision makers across a firm must be commonly directed. They try to understand the cause-and-effect connections within their firm to make a complete set of decisions that will keep costs as low as possible. Inefficient producers cannot pass higher costs to consumers through higher prices, are destined to realize disappointing profits, and are ultimately driven out of business.

In contrast to commodity-like markets, other industries are conducive to differentiation based on product features or customer service. For example, automobile makers compete on styling, dealer services, vehicle handling, acceleration, and safety in addition to price. Firms competing on product differences make different operating decisions than those competing on price. For examples, equipment needs and procurement choices differ according to a firm's competitive strategy. Successful product or service differentiation makes the firm a preferred seller and allows the firm to command higher prices and earn higher profits.

Some markets are *mature* and characterized by slowly growing sales and profits. These markets can be large and profitable but impose considerable pressure on sellers. Sellers aggressively protect each customer because new buyers are difficult to find. New buyers are gained by taking a customer away from a rival rather than selling to a new pur-

**Application Box 1.20**

In recent years telephone companies have offered cash incentives to households to switch service providers. While individual telephone companies seek new customers in the market, this behavior is an effort to steal market share from rivals.

chaser of the industry's product. Buyers recognize this market power and seek price or service level concessions. Sellers in these markets protect their sales, manage costs carefully, and consider redeploying assets to more favorable settings.

Other markets are *rapidly growing* and offer favorable selling conditions. These attractive selling circumstances conceal competitive differences. The rapid rate of growth of industry sales creates room for many competitors and allows firms that do not have a competitive advantage to sell products and be profitable. Sellers focus on gaining new customers, and the expanding markets create favorable settings for the entry of new competitors. However, rapid growth and favorable selling conditions do not last indefinitely. Firms that fail to develop strong products and distribution channels are the first to suffer when market conditions turn less favorable.

## Summary

This opening chapter defines the economic problem and presents the macro- and microeconomic responses to scarcity as environments within which firms and individuals make decisions and affect the outcomes of those choices. This chapter provides tools to describe a firm's macro- and microeconomic environments, allowing decision makers to align their choices with marketplace realities.

## Review Terms

| | |
|---|---|
| Business cycle indicators | Macroeconomics |
| Constrained maximum | Marginal analysis |
| Consumer Price Index | Market characteristics |
| Cost-benefit analysis | Microeconomics |
| Cyclical stocks | Opportunity costs |
| Economic systems | Present value |
| Expected value | Production cost chain |
| Five forces of competition | Rate of time preference |
| Fixed costs | Resource misallocations |
| Forecasting | Risk aversion |
| Gross domestic product | Scarcity |
| Horizontal reach | Scatter plots |
| Hurdle rate | Time value of money |
| Lagged relationships | Trade-offs |
| Least squares line | Vertical reach |

## Discussion Questions

1. Go to www.economagic.com. Under the "Stock Prices Indexes" section, print the daily closing of (1) "DJ Industrial Average Actual Daily Close (to 2001)" and (2) "DJ Transportation Average Daily Close (to 2001)." Click on "GIF Chart" and select the option to make the charts start from 1980. Use the display options to show the recession periods on the charts. Compare the volatility of the indexes.

2. Identify the costs and the benefits of enrolling in a graduate degree program, and outline a cost-benefit study. Consider how the risk and time to complete the degree complicate the assessment of the costs and the benefits.

3. Why is marginal analysis important for decision makers? Provide multiple examples.

4. With reference to your employer or a firm of your choice, review the five forces of com-

petition. What are the implications for the firm's competitive strategy? Then consider the market conditions within which the firm operates. Review the strategic implications. What do you suggest to the firm?

5. For the firm selected in question 4, provide examples of extending the horizontal and vertical reaches of the firm.

6. Using the data below, plot the relationship between the percentage change in sales at Holland Manufacturing and the percentage change in the number of people employed across the economy. Comment upon the relationship and provide guidance for the firm. What other factors may affect the firm's sales?

7. Provide examples of an entry barrier and discuss the effects of those barriers on the industry and on consumers.

8. Define the economic problem. Provide examples as the economic problem applies to society, a firm, and a household; discuss the decision-making problem and the methodology of cost-benefit analysis.

9. The table below shows a prospective MBA student's estimates of the probability of not graduating, earning the degree, and earning the degree with honors. The table also shows the present value of the gains in compensation associated with each outcome. The cost of the degree program is $20,000. Should the student enroll?

10. Using present-value tables, calculate the following.

   (a) What is the present value of $2 in one year at 5 percent interest?

   (b) What is the present value of $2 in two years at 5 percent interest?

   (c) What is the relationship between the present value of a fixed sum and the length of time to receipt of the sum?

   (d) What is the present value of $2 in two years at 7 percent interest?

   (e) Compare the answers to parts (b) and (d). What is the effect of the present value of a fixed sum at a higher interest rate?

| Prospective MBA Student's Decision Matrix | | |
|---|---|---|
| Outcome | Probability | Present Value of Earnings Increase |
| Do not graduate | .20 | $0 |
| Graduate | .50 | $30,000 |
| Graduate with honors | .30 | $50,000 |

| Holland Manufacturing | | |
|---|---|---|
| Quarter | Percentage Change in Sales | Percentage Change in Number Employed |
| 1 | 2.2 | 1.1 |
| 2 | 3.0 | 1.5 |
| 3 | 3.5 | 1.8 |
| 4 | 4.0 | 2.0 |
| 5 | 5.7 | 3.0 |
| 6 | 6.0 | 3.1 |
| 7 | 6.8 | 3.5 |
| 8 | 5.0 | 2.2 |
| 9 | 4.3 | 2.1 |
| 10 | 3.5 | 1.3 |
| 11 | 1.2 | −0.8 |
| 12 | 0.5 | −0.1 |
| 13 | −1.1 | −0.3 |
| 14 | −3.3 | −1.6 |
| 15 | −5.0 | −4.0 |
| 16 | 0.1 | −0.2 |
| 17 | 2.5 | 1.1 |
| 18 | 3.3 | 1.8 |
| 19 | 5.7 | 3.1 |
| 20 | 7.1 | 5.1 |

(f) Using your answer to (e), why are long-term bonds a riskier investment than short-term obligations?

11. Assume a world of two countries and two products. The production possibilities of the two goods, food and sunscreen, and the two countries, Heartland and Leisure Land, are shown below. Before specialization and trade, both countries produce at point B.

| Production Possibilities: Heartland | | | | |
|---|---|---|---|---|
| | Point A | Point B | Point C | Point D |
| Food | 300 | 200 | 100 | 0 |
| Sunscreen | 0 | 50 | 100 | 150 |
| Production Possibilities: Leisure Land | | | | |
| Food | 150 | 100 | 50 | 0 |
| Sunscreen | 0 | 100 | 200 | 300 |

(a) Before specialization, calculate world output.

(b) In Leisure Land, what is the opportunity cost of a unit of sunscreen in terms of food? In Heartland, what is the opportunity cost of a unit of sunscreen in terms of food? Where is the opportunity cost of food lower? Where is the opportunity cost of sunscreen lower?

(c) Assume specialization. Which country produces which product?

(d) Calculate world output after specialization. What are the gains in world output?

(e) Identify a trade rate between the two countries that is acceptable to both. Given the terms of trade, what are the gains in the number of units of products in each country?

## Notes

1. Campbell R. McConnell and Stanley L. Brue, *Economics: Principles, Problems, and Policies*, 16th edition (New York: McGraw-Hill, 2005), p. 3.

2. Robert Heilbroner, *The Worldly Philosophers* (New York: Simon and Schuster, 1953), pp. 42–73.

3. Arthur Okun, *Equality and Efficiency: The Big Tradeoff* (Washington, D.C.: Brookings Institution, 1975).

4. Kevin Stiroh, "Is There a New Economy?" *Challenge: The Magazine for Economic Affairs* 42 (July-August 1999), pp. 82–102.

5. Michael Porter, *Competitive Strategy: Techniques for Analyzing Industries and Competitors* (New York: Free Press, 1980), pp. 3–34.

# Appendix 1.1

# Regression Analysis

## Ordinary Least Squares Regression

In Chapter 1, the relationship between the sales of a hypothetical manufacturing firm and national income was plotted on a graph (see Figure 1.5). The graph shows that the firm's percentage change in sales is positively affected by a percentage change in national income. The reader was instructed to draw a line on the graph to indicate the effect of national income on sales. This line, created by simply eyeballing the data, was drawn by minimizing the distance between the actual points and the constructed line. While this is effective for a quick analysis, it is hardly a sophisticated methodology.

In this section, the method of regression analysis is presented as a rigorous method of determining the relationship between two variables. The emphasis is on the managerial implications and not on the derivation of mathematical equations. The student learns how to run a regression analysis in Excel and how to interpret the results.

The manufacturing firm's percentage change in sales is hypothesized to be dependent on the percentage change in national income. The percentage change in sales, then, is the *dependent* variable and is denoted by $Y$. The percentage change in national income is an *independent* variable, and it is denoted by $X$. Over a period of time the percentage change in sales is recorded along with the percentage change in national income during the same period. The process is repeated to create a series

*Table A1.1*
**True Regression Equation**

$$Y_i = A + BX_i + e_i$$

of corresponding data. Each observation pair of percentage change in sales and percentage change in national income is denoted using a subscript, so the $i$th observation of the pair is $X_i, Y_i$.

The method of regression analysis employed assumes that there is a true linear relationship between the percentage change in national income, $X$, and the percentage change in sales, $Y$. The objective of regression analysis is to estimate this relationship, which is represented by the equation in Table A1.1. The value of $B$ indicates the slope of the regression line, which is the effect each additional unit of $X$ has on $Y$. The value of $A$ is the Y-intercept, or the value of $Y$ when $X_i = 0$. A random effect is also assumed to be present in this relationship between $X$ and $Y$ and is denoted by $e_i$. The values of $e_i$ are assumed to be independent of each other, and their mean value is zero.

There is no way to know the true relationship between $X$ and $Y$. The best that one can do is use a sample of observed values to estimate the true relationship. This estimated regression line is constructed using observed data, and regression statistics are used to indicate the accuracy of the estimate. The estimated regression equation is displayed in Table A1.2. The variable $\hat{Y}_i$ represents

*Table A1.2.*
**Estimated Regression Equation**

$$\hat{Y}_i = a + bX_i$$

the value of the dependent variable predicted by the regression line, and $a$ and $b$ are estimators of $A$ and $B$.

The estimated regression line is constructed by finding the line that best fits the observed data. In the chapter, a line was constructed by hand to do this. A precise regression line can be constructed using the method of ordinary least squares (OLS). The OLS regression line is the line that minimizes the sum of the squared residuals between the observed values, $Y_i$, and the line's estimated values, $\hat{Y}_i$. Calculating the ordinary least squares regression line requires algebra and calculus techniques and is beyond the scope of this book. Instead, the spreadsheet program Microsoft Excel is used to calculate the estimators and create the OLS regression line.

## OLS Regression in Excel

Using the data from the chapter, Figure A1.1 shows the dialogue box in Excel used to create the regression equation. This dialogue box is found by using the Tools menu, selecting Data Analysis, and then choosing Regression.

### The Regression Coefficients

The regression output from Excel appears in Figure A1.2. The values of the coefficients $a$ and $b$ are calculated to be −0.232 and 1.983, respectively. The OLS estimate of the regression line is shown in Table A1.3.

The calculation means that if the percentage change in national income is zero ($X_i = 0$), then sales are predicted to decrease by 0.232 percent.

*Table A1.3.*
**OLS Regression Line**

$$\hat{Y}_i = -0.232 + 1.983X_i$$

*Figure A1.1.*
**Excel Regression Dialogue Box**

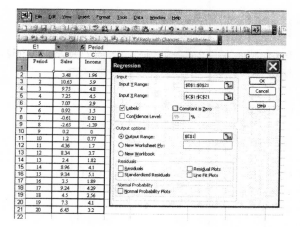

The firm's sales are positively correlated with national income. In fact, the firm's sales are predicted to increase by 198.3 percent of any increase in national income. If national income is up 10 percent, then sales are predicted to increase by 19.6 percent ($= -0.232 + (1.983 \times 10)$).

### R Square

It is important to know how well the OLS regression line fits the data. Certainly, a line with a better fit will provide a higher degree of confidence that the estimated line is close to the true relationship between the variables.

Figure A1.3 displays the OLS regression line in relation to the actual data for the example. As can be seen on the graph, the actual data points are very close to the line. The line appears to fit the data

*Figure A1.2.*
**Excel Regression Output**

| E | F | G | H | I |
|---|---|---|---|---|
| SUMMARY OUTPUT | | | | |
| | | | | |
| *Regression Statistics* | | | | |
| Multiple R | 0.971090835 | | | |
| R Square | 0.94301741 | | | |
| Adjusted R Square | 0.939651711 | | | |
| Standard Error | 0.95953769 | | | |
| Observations | 20 | | | |
| | | | | |
| ANOVA | | | | |
| | *df* | *SS* | *MS* | *F* |
| Regression | 1 | 274.2673486 | 274.26735 | 297.886 |
| Residual | 18 | 16.57282642 | 0.9207126 | |
| Total | 19 | 290.840175 | | |
| | | | | |
| | *Coefficients* | *Standard Error* | *t Stat* | *P-value* |
| Intercept | -0.232406131 | 0.375319368 | -0.619222 | 0.543529 |
| Income | 1.982804003 | 0.114882736 | 17.259373 | 1.21E-12 |

*Figure A1.3.*
**OLS Regression Line**

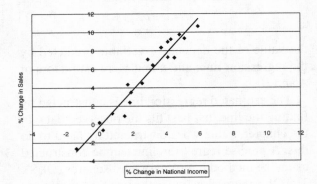

very well. The regression output in Figure A1.2 indicates that the coefficient of determination, or R square, is 0.94. R square is the most commonly used measure to determine how well a regression line fits the actual data. For the purpose of this book, it is not necessary to show the mathematical formula of R square because it is rarely calculated by hand. Instead, it is important to understand how R square explains whether the regression line fits the data.

The value of R square varies between 0 and 1. The closer it is to 1, the better the regression line fits the data. The closer it is to 0, the poorer the fit. Essentially, R square indicates the percentage of the variation in the $Y$ variable that can be explained by the $X$ variable. In the example, R square is 0.94. This means that 94 percent of the variation in the percentage change in sales is explained by the percentage change in national income. Consequently, 6 percent of the variation in the percentage increase in sales is not explained by the regression equation.

Figures A1.4 through A1.7 present various scat-ter plots of sales and national income. On each of the graphs, an OLS regression line is drawn along with the corresponding value of R square. As the R square value approaches 0, there is less confidence in the estimated regression line.

### Standard Error of the Regression

The R square measure is useful because its value is always between 0 and 1, and it is used to compare OLS regression equations. Another useful tool to determine how well the regression line fits the data is the *standard error of the regression*. In Figure A1.2, the standard error of the regression appears under Regression Statistics. Unlike the R square measurement, the value of the standard error depends on the data in the regression analysis.

The standard error is useful in constructing a prediction interval. Given a specific value for $X$, the prediction interval is the range within which there is a specified probability that the true value of $Y$ lies. The regression equation in Figure A1.2 predicts that when national income is up 10 percent, then sales are predicted to increase by 19.6 percent. The standard error of the regression is 0.96, so the range of values within which the true increase in sales lies, with 95 percent confidence,

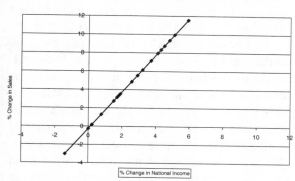

*Figure A1.4.*
**Sample Data with R squared = 1.00**

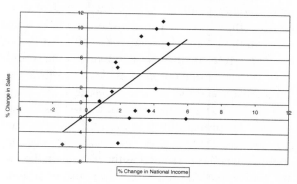

*Figure A1.6.*
**Sample Data with R squared = 0.30**

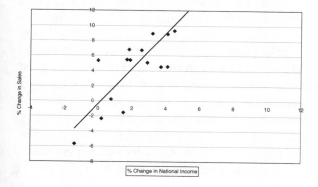

*Figure A1.5.*
**Sample Data with R squared = 0.72**

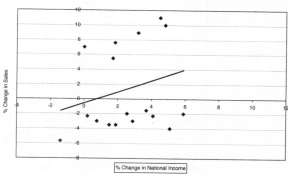

*Figure A1.7.*
**Sample Data with R squared = 0.05**

is 19.6% ± (2 × 0.96)% or 17.68% to 21.52%.[1] The greater the standard error of the regression, the less confident one would be in the predictive capability of the regression line.

### Standard Error of the Coefficient

The R square measurement and the standard error of the regression provide managers with information on the entire regression equation's ability to estimate the dependent variable. The *standard error of the coefficient*, displayed to the right of each coefficient in Figure A1.2, allows managers to eval-

uate the individual significance of the independent variable and the intercept term. The standard error of the income coefficient in Figure A1.2 is 0.115, so the range of values within which the true value of the coefficient lies, with 95 percent confidence, is 1.983 ± (2 × 0.115) or 1.753 to 2.213.

### The t-Statistic

The reason simple regression analysis is typically employed is to determine whether a significant relationship exists between two variables. The regression output in Figure A1.2 provides information that enables managers to determine whether or not there is a statistically significant relationship between the independent variable, sales, and the dependent variable, national income. If there was no relationship between these variables, then the coefficient in the true regression equation for national income would be 0. The regression output provides a *t-statistic* for the intercept and the income variable. Everything else equal, the larger the value of the t-statistic, the smaller the probability that the true value of the regression coefficient is 0. The probability that the coefficient is 0 is presented as the *p-value* in the regression output. Assuming that the manager prefers 95 percent confidence that the coefficient is not 0, the p-value must be less than 0.05. As a general rule of thumb, the absolute value of the t-statistic should be greater than 2 in order for the coefficient to be considered statistically significant.

### Multiple Regression Analysis

Regression analysis is also employed to analyze the relationship between any number of independent ($X$) variables and one dependent variable ($Y$). In Chapter 6, the relationship between a dependent variable, quantity demanded of a product, and various independent variables (price of the product, income, price of a substitute product) will be examined. Multiple regression analysis constructs an equation that identifies each independent variable's effect on the quantity of product demanded. The process of developing the regression equation is identical to the example shown in Figure A1.1 except for one minor exception: the X-range in the Excel regression dialogue box must encompass all of the columns of data for the independent variables.

To analyze the ability of the multiple regression equation to predict the true relationship among the $X$ and $Y$ variables, the manager examines the regression output in the same manner as with the simple regression model. The R square measure and the standard error of the regression both indicate the model's ability to accurately predict. The standard errors of the coefficients, the t-statistics, and the p-values indicate to the manager whether each of the independent variables is statistically significant. If one or more of the independent variables are found to be insignificant at a 95 percent confidence level (p-value is greater than 0.05), the manager should run another regression equation with that particular variable excluded from the model. Finding the model that is the best estimator of the dependent variable is an art, and it can be a time-consuming process.

Regression analysis is a tool managers employ to help them make better decisions. Often the relationship between two variables is determined by anecdotal information or limited experience. Regression analysis is a thorough statistical technique that uses data to identify whether significant relationships truly exist between variables. The technique provides the manager with better predictive and analytical capability.

### Note

1. The prediction interval for the standard error of the regression assumes that regression equation estimates from various samples are distributed normally (a bell-shaped curve). Within a normal distribution, 95 percent of the observations are within two standard deviations of the mean observation. Therefore, the prediction interval is the estimated value plus or minus two standard errors of the regression.

# Case Study 1.1
# Mountain Builders

## Introduction

Located in the Catoctin Mountains of Maryland and in close proximity to the presidential retreat at Camp David, Mountain Builders designs and erects residential properties and complete custom renovations and additions. The region offers rich opportunities. The Washington, D.C., corridor is expanding rapidly to the west, where land prices are lower. Further, as businesses locate west of the District, employees move further westward.

In Mountain Builders' geographic region, new construction activity has been running at double the national pace. Also, with the area's old farmhouses and pre–Civil War stone homes, restoration projects are abundant. Additionally, the District's population shift is raising the region's average income level. Over the last five years, Mountain Builders has enjoyed the luxury of choosing jobs. There has been more work than the company can handle.

## Seth Wevall

The Wevall family has lived in the area since the mid-1880s. Today, successful reunions gather 200 family members. The extended family comprises many skilled tradesmen, and Seth is the most financially successful. His prosperity is a result of the success of Mountain Builders and the family's judicious sale of agricultural land for residential development. As president of Mountain Builders, Seth abides by family values of hard work, craftsmanship that endures the test of time, fair prices, and precision.

## The Outlook

Seth is looking forward to retirement. Though still healthy and active, he is eager to spend more time hunting and fishing. Also, his two sons, Rick and Scott, are ready for greater decision-making and leadership responsibility in the business.

Seth recognizes that business has been excellent. Table C1.1 shows quarterly gross billings, the twenty-year fixed mortgage rate, and the county's population.

## The Concerns

Seth's wife, Mary, knows the business has provided for the family. Can the prosperity continue? Her concerns are as follows.

- The area has changed. Mountain Builders used to work for people who knew the company and its reputation for craftsmanship. Now buyers come from greater distances; they do not know the company, and the importance of the Wevall name is diminished.
- There are many more builders and renovators. Many advertise more aggressively. Also, the large retailers have diversified and not only

sell building materials but also link buyers with contractors.

- The prices of material have risen significantly and threaten profit margins.
- Mountain Builders now depends upon large national building supply companies for materials, and it is harder to obtain customized products.
- The company's ability to hire skillful tradesmen has diminished. Is the firm too demanding? Maybe there are too many opportunities for skilled personnel?
- Buyers are different. The company's best work is done for those who see their houses as a place to live and as long-term assets. Now, more and more, Mountain Builders does work for buyers who sell the property within three years. The enduring quality of the firm's work is less important to these buyers.
- The era of low long-term interest rates cannot last forever.
- Impending restrictions on residential development threaten the growth of the county's population. Environmental concerns, water and sewage capacities, and stresses on the road system, schools, police departments, and fire departments are expected to lead to stricter zoning, development impact fees, and denials of proposed housing developments.

## Discussion Questions

1. Plot the gross billing data over time and identify the trend. What is the approximate rate of increase over the time period? Do you observe any seasonal patterns?
2. Plot the gross billing data with the interest rate data. Estimate the intercept and slope and comment on the relationship between billing and mortgage rates. Repeat the task

*Table C 1.1*
**Historical Data**

| Time | Billings | County Population | 20-Year Mortgage Rate (Percent) |
|---|---|---|---|
| Year 1 | $ | | |
| Q I | 595,000 | 150,100 | 6.0 |
| Q II | 885,000 | 160,100 | 5.9 |
| Q III | 895,000 | 172,200 | 5.7 |
| Q IV | 605,000 | 185,000 | 5.6 |
| Year 2 | | | |
| Q I | 780,000 | 195,700 | 5.5 |
| Q II | 1,115,000 | 210,000 | 5.6 |
| Q III | 1,125,000 | 218,000 | 5.8 |
| Q IV | 790,000 | 229,000 | 5.9 |
| Year 3 | | | |
| Q I | 950,000 | 240,000 | 6.1 |
| Q II | 1,500,000 | 2251,000 | 6.1 |
| Q III | 1,600,000 | 260,000 | 6.2 |
| Q IV | 980,000 | 266,000 | 6.0 |
| Year 4 | | | |
| Q I | 1,200,000 | 276,000 | 5.9 |
| Q II | 1,926,000 | 281,000 | 5.8 |
| Q III | 2,160,000 | 288,000 | 5.8 |
| Q IV | 1,400,000 | 295,000 | 5.7 |

plotting gross billings and the county's population.

3. Forecast billings based on interest rates. Over the next four quarters the fixed-rate 30–year mortgage rate is projected to be 5.75 percent, 5.9 percent, 6.2 percent, and 6.5 percent.
4. Forecast gross billings over the next four quarters assuming the county's population to be 300,000, 306,000, 310,000, and 315,000.
5. Are you comfortable with the forecast based on interest rates? Are you more or

less comfortable with the forecast based on population growth? Why?

6. Describe each of the five forces of competition facing this firm. How do these forces affect the revenue and profit outlook for the firm?

7. Draw the production cost chain for Mountain Builders. What does it mean for the company to extend its vertical reach? What does it mean for it to extend its horizontal reach?

8. What are the critical variables that define the nature of the company's market?

9. Assume the role of Seth. What actions do you take? Why?

10. Use multiple regression techniques developed in Appendix 1.1. Test the importance of the independent variables. Forecast gross billings based on the population data from question 4 and the interest rate data in question 3. Comment on the results.

# 2

# Aggregate Output, Prices, and Economic Indicators

This chapter develops a model of a free market economy, contributes to our understanding of the macroeconomic environment, and examines the determination of the economy's aggregate output. Economic indicators are presented to help decision makers monitor the state of the economy and to align choices with the realities of the marketplace.

---

**Learning Objectives**

The successful reader understands:

- The nature of free market economies
- The role of aggregate demand in the determination of aggregate output
- How to use economic indicators to monitor the macroeconomy
- The multiplier and the interactions between components of aggregate demand
- The concept of aggregate supply and the relationship between aggregate supply, employment, and inflation
- Fiscal policy and supply-side economic policy
- How the macroeconomy affects business and personal decisions

---

## The Circular Flow of Income

Figure 2.1 depicts a two-sector (households and businesses) market economy. Both participants are defined by their activities. Households own the resources used in the production process and express a force of supply in the resource market, and they use the income earned in the resource market to express a force of demand in the goods market. Businesses express a force of demand in the resource market based on the expectation of producing a good or service salable for profit, and they express a force of supply in the goods market to sell their products.

The circular flow model is a useful tool in microeconomics. It shows the interactions between buyers and sellers and the role of the goods market and the resource market. The model assumes both households and businesses are motivated by self-interest. Households seek the highest possible payment for their resources and the lowest possible price for goods and services. Businesses have opposing objectives, seeking to pay the least for the resource inputs while realizing the highest price for their good or service. The interactions of the forces of supply and demand (examined more closely in Chapter 4) mediate the differences between buyers and sellers and lead to voluntary transactions. In macroeconomics the model shows the linkage from producing and earning income to the purchase of goods and services.

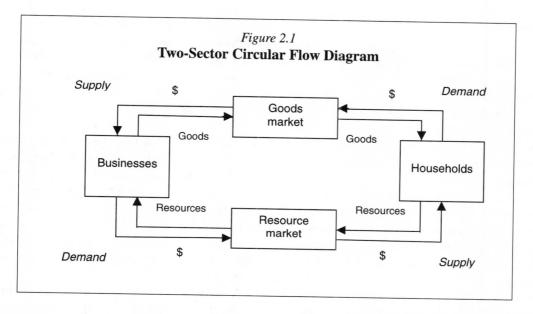

Figure 2.1
**Two-Sector Circular Flow Diagram**

### The Risk Takers

The risk-taking function of business is vital to creating output, jobs, and income, and entrepreneurial risk taking is the first step in the circular flow of income and wealth. In considering a new business venture, the owner assesses risks and rewards. If the assessment is favorable, the business purchases resource inputs with the expectation of assembling a good or service for sale and profit. The business owners accept financial obligations upon entering contractual agreements with the owners of the resource inputs, and these obligations are incurred prior to the production and sale of a good or service. These obligations create jobs, income, and households' abilities to purchase goods and services.

The acceptance of risk is evident for a new business, but it recurs for ongoing enterprises. Consider a clothing retailer who has operated successfully for many years. Months in advance of the fall selling season, the retailer orders inventory. The financial obligations are accepted by the retailer, who is immediately vulnerable to

changing consumer preferences and rivals' prices and merchandise selections. The risks of business ownership are continuous.

The important role of risk taking in a free market economy has political implications. For example, the taxation of business profits and the imposition of safety and environmental regulations adversely affect the risk/reward assessment. All else equal, higher taxes and regulations discourage risk taking and are detrimental to the creation of output, jobs, and income. However, society balances its need for tax collections to pay for publicly provided goods and to protect workers, consumers, and the environment against the desirability of preserving entrepreneurial initiatives.

---

**Exercise 2.1**

Present your views on the effect of taxes and regulation of entrepreneurial risk taking. How do your views affect the party you vote for? What public policy recommendations do you offer?

### The Markets

In the *goods market*, businesses express a force of supply when placing goods and services on the market for sale to households. Households express a force of demand when making voluntary purchases based on prices, preferences, and income. Business owners who surpass profit expectations in one period have an incentive to produce more in the following period, and new businesses are attracted to profitable industries. In contrast, owners who fail to meet profit expectations exit the marketplace. This free mobility of resources from one industry to another leads the economy to produce the mix of goods and services most desired by those who are willing and able to pay. While the free mobility of resources is advantageous for society as a whole, successful firms and industries seek to build barriers to entry to prevent the entry of new competitors to protect their markets and profitability.

Businesses express a force of demand for the resources market, and the demand is derived from the resources' expected contribution to the production of goods and services salable for profit. In the resource market, compensation for work and the distribution of income are based on a meritocracy. Those workers who are the most productive making goods and services that are profitable earn the highest wages. Those with lesser productivity and those who contribute to the production of less-profitable goods and services earn less. The merit-based reward system encourages individuals to acquire skills valued in the marketplace, motivates hard work, and directs resources toward the production of the most highly valued goods and services.

Incomes earned in the resource market determine a household's ability to purchase goods. Those who make the greatest contribution to the production process enter the goods market with the largest purchasing power and exert the largest influence on the mix of goods produced. The distribution of income and the pursuit of profit by risk takers explain why high-priced luxury items are produced while some people struggle with inadequate food, clothing, and shelter.

### Income Equals Output

The primary task of this chapter is to explain the determination of aggregate output and employment. The first step establishes the equality between income and output. Consider an economic system within which employees are paid in units of the product they produce. In this hypothetical barter economy, workers and others who have claims against a company are paid on the last day of the year.

As production occurs over the year, units of output accumulate in a storage area. On the last day of the year, workers and other claimants meet with the business owner to be paid. The owner distributes the products based upon contractual agreements. The payments fall into different categories. Workers are paid wages, sellers of land resources are paid rent, and lenders of financial resources are paid interest. As each claimant is paid, the stockpile of output diminishes. After all contractual claimants are paid, the residual belongs to the owner. This income is designated as profit. All output is either distributed to those with contractual obligations or claimed by the owner: *income equals output.*

Introducing money does not change the underlying relationship between income and output. Employers enter into contractual agreements with owners of the factors of production based upon the expected market value of their contribution to the production process. Payment is made with money. After the goods are sold for money and the contractual claimants paid, the owner claims the residual. The residual is the difference between sales receipts and contractual obligations plus any unsold goods.

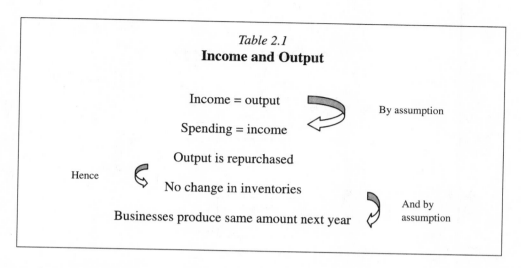

Table 2.1
**Income and Output**

Income = output

Spending = income

By assumption

Output is repurchased

Hence

No change in inventories

Businesses produce same amount next year

And by assumption

The equality between income and output means that the process of production creates enough income to repurchase what has been made.

## Model 1: Two-Sector Circular Flow (No Savings)

The equality between income and output is key to understanding how the aggregate level of output and employment is determined. Several assumptions are made in this initial look at the macroeconomy. (1) Only households and businesses are included. Government and international transactions are added later in the chapter. (2) Income earners do not save. All income is spent on consumer goods; no resources are available for businesses to produce new tools or machines for sale to other businesses. Savings and business investment in new machinery are added later. (3) In the aggregate, businesses produce an amount equal to the level of sales in the prior period.

Table 2.1 summarizes an initial look at the macroeconomy. (1) Income is equal to output. (2) By assumption, spending and income are the same; therefore, spending equals output. (3) All of the goods produced are sold. (4) By assumption, busi-

nesses in the aggregate produce in the next period the amount sold in the current period.

The equality between spending and output does not imply that businesses produced the mix of goods desired by consumers. As buyers express their preferences for particular goods through their spending patterns, the demand for some products is strong, and their prices rise. For other products, the demand is weaker and prices fall. In the ensuing period, risk takers respond to the price changes and produce more of some goods and less of other goods. Though the mix of goods changes, the aggregate value of the output (which equals income) remains unchanged.

## Model 2: Savings with No Business Investment

In this model, households save. Figure 2.2 shows savings as a *leakage* from the circular flow of income. Savings are a leakage because they are a part of current income that is not used by the income recipient to purchase goods and services. To isolate the effect of savings, it is assumed that businesses do not buy new facilities or tools.

Given the equality of income and output, if some

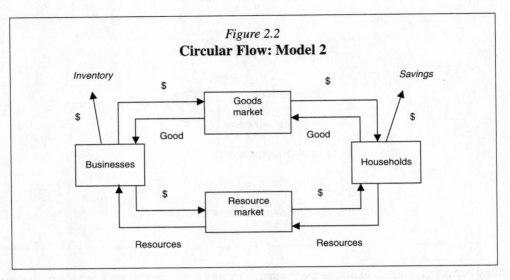

*Figure 2.2*
**Circular Flow: Model 2**

income is not spent on goods and services (savings), some currently produced goods are not sold. The unsold goods accumulate in inventory, and the dollar amount saved equals the market value of the accumulated inventory. This accumulation of inventory prompts businesses to produce fewer units in the following period, and output, employment, and income decline. In contrast, if households deplete savings, previously accumulated inventories decrease. Businesses respond by producing more in the following period. Output, employment, and income rise. Therefore, an economy's output, employment, and income grow or decline based upon the purchase of goods and services and the changes in inventory levels.

### Aggregate Demand

This model highlights the importance of the purchase of goods and services and the role of changes in inventories in business expansions or contractions. Table 2.2 summarizes the relationships between spending, income, inventory changes, and the expansion or contraction of aggregate output and employment. If spending is less than income, inventories grow. Businesses respond by producing

fewer goods, and the economy shrinks. If spending exceeds income, inventories decline. Businesses respond by increasing production, and the economy expands. If spending equals income, inventories neither grow nor shrink. The aggregate production rate is validated, and businesses produce the same aggregate amount in the next period.

In this model the only component of spending is household consumption. In ensuing pages, business investment, government, and exports are added as components of aggregate demand. In the contemporary U.S. economy, consumer spending constitutes approximately two-thirds of the aggregate demand. The remaining one-third is made up of business investment spending, government spending on goods and services, and the net export of goods and services. Household consumption is the dominant spending force in the economy, and to forecast the macroeconomy it is important to monitor households' willingness and ability to spend.

### Economic Indicators: An Introduction

The term *macroeconomic indicators* refers to measures of aggregate economic activity and includes

### Table 2.2
### Income, Spending, Inventory, and Aggregate Output

If

Spending < income

Inventory rises

Economy contracts

If

Spending > income

Inventory falls

Economy expands

---

### Application Box 2.1

Alan Greenspan, before serving as chairman of the Federal Reserve, ran a consulting business. One leading indicator he used to forecast future economic growth was the sale of corrugated boxes. The increasing sale of boxes, he surmised, meant business was gearing up to produce and ship more goods.

*Source:* Justin Martin, *Greenspan* (Cambridge, Mass: Perseus Press, 2000), p. 57.

### Table 2.3
### Selected Economic Indicators

| Leading Indicators | Concurrent Indicators |
|---|---|
| Index of Consumer Confidence | Unemployment rate |
| New orders for durable goods | Payroll |
| Inventory-to-sales ratio | Industrial production |
| Building permits | Retail sales |
| Debt-to-income ratio | Car sales |
| Stock market valuations | New home sales |
| Inches of newspaper help-wanted advertisements | Sales of durable goods |

---

employment, production, and sales data. Many indicators are reported in the popular press and are available on the Internet. The indicators allow decision makers to monitor the macroeconomy and to align choices with the realities of the marketplace.

Macroeconomic indicators fall into three categories. *Concurrent indicators* measure the current level of macroeconomic activity and include output, employment, income, and sales data. *Leading indicators* predict the future. For example, new unemployment compensation claims are a leading indicator, whereas employment is a concurrent indicator; consumer confidence is a leading indicator; retail sales and home purchases are concurrent indicators; the number of building permits is a leading indicator; new housing starts and construction employment are concurrent indicators; the ratio of inventory to sales is a leading indicator; and employment and industrial production are concurrent indicators. Table 2.3 lists leading and concurrent indicators relevant to models 1 and 2. The discussion of *lagging indicators* is deferred until later in this chapter.

The macroeconomic model is expanded in the following pages to include business investment, government spending, and international transactions. In turn, the list of macroeconomic indicators is lengthened. In Chapter 3, the discussion of money and the financial system adds interest rate and money supply indicators.

---

**Exercise 2.2**

Go to www.economagic.com and click on "Most Requested Series."

Showing the recession periods and plotting data from 1980 to the present, print the following GIF charts:

(a) Total industrial production
(b) Unemployment rate
(c) Percentage change in the real gross domestic product
(d) S&P 500 total returns

Describe the commonalities of the data patterns. Explain.

---

## Model 3: Savings and Business Investment

This model introduces investment spending. In gross domestic product accounting, investment spending is *gross private domestic investment*. This category includes business investment in plant and equipment and software, residential construction, and inventory investment. Before proceeding with this model, investment spending and financial investments are carefully distinguished. Investment spending purchases a tangible product, including a tool, machine, or structure. It is a component of aggregate demand along with consumption. In contrast, financial investment is an act of saving; no good or service is purchased, but purchasing power is transferred from the saver to the borrower. Financial investment is not a component of aggregate demand.

Four points are made. (1) Gross private domestic investment is distinguished from net private domestic investment, which subtracts depreciation. Net investment grows the nation's capital stock.

(2) Gross private domestic investment does not include public sector investment spending on roads and other aspects of infrastructure; these items are recorded as government purchases. (3) Gross private domestic investment spending is a volatile component of aggregate demand because these costly purchases are sensitive to business expectations and can be postponed. (4) Gross private domestic investment is the way an economy builds its capital base and expands its production potential.

Figure 2.3 includes investment spending in the circular flow model. Households earn income in the resource market. Some of the income is used for consumption and some is saved. Savings are a leakage (income earned not currently spent by the income recipient), and business investment is an *injection* (spending on goods and services beyond currently earned income). In Figure 2.3, households direct savings dollars into the financial system (banks, the stock market, etc.), which facilitates the transfer of funds for businesses to make investments. Figure 2.3 makes two simplifying assumptions. First, the figure shows investment spending by businesses in plant and equipment, but investment spending in residential construction is not shown. Second, the figure shows all savings originating from households, yet business and government units also save. Both assumptions minimize the complexity of Figure 2.3.

As seen in Figure 2.3, household savings are a leakage. Leakages, all else equal, lead to inventory accumulation and, in turn, to less output, employment, and income in the following period. However, the unemployed resources are available to produce machines and tools for sale to other businesses. Entrepreneurs choose to produce machines and tools, which are investment products for sale in the goods market.

The financial system plays an important role in facilitating the transfer of funds from savers to support investment. Structures and equipment

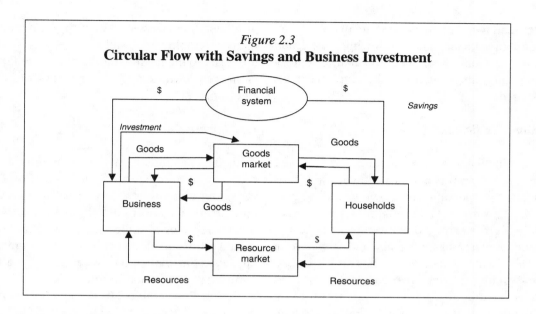

*Figure 2.3*
**Circular Flow with Savings and Business Investment**

have multiyear lives and are paid for over their useful life. Therefore, businesses that purchase capital equipment turn to the financial system to acquire purchasing power. Businesses acquire financing through, for example, a bank loan, a bond issue, or the sale of new shares of stock. Those who save and those who make business investments are not the same. Therefore, a well-developed system of financial institutions and markets facilitates the transfer of purchasing power from savers to borrowers.

The amount households save and the amount businesses want to invest are not necessarily the same, and Table 2.4 summarizes the effect on the economy. If savings exceed business investment, inventories accrue and output and employment shrink in the following period. If business investment spending is greater than savings, previously accumulated inventories are depleted. Businesses respond by increasing output and employment in the following period.

Given that income equals output, Table 2.4 indicates that (1) if aggregate demand (consump-

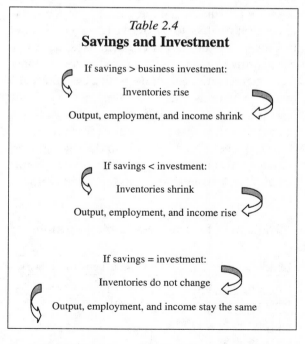

*Table 2.4*
**Savings and Investment**

If savings > business investment:

Inventories rise

Output, employment, and income shrink

If savings < investment:

Inventories shrink

Output, employment, and income rise

If savings = investment:

Inventories do not change

Output, employment, and income stay the same

tion plus investment, C + I) is less than income, inventories accumulate, and the economy contracts in the following period, (2) if aggregate demand is greater than income, inventories are depleted, and the economy expands in the following period, and (3) if savings and investment are equal, inventory levels remain unchanged and the output remains unchanged.

### Economic Indicators

With the inclusion of investment spending in the model, leading and concurrent economic indicators of investment spending are shown in Table 2.5.

The current level of business investment spending, gross private domestic investment, is a component of aggregate demand and a concurrent indicator. Leading indicators of business investment spending fall into two categories. One set of measures reflects the need for additional tools, machinery, and workspace and includes the rate of capacity utilization and the outlook for economic expansion relative to capacity. The second set of leading indicators refers to businesses' ability to finance investment spending and includes long-term interest rates, corporate profits, cash flow, and equity valuations. Because investment spending also includes residential construction, building permits are included as a leading indicator.

These leading indicators help decision makers monitor and anticipate the level of macroeconomic activity. If leading indicators appear favorable,

### Table 2.5
### Indicators for Business Capital Spending

| Leading Indicators | Concurrent Indicators |
| --- | --- |
| Capacity use rate | Gross private domestic investment |
| Business outlook | |
| Corporate profitability | |
| Cash flow | |
| Equity valuations | |
| Building permits | |

producers accelerate production schedules and increase employment and income. Equity investors react to the leading indicators by anticipating earnings growth and push the prices of cyclical stocks higher.

### Equilibrium Income

Table 2.6 is a numeric model that highlights macroeconomic interactions and fluctuations. Two important conditions are cited before examining the numeric model. By definition, the *equilibrium income* level, once achieved, is repeated until disturbed by an outside force. Also, it is assumed that businesses in the aggregate produce the amount purchased in the prior period.

Period 1 (see Table 2.6) is an equilibrium condition, as evidenced by the following: (1) Income equals aggregate demand (consumption plus business investment). Government spending, tax, imports, and exports are added as components of aggregate demand later in this chapter. For now, tax, government spending, imports, and exports are recorded with zeros. (2) Leakages (savings) and injections (investment) are equal. (3) There is no change in the level of inventory.

In period 1, aggregate income (equal to output) is $100. Because government is not yet included in the model, there are no taxes, and there is no government spending. Income and disposable income (income less tax) are the same. Households use $90 of their income for consumption and save $10. Imports and exports are zero because the international sector has not yet been introduced. Investment spending is $10. Aggregate demand (C + I) equals income, and there is no change in inventory. By assumption, business produces in period 2 the amount sold in period 1. The macroeconomy is in equilibrium.

In period 2, income is unchanged at $100. Household consumption spending and savings do

*Table 2.6*
## National Income Determination

|  | Period 1 | Period 2 | Period 3 | Period 4 | New Equilibrium |
|---|---|---|---|---|---|
| Income | $100 | $100 | $110 | $118 | $150 |
| Tax | 0 | 0 | 0 | 0 | 0 |
| Disposable income | 100 | 100 | 110 | 118 | 150 |
| Consumption | 90 | 90 | 98 | 104.4 | 130 |
| Savings | 10 | 10 | 12 | 13.6 | 20 |
| Government | 0 | 0 | 0 | 0 | 0 |
| Imports | 0 | 0 | 0 | 0 | 0 |
| Exports | 0 | 0 | 0 | 0 | 0 |
| Investment | 10 | 20 | 20 | 20 | 20 |
| Aggregate demand | 100 | 110 | 118 | 124.4 | 150 |
| Change in Inventory | 0 | −10 | −8 | −6.4 | 0 |

not change. By assumption, investment spending increases to $20. In turn, aggregate demand (C + I) rises to $110; spending exceeds income, injections exceed leakages, and inventories decline by $10. The equilibrium income is disturbed by the increase in investment spending. Businesses respond to the decline in inventories by increasing the aggregate production in period 3.

To track the consequences of the inventory depletion in period 3 and beyond, it is necessary to introduce the *multiplier.*

### The Multiplier

The multiplier process is initiated by the increase in investment spending of $10 in period 2. In period 2, aggregate demand rises to $110 and exceeds income. Businesses respond to the increase in aggregate demand and the decline in inventory by producing in period 3 an amount equal to period 2's aggregate demand. In period 3, income is $110.

Because there are no taxes, disposable income rises to $110 in period 3. How do households respond to the increase in their income?

To answer the question, the *marginal propensity to consume* (MPC) is introduced. The MPC is the proportion of an additional dollar of income that is used for consumption. In Table 2.6 it is assumed the MPC is 0.8. This value indicates that households increase their consumption by $0.80 for each additional dollar of income. Correspondingly, the *marginal propensity to save* (MPS) is 0.2 because the amount not used for consumption is saved. In period 3, households increase their consumption by $8, to $98. Savings rise to $12.

In Table 2.6, period 3 is not an equilibrium condition. Aggregate demand (C + I = $118) is greater than income ($100), leakages (S = $12) are less than injections (I = $20), and inventories are depleted by $8. Businesses respond in period 4 and produce an amount equal to the aggregate

*Table 2.7*
**The Multiplier**

$$\text{Multiplier} = k = \frac{1}{1 - \text{MPC}}$$

where MPC $= 0.8$

$$k = \frac{1}{1 - 0.8} = \frac{1}{0.2} = 5.0$$

demand in period 3. In period 4, income and output rise to $118. Households respond to the increase in income, and consumption rises by 80 percent of the increase in income. Consumption in period 4 is $104.40 (= $98 + (0.8 × $8)). Savings rise to $13.60 (= $12 + (0.2 × $8)). The economy is not in equilibrium, but the decline in inventories is getting smaller in successive periods as households save a portion of each increase in income.

The multiplier is unfolding. The initial change in investment spending sets off a chain reaction of increases in income that spark increases in consumption, which increase income and, again, increase consumption. Importantly, consumption spending rises by only a portion of the increase in income (the MPC is less than 1); therefore, in successive rounds the increases in income and consumption shrink and approach zero. The increase in income attributable to the initial increase in investment spending is the multiplier, and the size of the multiplier depends upon the value of the MPC. The higher the MPC, the greater the sequential impact on consumption spending, the larger the multiplier, and the greater the increase in income.

Table 2.7 calculates the multiplier $k$.

Table 2.7 shows a marginal propensity to consume of 0.8, and the multiplier is 5. The multiplier means that the $10 initial increase in spending (see Table 2.6) has a fivefold impact

**Application Box 2.2**

The example in Table 2.6 indicates the critical roles of aggregate demand and changes in inventory as drivers of the macroeconomy.

In recent years changes in technology have allowed businesses to react more quickly to changes in demand, thereby preventing large increases in inventory levels. One consequence is that the intensity of swings in the business cycle may be damped. While year-to-year business cycle volatility may be muted, there may also be greater month-to-month volatility.

*Source:* David Leonhardt, "Have Recessions Absolutely, Positively Become Less Painful?" *New York Times,* October 8, 2005.

on income. The change in the equilibrium level of income prompted by the initial change in investment spending is $50 (see Table 2.6). The resultant equilibrium income in the final period is $150.

Following Table 2.6, the final period is calculated as followed. The new equilibrium level of income is $150 (= $100 + (5 × $10)) where the multiplier is equal to 5 and the initial increase in spending is $10. Taxes do not change, and the disposable income is $150. From the initial period, disposable income rises by $50. Households increase consumption by 80 percent of the increase in disposable income, and consumption rises from $90 to $130. The $50 increase in disposable income, with the MPS at 0.2, leads to a $10 increase in savings to $20. At an income level of $150, aggregate demand equals income at $150, leakages (savings) equal injections (investment) at $20, and there is no change in the level of inventory. The macroeconomy is in equilibrium.

## Local and Microeconomic Effects of the Multiplier

The multiplier process has local and microeconomic effects on a firm's environment. Consider a municipality examining the use of tax dollars to build a new sports complex for a major league team. The construction spending creates new jobs and income, which set off a multiplier process. Higher incomes lead to more consumption spending and, in turn, to higher income. Further, games and other events attract visitors to the community, who stay in hotels, park vehicles, eat in restaurants, and purchase items from the concessions. These outlays spark the multiplier. If the multiplier is sufficiently large, the increase in income and associated increase in tax collections pays for the initial investment in the sports complex.

The analysis of local projects such as a sports complex, industrial park, or airport necessitates distinguishing between the multiplier and the *local multiplier*. Consider the sports complex. If the architectural firm that designs it is hired from outside the local community, if materials are purchased from outside the community, or if workers reside or spend their income elsewhere, income and spending increases occur beyond the community's boundaries. The local multiplier is determined by how much of the successive increases in income are earned and spent locally. The local multiplier is smaller as more purchases are made outside of the community.

### Application Box 2.3

Advocates for the building of the Arizona Diamondbacks' baseball stadium in Phoenix used economic impact statements to make their case to the public. The studies promised a large multiplier effect for the city of Phoenix. Most trained economists criticized the studies, saying that the local multiplier was actually much smaller, as most income would be spent outside of the city. Taxpayers sided with the economists and voted no to the building of the new stadium. The city council then changed the law that required taxpayers to vote and had the stadium built with public monies anyway.

*Source:* Len Sherman, *Big League, Big Time: The Birth of the Arizona Diamondbacks, the Billion-Dollar Business of Sports, and the Power of Media in America* (New York: Simon and Schuster, 1998).

### Application Box 2.4

The multiplier also works in reverse and is a reason why the closure of a military base threatens the vitality of a local economy. A closure leads to termination of contracts with local suppliers and removes disposable income from the community. As local retail expenditures by military personnel and their suppliers are reduced, other incomes in the community fall; jobs are also lost, which causes further reductions in spending and income.

The multiplier also has important microeconomic implications. For example, assume a business purchases a new forklift. The manufacturer of the forklift hires more workers and purchases additional materials. The new workers receive income and spend a portion of it within their hometown. The sequential income recipients spend a portion of their increased income locally. In contrast, assume the initial change in spending involves the purchase of a new computer or communications system. A different set of industries, suppliers, employees, and geographic regions is affected. The microeconomic effects of the multiplier differ because different firms participate in the production cost chains and because different geographic regions are affected. Firms and their employees must anticipate their participation in multiplier processes and align their decisions with the realities of their particular circumstances.

### The Accelerator

In Table 2.6, the initial increase in investment spending prompts sequential increases in income and consumption, and the resultant change in income is a multiple of the initial increase in business investment spending. In Table 2.6 the initial increase in business investment spending is sustained at the higher level. If businesses reduce investment spending to the original level, the economy returns to its initial equilibrium income. Further, in Table 2.6, the successive increases in consumption increase output, but businesses do not add to their plant and equipment. It is, however, reasonable that businesses need to add plant and equipment to produce more. Therefore, as increases in income prompt increases in consumption, there are also increases in business investment. The increase in investment spending increases the multiplier, and the change in investment spending based on changes in the economy's aggregate output defines the *accelerator*.

Table 2.8 expands the multiplier by introducing the *marginal propensity to invest* (MPI). The MPI is the change in investment spending relative to the change in income. An MPI of 0.1 means that a $10 increase in income prompts a $1 increase in investment spending. An increase in aggregate demand now leads to an increase in consumption plus an increase in investment spending. The multiplier gets larger; the calculation is shown in Table 2.8.

With the assumption that the MPC is 0.8 and the MPI is 0.1, the multiplier effect is ten times the initial increase in spending. Table 2.9 shows

*Table 2.8*
### Expanded Multiplier

$$\text{Multiplier} = k = \frac{1}{1 - \text{MPC} - \text{MPI}}$$

where:
$$\text{MPC} = 0.8$$
$$\text{MPI} = 0.1$$

$$\text{Multiplier} = k = \frac{1}{1 - 0.8 - 0.1}$$

$$\text{Multiplier} = k = 10.0$$

the effect of the expanded multiplier. The initial equilibrium conditions are the same as in Table 2.6, and the increase in investment spending in the second round is the same as shown previously.

In period 2, the equilibrium is disrupted by the $10 increase in business investment spending, and inventory levels are depleted by $10. In period 3, income and output rise by $10 as businesses produce the level of aggregate demand in the prior period. The $10 increase in income has two effects. First, it prompts an $8 increase in consumption based on the marginal propensity to consume. Second, it prompts businesses to increase their spending on plant and equipment by $1 above the prior period level. Investment spending rises to $21. In period 3, aggregate demand is $119 and inventories decline by $9. Compared to Table 2.6, the expansion of the economy is larger. Firms engaged in the production and sale of investment products carefully monitor leading indicators of investment spending to meet the changing demand for new plant and equipment.

In period 4, businesses respond by producing $119. There is a $9 increase in income and disposable income. Households spend 80 percent of the increase in income (MPC = 0.8), and consumption rises to $105.20. Savings rise to $13.80. Importantly, invest-

*Table 2.9*
**National Income Determination with the Accelerator**

|  | Period 1 | Period 2 | Period 3 | Period 4 | New Equilibrium |
|---|---|---|---|---|---|
| Income | $100 | $100 | $110 | $119 | $200 |
| Tax | 0 | 0 | 0 | 0 | 0 |
| Disposable income | 100 | 100 | 110 | 119 | 200 |
| Consumption | 90 | 90 | 98 | 105.20 | 170 |
| Savings | 10 | 10 | 12 | 13.80 | 30 |
| Government | 0 | 0 | 0 | 0 | 0 |
| Imports | 0 | 0 | 0 | 0 | 0 |
| Exports | 0 | 0 | 0 | 0 | 0 |
| Investment | 10 | 20 | 21 | 21.10 | 30 |
| Aggregate demand | 100 | 110 | 119 | 127.30 | 200 |
| Change in inventory | 0 | −10 | −9 | −8.30 | 0 |

**Application Box 2.5**

The assumption that businesses produce an output equal to the prior period's aggregate demand simplifies the analysis. However, the assumption negates business expectations that are a source of macroeconomic instability. Consider, for example, an expanding economy. With expectations of rising sales, businesses produce an output in excess of the prior period's aggregate demand, and the economy grows faster. However, if the expectations were overly optimistic, businesses experience inventory accumulations. The following decline in economic activity is intensified as business expectations turn decidedly negative.

ment spending continues to increase by 10 percent of the change in income (MPI = 0.1), and investment spending rises to $21.10. Aggregate demand equals $127.30, and the decline in inventory is $8.30.

The resulting equilibrium level of income is $200. The initial change in investment spending of $10 sets off a multiplier process, and the multiplier is 10 (see Table 2.8). Hence, income rises by $100 from the initial equilibrium. Household consumption rises by $80 (MPC = 0.8) to $170; savings rise by $20 (= 0.2 × $100) to $30. In the new equilibrium, aggregate demand equals income, and inventory levels do not change; leakages (S = $30) equal injections (I = $30).

## Model 4: Three-Sector Circular Flow

This model introduces government spending (G) and taxation (T) (see Figure 2.4). For simplicity, Figure 2.4 does not show the savings and investments flows.

In Figure 2.4 taxes are a leakage and analogous to savings. Taxes are a portion of currently earned income not directly used to purchase goods and services. Government may spend the tax dollar on

**Exercise 2.3**

Complete the table using the following assumptions:

  (a)  MPC = 0.7
  (b)  MPS = 0.3
  (c)  MPI = 0.2
  (d)  Investment spending rises to $40 in period 2

National Income Determination

|  | Period 1 | Period 2 | Period 3 | Period 4 | New Equilibrium |
|---|---|---|---|---|---|
| Income | $200 | | | | |
| Tax | 0 | | | | |
| Disposable income | 200 | | | | |
| Consumption | 170 | | | | |
| Savings | 30 | | | | |
| Imports | 0 | | | | |
| Exports | 0 | | | | |
| Government | 0 | | | | |
| Investment | 30 | 40 | | | |
| Aggregate demand | 200 | | | | |
| Change in inventory | 0 | | | | |

Check your results. Show for the new equilibrium:
   (a)  Aggregate demand equals income
   (b)  Injections equal leakage

defense or roads, but the payment of tax is separate from the government's purchases. Government spending is an injection and analogous to investment spending. Both are components of aggregate demand. Investments are paid for by acquiring (through loans, the sale of bonds, or the sale of new stock) the savings of income earners. Government spending is paid for through tax collections or borrowing. Figure 2.4 does not show how the government finances a budgetary deficit or disposes of a budgetary surplus. These topics are deferred until Chapter 3.

Government spending is differentiated from government outlays, which include payments that shift purchasing power from one household to another. For example, one household pays tax and another receives a welfare or social security payment. The outlay is the social security or welfare payment. The transfer recipient's purchases are recorded as consumption. In contrast, the government's purchase of a jet fighter buys a product and is part of the aggregate demand for goods and services.

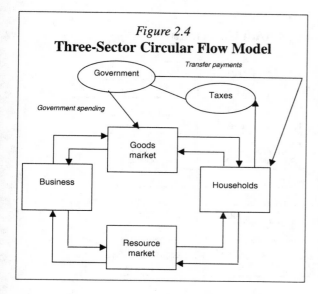

*Figure 2.4*
**Three-Sector Circular Flow Model**

## Fiscal Policy

In Table 2.10, period 1 is an equilibrium condition: aggregate demand (consumption + investment + government = $150) equals income, leakages (savings + taxes = $30) equal injections (government + investment), and inventory levels are unchanged. By assumption, the full employment level of income is $250. There is need to stimulate the economy to full employment. With the MPC = 0.8 (the multiplier equals 5), government stimulates the economy by raising its spending level in period 2 to $40. Two points are emphasized. First, the increase in aggregate demand disrupts the equilibrium, and inventory is depleted by $20 in period 2. Second, the $20 increase in government spending, given that the multiplier is 5, boosts the equilibrium by $100, from $150 to $250, and leads to full employment.

With government in the model, two observations are noted: (1) Income earners pay taxes. For simplicity, taxes are a fixed dollar amount ($10) and do not vary with income. Income minus tax is disposable income, and changes in consumption are prompted by changes in disposable income. In Table 2.10, the marginal propensity to consume is 0.8, and investment spending does not rise with increases in income. (2) Government in Table 2.10 refers to spending on goods and services and excludes transfer payments. International transactions are not included; imports and exports are shown with zeros.

The depletion of inventory (by $20) in period 2 induces business to expand production, and income rises to $170 in period 3. Businesses (by assumption) produce the level of aggregate demand in the prior period. Taxes remain unchanged, and disposable income rises to $160. The $20 change in disposable income leads to a $16 increase in consumption (= 0.8 × $20) and a $4 increase in savings (= 0.2 × $20). Aggregate demand (C + I + G) is $186, and inventories are depleted by $16 in period 3.

The new equilibrium level of income is $250. The increase in the equilibrium level is the multiplier (here, 5) times the increase in government spending ($20). There is no accelerator in this model; by assumption, investment spending does not rise with the increase in aggregate demand. With the $100 increase in income, taxes do not change; hence, disposable income rises by $100 and consumption increases by $80 to $200. Savings increase by $20, equal to the marginal propensity to save (0.2) multiplied by the change in income ($100). Imports and exports remain at zero; government spending stays at the higher level, and investment spending is unchanged. Aggregate demand (C + I + G) equals $200; leakages (S + T) equal injections (I + G), and the change in inventory is zero.

In the new equilibrium, government is in *budgetary deficit* by $30. Spending is $40 and taxes are only $10. This deficit is justifiable because the economy needed a boost to full employment. How the government finances this deficit is an

*Table 2.10*
**National Income Determination with Government**

|                     | Period 1 | Period 2 | Period 3 | Period 4 | New Equilibrium |
|---------------------|----------|----------|----------|----------|-----------------|
| Income              | $150     | $150     | $170     | $186     | $250            |
| Tax                 | 10       | 10       | 10       | 10       | 10              |
| Disposable income   | 140      | 140      | 160      | 176      | 240             |
| Consumption         | 120      | 120      | 136      | 148.8    | 200             |
| Savings             | 20       | 20       | 24       | 27.2     | 40              |
| Imports             | 0        | 0        | 0        | 0        | 0               |
| Exports             | 0        | 0        | 0        | 0        | 0               |
| Government          | 20       | 40       | 40       | 40       | 40              |
| Investment          | 10       | 10       | 10       | 10       | 10              |
| Aggregate demand    | 150      | 170      | 186      | 198.9    | 250             |
| Change in inventory | 0        | –20      | –16      | –12.8    | 0               |

important question, but the analysis is deferred to Chapter 3.

Table 2.10 shows the expansion of the economy based on an increase in government spending. An alternative expansionary policy is to lower taxes. Lower taxes increase disposable income, stimulate consumption spending, and raise aggregate demand. However, the effects of a tax cut are smaller than an equal dollar increase in government spending. For example, a $10 increase in government spending raises aggregate demand by that amount and prompts the multiplier process. A $10 tax cut leads to an increase in spending by less than $10 because the marginal propensity to consume is less than 1. Only a portion of a change in income is used for consumption, and the initial economic stimulus that sets off the multiplier is smaller.

The microeconomic effects of tax and spending are different. Government purchases are different from those of households; hence, different industries, firms, employees, suppliers, regions, and stockholders are affected. The effect of tax cuts may extend beyond the consequences of aggregate demand. If lower tax rates spur entre-preneurial risk taking, the economy's ability to produce expands.

Table 2.10 is an example of expansionary fiscal policy. Fiscal policy also works in reverse. When private sector aggregate demand is in excess of the economy's ability to produce, market conditions allow sellers to raise their prices. This circumstance is *demand-pull inflation*. To reduce aggregate demand and damp inflation, government reduces spending and prompts a multiplier process that

**Application Box 2.6**

If lower-income households have a greater marginal propensity to consume than higher-income households, tax cuts for the poor have a larger multiplier effect than tax cuts for the rich.

The effects of tax cuts also include greater incentives to work and to accept business risks. Lower taxes may prompt the formation of new businesses and increases in employment and income.

*Exercise 2.4*

Refer to Table 2.6 and complete the following table, indicating by period whether the selected economic indicators are rising or falling. Indicate if the variable is a leading or a concurrent indicator.

| Indicator | Period 3 | Period 4 | Period 5 | Leading or Concurrent Indicator |
|---|---|---|---|---|
| Consumer confidence | | | | |
| Industrial production | | | | |
| Orders for durable goods | | | | |
| Retail sales | | | | |
| Unemployment rate | | | | |
| New home sales | | | | |
| Building permits | | | | |
| Car sales | | | | |

reduces consumption spending. Equilibrium is restored at a lower level of aggregate demand.

*Effectiveness of Fiscal Policy*

The numeric calculation of the effects of fiscal policy does not consider two problems. First, the implementation of fiscal policy occurs through the political process at the federal level. Congress makes spending and tax decisions. Expansionary fiscal policy (spending increases and tax decreases) wins votes. Spending cuts and tax increases are less popular. Therefore, fiscal policy is more likely applied to stimulate the economy than to restrain it. Second, fiscal policy needs time to affect the economy. In the numeric model, government spending increases in period 3 and the multiplier process is prompted in period 4. In the real world, there is a *recognition lag*, an *action lag*, and an *operational lag:* the unemployment must be recognized and a spending or tax bill proposed, passed, and implemented before the multiplier begins. The lag effect of fiscal policy creates problems. Policy makers must forecast future economic conditions and initiate policy before macroeconomic problems occur. Once policy initiatives are undertaken, it takes time for those actions to affect the macroeconomy.

*Supply-Side Economics*

Table 2.10 traces the macroeconomic effects of expansionary fiscal policy. However, from Table 2.10 it is not possible to determine if the increase in equilibrium income is attributable to more output, higher prices, or some combination of the two. To make the determination and to introduce *supply-side economics* the concept of the *aggregate supply curve* is introduced.

The aggregate supply curve shows the relationship between the price level (on the vertical axis) and the economy's real output (on the horizontal axis) (see Figure 2.5). On the left-hand side of Figure 2.5, the aggregate supply curve is horizontal up to full employment and then vertical. The shape of the curve reflects pricing decisions across the economy. Along the horizontal section

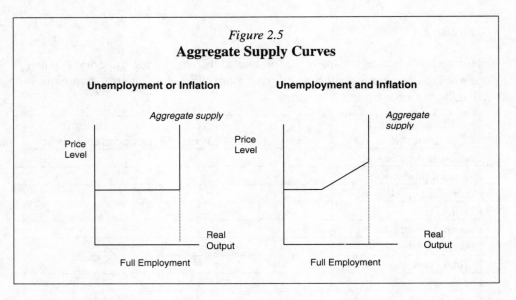

*Figure 2.5*
**Aggregate Supply Curves**

of the aggregate supply curve, businesses respond to increases in aggregate demand by producing more output. They do not raise prices, perhaps a result of intense interfirm competition. The vertical portion of the curve occurs at full employment production. At full employment, more output cannot be produced. In response to increases in aggregate demand, businesses raise their prices. This section of the aggregate supply curve reflects demand-pull inflation: aggregate demand exceeds the economy's ability to produce and leads to higher prices.

This formulation of the aggregate supply curve leads to an interesting conclusion. Unemployment is the result of too little aggregate demand, and inflation is the result of aggregate demand in excess of the economy's ability to produce. With this aggregate supply curve, an economy experiences either inflation or unemployment, but not both at the same time.

The aggregate supply curve on the right-hand side of Figure 2.5 reflects different pricing behaviors. The critical difference is the upward-sloping portion of the aggregate supply. This portion of the

aggregate supply curve indicates that firms raise their prices and increase output as the economy approaches full employment. One consequence is that inflation occurs before the economy expands to full employment production. The prior conclusion that either inflation or unemployment occurs is revised. Rising prices are associated with declining unemployment; less inflation is associated with higher unemployment.

There are several reasons why prices increase prior to full employment, thereby causing the upward-sloping portion of the aggregate supply curve. (1) Full employment refers to the economy as a whole. However, some firms reach their capacity to produce and some resources are fully utilized before the economy as a whole reaches full employment. Shortages of particular labor skills or natural resources and capacity limitations in some industries lead to higher prices. (2) As the economy moves closer to full employment, production costs rise. It is increasingly expensive to attract and retain employees. Firms pay overtime wages to meet orders for their products, passing the higher costs forward to buyers through higher

**Application Box 2.7**

The historical pattern of inflation and unemployment is shown in the Phillips curve. The Phillips curve is drawn by plotting annual inflation and unemployment rates and drawing a curve that describes the pattern of data points.

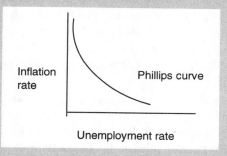

The downward slope of the Phillips curve confirms that lower inflation is realized when the unemployment rate is higher, and higher rates of employment coincide with more rapid price increases.

prices. (3) In markets characterized by monopoly-like selling conditions, firms raise prices as the economy expands toward full employment. (4) As the economy expands toward full employment, the rising pressure on prices is reflected in *lagging economic indicators*. As production strains capacity, the prices of industrial commodities rise, unit labor costs increase, and vendor deliveries slow.

The upward-sloping portion of the aggregate supply curve creates a dilemma for policy makers. Expansionary fiscal policy (spending increases and tax cuts) to stimulate the economy and reduce unemployment leads to inflation. Contractionary fiscal policy (less spending and higher taxes) reduces inflation at the expense of higher unemployment. The goal of full employment without inflation is elusive.

On the upward-sloping portion of the aggregate supply curve, fiscal policy is unable to achieve full employment and stable prices at the same time.

*Supply-side economic policies* supplement fiscal policy. The goal of supply-side policies is to alter the trade-off between inflation and unemployment. With successful supply-side policies, the economy achieves higher levels of employment with lower rates of inflation. Supply-side policies change businesses' pricing and production decisions. By encouraging more output rather than higher prices, supply-side policies flatten the aggregate supply curve and reduce the rate of price increases as the economy expands to full employment.

**Application Box 2.8**

The Laffer curve shows the relationship between tax rates and tax revenues collected. The concept of the Laffer curve is that tax rates have two effects on the amount of revenue collected. First, per dollar of tax base, higher or lower tax rates raise or lower collections. The second concept is more intriguing: lower tax rates may have the effect of increasing the tax base by providing greater incentives for work, employment, and output.

The Laffer curve suggests the possibility that lower tax rates could stimulate enough additional economic activity to actually increase the revenues collected.

Supply-side economic policy relies upon improving incentives to produce, and so it includes tax cuts to promote new investments in plant and equipment and new business formation, the reduction of regulations to encourage increased output, antitrust policies to foster competition among rival sellers, and policies to reduce barriers to entry, encourage new business formation, and encourage increases in output.

---

*Exercise 2.5*

Engage in Internet research on the following topics and discuss your findings as examples of supply-side economic policy.

(a) The deregulation of the airline, interstate trucking, and long-distance phone industries
(b) The antitrust actions against Microsoft in the 1990s

---

**Model 5: Imports and Exports**

This model introduces imports and exports (see Figure 2.6). Imports are a leakage along with savings and taxes. Each is current income not directly used to purchase domestic products, and each leads to the accumulation of inventory. Exports are an injection along with government and investment spending. Each involves the purchase of goods and services without the prior act of earning (domestic) income. To simplify Figure 2.6, the savings and investment flows and the tax and government outlays are not shown.

The inclusion of foreign transactions changes the numeric example. The following assumptions are made. First, households spend $0.80 of each additional dollar of income (MPC = 0.8). However, $0.70 is used for the purchase of domestic goods and $0.10 is used to purchase foreign goods. This defines the *marginal propensity to import* (MPM = 0.1), which is the proportion of a change in income used to purchase foreign-made products. Because each increase in income creates an additional leakage, the multiplier is smaller (see Table 2.11). Second, exports are a constant.

Table 2.12 applies the multiplier to a numeric model.

Period 1 is equilibrium: aggregate demand (consumption + investment + government + exports) equals income at $100, leakages (savings + tax + imports) equal injections (investment + government + exports) at $30, and there is no change in inventories. The equilibrium is disturbed in period 2 with the increase in investment spending to $20. In period 2, aggregate demand is greater than income; inventory is depleted, and income and output grow to $110 in period 3.

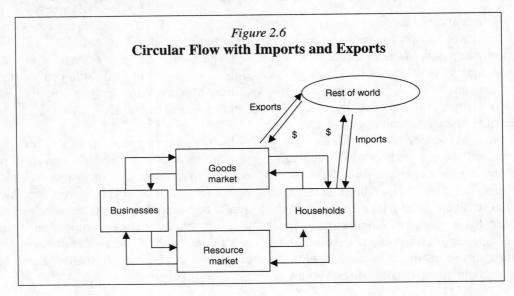

*Figure 2.6*
**Circular Flow with Imports and Exports**

Table 2.11
**Expanded Multiplier with Imports**

$$k = \frac{1}{1 - MPC + MPM}$$

where:
MPC = 0.8
MPI = 0.1

$$k = \frac{1}{1 - 0.8 + 0.1}$$

$$k = \frac{1}{0.3}$$

$$k = \frac{1}{0.3} = 3.3$$

In period 3, income is $110 and taxes, by assumption, do not change. Disposable income rises by $10. The increase in disposable income is used as follows: consumption spending on domestic goods rises by $7 (= 0.7 × $10), to $77; savings increase by $2 (= 0.2 × $10), to $12; and imports rise

by $1 (= 0.1 × $10) to $11. In period 3, disposable income is $100, of which $77 is consumption of domestic goods, $12 is savings, and $11 is imports. Period 3 is not an equilibrium condition because aggregate demand (consumption + investment + government + exports = $117) exceeds income (= $110). Also, injections (investment + government + exports = $40) exceed leakages (savings + tax + imports = $33). In period 4, business produces $117, an amount equal to the period 3 aggregate demand.

In period 4, income is $117 and taxes do not change. Disposable income is $117, and the $7 increase in disposable income is used as follows: the consumption of domestic goods rises by $4.90 (= 0.7 × $7), imports rise by $.70 (= 0.1 × $7), and savings rise by $1.40 (= 0.2 × $7). Aggregate demand exceeds income; injections exceed leakages, and the economy continues to expand.

The new equilibrium is $133. The $33 increase in equilibrium income is the product of the multiplier (k = 3.33; see Table 2.12) and the $10 increase in investment spending. In the new equilibrium, taxes do not change and the disposable income

Table 2.12
**National Income Determination with Imports and Exports**

| | Period 1 | Period 2 | Period 3 | Period 4 | New Equilibrium |
|---|---|---|---|---|---|
| Income | $100 | $100 | $110 | $117 | $133 |
| Tax | 10 | 10 | 10 | 10 | 10 |
| Disposable income | 90 | 90 | 100 | 107 | 123 |
| Consumption (domestic) | 70 | 70 | 77 | 81.9 | 93.1 |
| Savings | 10 | 10 | 12 | 13.4 | 16.6 |
| Government | 10 | 10 | 10 | 10 | 10 |
| Imports | 10 | 10 | 11 | 11.7 | 13.3 |
| Exports | 10 | 10 | 10 | 10 | 10 |
| Investment | 10 | 20 | 20 | 20 | 20 |
| Aggregate demand | 100 | 110 | 117 | 121.9 | 133 |
| Change in inventory | 0 | −10 | −7 | −4.9 | 0 |

level is $123. The $33 increase in disposable income is used as follows: the consumption of domestic goods rises by $23.10 (= 0.7 × $33) from the initial period, savings rise by $6.60 (= 0.2 × $33) from the initial period, and imports rise by $3.30 (= 0.1 × $33) from the initial period. By assumption, government spending and imports do not change. The new equilibrium is confirmed at $133 because income and aggregate demand are equal ($133) and the sum of the leakages equals the sum of the injections ($40).

### The Balance of Payments

In Table 2.12, the economy realizes a *balance of trade* deficit. Imports exceed exports. However, money leaked out through imports tends to return in the form of financial investments. This additional transaction requires understanding the two components of the balance of payments: the *current account* and the *financial account*.

The current account includes (1) the balance on the trade of goods, (2) the balance on the trade of services, (3) income received or paid on foreign investments, and (4) unilateral transfers between countries. The financial account includes (1) direct investments and other long-term financial flows between countries, (2) short-term non-official financial flows between countries, and (3) changes in reserve assets of central banks. Together, these accounts measure the total flow of funds between countries.

In Table 2.12, the United States experiences a net trade imbalance. Assume the cause of the imbalance is large textile imports from China. What do the Chinese do with their accumulation of dollars? The Chinese accept money from the United States because they see a use for it. They accept U.S. dollars beyond the levels needed to purchase U.S. goods and services, investing those additional dollars in U.S. financial assets, including government debt, stocks, bonds, real estate, and other

---

**Application Box 2.9**

In the third quarter of 2005, the United States' net imbalance in trade with the rest of the world was about $730 billion, seasonally adjusted at an annual rate. That figure is more than 5 percent of the U.S. gross domestic product. Total imports in that quarter amounted to $2,045 billion.

*Source:* Bureau of Economic Analysis, U.S. Department of Commerce, www.bea.gov/bea/newsrelarchive/2005/gdp305f.htm.

---

investment goods. The willingness of the Chinese who hold U.S. dollars to return the funds to the United States in the form of financial and other investments affects the availability of funds for domestic borrowers, interest rates, equity valuations, and the valuation of other domestic assets.

### Foreign Exchange Markets

Payments for a good or service are usually made in the exporting country's currency, unless the exporter requests payments in some other currency. For example, a retailer in the United States imports electronic equipment from Japan, and the payment is made in yen. The importer purchases yen in the foreign currency market to purchase the equipment. The price of the yen in terms of dollars is the *exchange rate*. The exchange rate is also stated in reverse: the number of yen needed to purchase a dollar. Exchange rates are determined by the interaction of supply and demand; the analysis is deferred to an appendix to Chapter 4.

Table 2.13 shows a hypothetical exchange rate between the yen and dollar and the effect of changes in the exchange rate on imports and exports.

In the upper portion of Table 2.13, the exchange

### Table 2.13
### Dollar-Yen Exchange Rate

| $1 = 100 yen | |
|---|---|
| In United States | In Japan |
| Japanese good costing 1,000 yen | U.S. good costing $10 |
| Price = $10 | Price = 1,000 yen |
| $1 = 90 yen | |
| (dollar devaluation and an increase in value of yen) | |
| Japanese good costing 1,000 yen | U.S. good costing $10 |
| Price = $11.11 | Price = 900 yen |

rate is $1 = 100 yen. For a U.S. buyer, the cost of a Japanese good priced at 1,000 yen is $10. A $10 U.S. good costs 1,000 yen in Japan. The lower portion of the table assumes a *devaluation of the dollar* relative to the yen. A dollar purchases only 90 yen. In reverse, this currency exchange rate is an appreciation of the yen relative to the dollar. A dollar costs only 90 yen.

Following the devaluation of the U.S. dollar relative to the Japanese yen, the dollar cost of Japanese imports rises. The 1,000-yen Japanese product costs a U.S. purchaser $11.11. The devaluation of the dollar discourages imports of Japanese goods to the United States. At the same time, the devaluation of the dollar encourages exports to

Japan by lowering the cost of U.S. goods in terms of yen. The yen cost of the U.S. import falls from 1,000 yen to 900 yen. Also, the increase in the cost of imports to the United States from Japan creates an opportunity for U.S. sellers to sell more units domestically while also raising their domestic prices. A country may purposely pursue a policy to devaluate its currency to encourage exports and discourage imports.

**Application Box 2.11**

In the early 1990s, the Japanese yen appreciated significantly relative to the U.S. dollar. Japanese exports became increasingly more expensive for U.S. buyers, and Japanese businesses struggled. The Japanese tenet that products were made best using Japanese labor and materials also became expensive. The Japanese central bank, in conjunction with other G-7 nations, made an agreement with the United States to depreciate the yen relative to the dollar. The Japanese aggressively pursued a weak yen to boost their export-driven economy.

**Application Box 2.12**

The Japanese devaluation of the yen in the mid-1990s had a significant worldwide impact and triggered the Asian financial crisis of the late 1990s. As the dollar strengthened relative to the yen, other currencies fixed to the U.S. dollar, such as Thailand's baht, also began to appreciate relative to the yen. Currency traders and speculators did not believe the baht was as valuable as the fixed exchange rate, and they began trading their baht for U.S. dollars. The result was panic, and Thailand's central bank began to run out of U.S. dollars to trade. Thailand was forced to devalue the baht, and the country was driven into recession.

## Stock Prices and the Macroeconomy

This section presents an economic fundamentals approach to stock valuations, and the purpose of this section is to build a bridge between macroeconomic analysis and the behavior of the financial markets. The economic fundamentals approach is only one method to explain the prices of stocks and stock market variations. To keep the analysis simple, it is assumed that firms pay stockholders 100 percent of earnings in dividends.

A share of stock represents a portion of ownership in the company, and the value (price) of a share is equal to the present value of the expected stream of earnings (assuming earnings equal dividends; see Table 2.14).

The numerator is the investor's expectations of the company's future earnings (and dividends) by period. Because equities never mature, the expectations extend through perpetuity, designated as period $n$. Different investors have different expectations about a company's future, and the more optimistic investor aggressively buys a stock while the less optimistic investor willingly sells. Also, because the future earnings are expected, events that change expectations lead to changes in stock prices. For example, the anticipation of the release of a new drug leads to an increase in the stock price of the pharmaceutical firm. The actual release of the drug does not affect the stock price if investors' expectations were correct. Sales and profits that are either stronger or weaker than expectations do, however, affect the stock price. Finally, performance of the macroeconomy affects the firm's selling environment, and the economic outlook is one important variable that shapes expected earnings. Potential investors are, therefore, careful observers of economic indicators because those indicators create expectations about the firm's selling environment and its future earnings.

The denominator of the equation (see Table

*Table 2.14*
### Stock Valuation Equation

$$Price = \frac{D_1}{(1+r)} + \frac{D_2}{(1+r)^2} + \frac{D_3}{(1+r)^3} + \frac{D_n}{(1+r)^n}$$

where:

$D$ = dividend by time period per share

$r$ = investors' required rate of return as a decimal

2.14) is the investor's required rate of return, and this rate discounts the expected future earnings to present value. The investor's required rate of return comprises three components: the risk-free interest rate (perhaps the yield on a three-month Treasury bill), a risk premium above the risk-free interest rate as compensation for the risk of entering the equity market, and a company-specific risk premium. Investors purchase a debt or equity instrument if the expected return is greater than or equal to the required rate of return.

Following Table 2.15, assume an investor expects a firm to earn $2 per share for perpetuity and pay the full amount of the earnings in dividends. The stock price is the present value of the stream of $2 dividends. Assuming the investor has a required rate of return of 11 percent, the stock price is $18.18. This stock sells at a *ratio of price to earnings* of 9.09 (= $18.18 ÷ $2). If the investor's required rate

*Table 2.15*
### Stock Price: Constant-Dividend Firm

$$Price = \frac{Dividend}{k}$$

where $k$ = investors' required rate of return

$$= \frac{\$2}{0.11}$$

$$= \$18.18$$

*Table 2.16*

**Stock Price: Constant-Growth Firm**

$$\text{Price} = \frac{\text{Dividend}}{k - g}$$

where:

$k$ = investors' required rate of return with the percentage expressed as a decimal

$g$ = expected constant growth rate with the percentage expressed as a decimal

$$= \frac{\$2}{0.11 - 0.7}$$

$$= \$50$$

of return is 15 percent, a share of the stock sells at $13.33 and the price-to-earnings ratio falls to 6.66 ($13.33 ÷ $2). All else equal, the higher the risk-free interest rate, the higher the investors' required rate of return and the lower the ratio of price to earnings; in reverse, lower interest rates and a lower required rate of return lead to high price-to-earnings ratios.

Table 2.16 shows the valuation of a share in a firm whose earnings and dividends are expected to grow at a constant rate. The table assumes current earnings are $2 per share, the expected growth in earnings is 7 percent per year, and the investors' required rate of return is 11 percent.

The share of stock in Table 2.16 sells for $50 and the price-to-earnings ratio is 25. Several things follow: (1) If, all else equal, interest rates and the investors' required rate of return rise to 15 percent, the stock price falls to $25. The price-to-earnings ratio declines to 12.5 (= $25 ÷ $2). All else equal, higher interest rates lead to lower stock prices and lower price-to-earnings ratios. (2) Assuming the investors' required rate of return is 7 percent but investors' expectations of the future growth in earnings rise to 9 percent, the stock price is $100 and the price-to-earnings ratio rises to 50 (= $100 ÷ $2). All else equal, the higher the expected growth

rate, the higher the stock price and the higher the price-to-earnings ratio.

Equity investors carefully monitor the macroeconomy and time their purchase or sale of shares in accordance with the macroeconomic outlook. Those investors with a long-term investment horizon ignore short-term fluctuations in the macroeconomy and invest in a company's earnings prospects.

## Summary

This chapter provides a simplified look at the forces that determine an economy's aggregate output. By understanding the forces of aggregate demand, decision makers are able to monitor leading economic indicators and make informed judgments about their firm's future economic environment. Importantly, this chapter provides an income-and-expenditures approach to explaining swings in the macroeconomy.

### Review Terms

| | |
|---|---|
| Accelerator | Injections |
| Aggregate demand | Inventory-to-sales ratio |
| Aggregate supply | Lagging economic indicators |
| Balance of payments | Leading economic indicators |
| Concurrent economic indicators | Leakages |
| Debt | Phillips curve |
| Demand-pull inflation | Multiplier |
| Derived demand | Public debt |
| Equality of income and output | Risk |
| Equilibrium income | Role of changes in inventory |
| Exchange rates | Stock price valuation |
| Fiscal policy | Supply-side economics |

## Discussion Questions

1. Calculate the multiplier assuming the marginal propensity to consume is 0.7.
2. Calculate the multiplier assuming the marginal propensity to consume is 0.7 and the marginal propensity to invest is 0.1.
3. Assume:

   (a) The multiplier is 10.
   (b) Equilibrium income is $500.
   (c) Full employment income is $600.

   By how much should government increase spending to achieve full employment?
4. Go to www.economagic.com and print a graph of the ratio of inventory to sales from 1980 to the present. Include the recession periods on the chart. Explain what you see about the relationship between the inventory ratio and economic recessions.
5. Complete the following exercise using the assumptions below.
   Assume:

   (a) The marginal propensity to consume domestic goods is 0.7.
   (b) The marginal propensity to invest is 0.1.
   (c) The marginal propensity to import is 0.1.
   (d) Full employment output is $500.

6. Indicate the direction of change (up or down) of each of the following economic indicators, given the conditions in the macroeconomy.
7. Calculate the price of a share of stock under the following assumptions.

   (a) The current dividend (and earnings) is $2 per share.
   (b) The investors' required rate of return is 9 percent.

*Table D2.1*

|  | Period 1 | Period 2 | Period 3 | Period 4 | Final Period |
|---|---|---|---|---|---|
| Income | 200 |  |  |  |  |
| Tax | 20 |  |  |  |  |
| Disposable income | 180 |  |  |  |  |
| Consumption (domestic) | 140 |  |  |  |  |
| Savings | 20 |  |  |  |  |
| Government | 20 | 30 |  |  |  |
| Imports | 20 |  |  |  |  |
| Exports | 20 |  |  |  |  |
| Investment | 20 |  |  |  |  |
| Aggregate demand | 200 |  |  |  |  |
| Change in inventory | 0 |  |  |  |  |

*Table D2.2*

| Economic Indicators | Economic Expansion | Recession |
|---|---|---|
| Unemployment rate |  |  |
| Vendor delivery (faster or slower) |  |  |
| Producer Price Index |  |  |
| Car sales |  |  |
| Purchasing Managers Index |  |  |
| Industrial production |  |  |
| Orders for durable goods |  |  |
| Unit labor costs |  |  |
| Building permits |  |  |
| Payroll employment |  |  |

(c) The expected rate of growth in earnings and dividends is 5 percent.

Calculate the price-to-earnings ratio.

8. Repeat problem 7 changing one assumption: the expected growth rate in earnings (and dividends) is 7 percent. Recalculate the price-to-earnings ratio.

9. Repeat problem 7 changing one assumption: due to increased uncertainty, investors raise their required rate of return to 10 percent. Recalculate the price-to-earnings ratio.

10. Assume $1 purchases 50 yen.

   (a) What does it cost a dollar holder to purchase a product priced at 200 yen?
   (b) What does it cost a yen holder to purchase a product price at $50?
   (c) Repeat the problems above assuming $1 purchases 75 yen.
   (d) Did the dollar appreciate or depreciate in value?

   (e) Which country will experience an increase in imports?

11. Calculate the price of a share of stock and the price-to-earnings ratio under each of the following conditions.

   (a) The dividend is constant at $2 per share and investors have a required rate of return of 7 percent.
   (b) The dividend is constant at $2 per share and investors have a required rate of return of 9 percent.
   (c) The dividend is $3 per share and is expected to grow by 5 percent per year; investors have a required rate of return of 9 percent.
   (d) The dividend is $3 per share and is expected to grow by 6 percent per year; investors have a required rate of return of 9 percent.

# Case Study 2.1

# Kauffman's Management Consulting

Kauffman's Management Consulting has gross billings of about $650,000 per year. Consider how each of the decisions in Table C2.1 is affected by an expanding or contracting economy.

*Table C2.1*
### Decisions at Kauffman's Management Consulting

| Decision | Expanding Economy | Slowing or Contracting Economy |
|---|---|---|
| Hiring | | |
| Lease new office space | | |
| Increase marketing | | |
| Buy new computers | | |
| Issue new stock | | |
| Conserve cash | | |

# 3

# Money and the Financial Markets

The previous chapter develops a model of the economy that explains short-term macroeconomic fluctuations through an income and expenditures approach. The prior chapter does not consider (1) the role of money in facilitating transactions in the goods or resource markets, (2) interest rates, monetary policy, and economic fluctuations, (3) the process by which funds flow from savers to investors, or (4) the mechanics of financing government budgetary deficits. This chapter fills the gaps.

---

**Learning Objectives**

The successful reader understands:

- The structure and operations of the money and financial systems and the role of money and interest rates in the economy
- Monetary policy and its effects on a firm's operating environment
- The money and financial system as environments within which business and personal investment occur

---

An understanding of how money and credit interact with real economic activity is fundamental to management responsibilities. Business decisions dependent upon money and credit conditions include the management of a firm's cash position, extending and receiving credit, establishing the appropriate debt-to-equity ratio, and planning for the firm's long-term physical and financial capital needs. However, the importance of money and credit extends well beyond financial management decisions. The demand for many products is sensitive to the price and availability of credit, and decisions in production, procurement, hiring, and inventory control are made within the monetary and financial environments. Further, personal financial planning and investment decisions are made within these environments and include the timing of buying goods on credit, choosing a fixed- or variable-rate mortgage, selecting stocks, and choosing the maturity of financial investments.

Two sets of issues are covered in this chapter. The flow of funds section of this chapter examines the institutions and markets that facilitate the transmission of foreign and domestic savings to companies for investment in plant and equipment, to government to finance public debt, and to households for purchases of homes, cars, and other durable products. The second section of this chapter examines the role of money in the economy, monetary policy, and interest rates.

## The Flow of Funds

In the macroeconomic model developed in Chapter 2, leakages include savings, taxes, and imports. The injections are investment spending, government, and exports. Two considerations arise. First, those who save are not the same as those who invest. How does

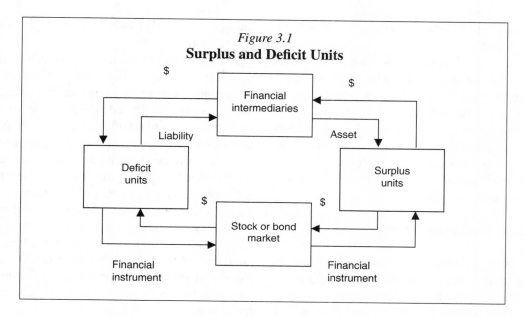

*Figure 3.1*
**Surplus and Deficit Units**

the money flow from those who save to those making investments? Second, if the government's budget is in deficit, from where does the money come to cover the expenditures? Alternatively, if the government's budget is in surplus, where does the money go?

Figure 3.1 describes the financial system. The principal players are *surplus units* and *deficit units.*

Surplus units are the sources of funds in the financial system. Surplus units include households that save, and savings consist of take-home pay that is not spent on goods and services as well as payroll deductions and employer contributions to retirement programs. Businesses are surplus units during periods of positive cash flow and when earnings are retained. Federal, state, and municipal governments are surplus units during periods of positive cash flow and when budgets are in surpluses. Surplus units include net foreign investments in U.S. financial markets and institutions. The sources of funds also include new money created by the Federal Reserve; this topic is deferred until later in this chapter.

Surplus units make financial investment decisions based on their particular needs, including investment income, safety, and liquidity. Their options include stocks, bonds, and bank deposits. For example, a retiree seeks predictable and periodic interest or dividend income. A new entrant into the workforce chooses long-term capital appreciation in lieu of current income. A business or government unit with a temporary surplus of funds seeks short-term interest income.

Deficit units, which include households, government, businesses, and foreign units, acquire the surplus units' funds. Households acquire surplus units' monies to purchase homes, cars, vacations, and education. Businesses raise funds to purchase plant and equipment, acquire new inventory, or meet temporary cash flow needs. Federal, state, and municipal governments acquire funds to finance budgetary deficits or to meet temporary cash flow needs. State and municipal government units raise funds to finance capital projects such as bridges, roads, airports, schools, and industrial parks. Deficit units include foreign governments, businesses, and individuals who raise funds in the United States.

Deficit units have short- and long-term needs for external funds. For example, a retailer needs short-term credit to purchase inventory for the upcoming selling season. A new business seeks long-term funds to acquire production equipment, and a household needs long-term funds to purchase a home. Deficit units compete for funds by offering various combinations of yield, level of liquidity, risk, and taxability of earnings.

### Financial Markets and Institutions

Financial markets and institutions facilitate the flow of funds from the surplus units to the deficit units. Figure 3.1 shows two routes for surplus units' funds to flow to deficit units. One route is *indirect finance*, in which funds flow through financial intermediaries, including commercial banks, savings and loan associations, credit unions, and insurance companies. The second route is *direct finance*, in which funds flow through debt and equity markets.

Financial intermediaries conduct indirect finance by issuing claims against themselves to gather monies from the surplus units. For example, a bank offers a certificate of deposit for a fixed period of time at a fixed interest rate. The household that purchases the certificate of deposit holds a claim against the issuing bank. The bank accepts the liability to lend the funds to deficit units who want to purchase a car, home, inventory, or equipment. Financial intermediaries also extend credit to the federal government to finance a budget deficit and to state and municipal governments to cover capital projects such as a bridge, road, or stadium. Financial institutions profit through the yield spread between the rate charged on the loan and the rate paid to depositors.

Financial intermediaries offer significant benefits to both surplus and deficit units. (1) Many financial intermediaries are conveniently located. (2) Intermediaries are highly regulated (and often insured) to protect the assets of savers. (3) By pooling the funds of surplus units, financial intermediaries possess the size to research financial investment opportunities and to build diversified investment portfolios. (4) Financial intermediaries specialize, so both surplus and deficit units can find an intermediary to accommodate their needs. For example, life insurance companies gather surplus funds through premiums, and by virtue of their long-term liabilities acquire long-term assets. In contrast, commercial banks issue liabilities (checking accounts) that are payable on demand, and commercial banks make shorter-term extensions of credit. (5) Financial intermediaries pool the funds of surplus units, and pooled funds are less likely to be withdrawn at the same time. With this protection, financial intermediaries acquire less-liquid (and higher-yield) assets than would an individual surplus unit.

### Application Box 3.1

The savings and loan crisis of the 1980s was the result of a mismatch between short-term liabilities and long-term assets. Savings and loans associations hold liabilities in the form of deposits payable on demand. Their asset portfolio is dominated by long-term mortgage loans. When long-term interest rates are higher than short-term rates, the savings and loan associations profit from the rate differential. In the 1980s short-term interest rates rose above long-term rates. The savings and loans experienced a profit squeeze, and depositors withdrew funds in search of even higher yields. The solvency of the associations was threatened.

## Application Box 3.2

It is useful to distinguish between a loan originator and the ultimate holder of the loan. For example, a commercial bank issues a mortgage loan, but the duration of the loan is a mismatch with the bank's deposits, which are payable on demand. To rectify this, the issuing bank sells the mortgage, thus serving as a mortgage originator. Buyers of the mortgages are long-term investors and include life insurance companies and federal government agencies. Fannie Mae, for example, buys and holds many home mortgages. The agency sells long-term debt to raise the money to purchase the mortgages, thus restoring liquidity to financial intermediaries, which allows new mortgage loans to be issued.

Financial intermediaries are regulated by government and government agencies to protect depositors' assets. The Federal Reserve System, for example, supervises commercial banks. It periodically audits banks to ensure compliance with regulations on investment and operating practices. Financial institutions offer insured accounts, and the deposit insurers provide an additional layer of regulation. The Federal Deposit Insurance Corporation (FDIC) and the National Credit Union Association (NCUA) are insurance agencies that impose rules and procedures to ensure prudent operating and investment practices.

Direct finance is an alternative route for funds to flow from surplus units to deficit units. In direct finance, the surplus unit holds a claim against the deficit unit and not against a financial intermediary. For example, a surplus unit purchases a bond issued by a corporation that needs funds to expand its production capability. A different surplus unit buys shares of stock newly issued by a start-up computer software company, and another surplus unit purchases a municipal bond that is guaranteed by a municipality that pledges revenues from a new toll road.

A direct finance transaction involves the sale and purchase of a debt or equity instrument. Equity holdings represent shares of ownership in a corporation, whereas debt instruments are promises to make interest payments and to return the principal on a predetermined schedule. Debt instruments differ by the duration of time to maturity, the risk level of the issuing unit, and the tax status of interest income. Equity holders have a residual claim on the assets of the issuing corporation and carry a higher level of risk. Correspondingly, firms with a lot of debt pay an additional risk premium when borrowing additional sums. Similarly, excessive debt depresses a firm's stock price as potential investors recognize prior claimants to the firm's assets and pay less for a share of stock.

## Application Box 3.3

There are two sides of the debt and equity markets. The supply side consists of the surplus units, which are engaged in the management of their asset portfolios. Each surplus unit has a tolerance for risk and a preference for current or deferred income. The investment decisions made by surplus units are based on personal and institutional financial needs.

The demand side of the debt and equity markets consists of deficit units, which seek external funds to pay for short- and long-term needs. The decisions made by deficit units are financial management choices.

Many different financial instruments, including short-term Treasury debt and corporate bonds, are traded to help meet the diverse needs of surplus and deficit units.

Direct finance occurs in debt and equity markets and is conducted by brokers and dealers. Dealers purchase securities from government and business units, hold them temporarily in their own accounts, and resell the securities to surplus units. Dealers profit from the spread between the purchase price and the resale price, any capital appreciation of the asset over the time from the purchase to the resale, and net income earned while holding the asset. In contrast, brokers do not purchase securities for their own accounts. Brokers use their distribution networks to find buyers for the securities, and they profit from transaction fees.

Equities are shares of ownership in corporations, and well-established equity markets facilitate the purchase and sale of stocks. The initial issue of a firm's stock occurs in a *primary market*. Most of the day-to-day equity market activity involves *secondary market* transactions in which previously issued shares of stock are resold. The corporation that initially issued the stock is not involved in the secondary market transaction, but it carefully monitors its stock price as a reflection of investor confidence and as a predictor of the cost of raising new funds.

Stock market indexes reflect changes in the prices of a group of stocks. For example, the Dow Jones Industrial Average is a composite measure of the prices of thirty major U.S. industrial firms. The day-to-day variations in the Dow reflect changes in the prices of this limited group of stocks, not necessarily the patterns of all stocks. The valuation of a share of stock is discussed on pages 70 and 99.

In debt markets, borrowers (deficit units) issue promissory notes. Debt instruments do not represent shares of ownership, and debt instruments differ by risk, maturity, and the tax status of the interest paid. Short-term promissory notes mature in a year or less and include U.S. Treasury bills and commercial paper. Longer-term notes and bonds are issued by corporations, the Treasury, government agencies, and state and municipal govern-

**Application Box 3.4**

Individual investors have different tolerances for risk, different needs to convert financial investments to cash, and different expectations about a corporation's future earnings. Each investor values a stock or bond differently. These different valuations explain why buyers and sellers are willing to make trades in the financial markets.

ment units. Long-term corporate debt carries a risk rating. Standard and Poor's and Moody's Investor Services are two major credit rating agencies.

*Valuation of Debt Instruments*

The price an investor willingly pays for a debt instrument is determined by present value calculations. For example, consider a financial obligation that promises the return of the $100 principal in two years with no interest paid over the period. This is a *zero-coupon* note because there are no periodic interest payments. If the interest rate is 7 percent, the price is $87.34 (= $100 ÷ (1.07 × 1.07)). If the interest rate rises to 8 percent, the $100 promissory note with a two-year maturity sells for $85.73 (= $100 ÷ (1.08 × 1.08)). All else equal, the higher the interest rate, the lower the price of the debt instrument. This inverse relationship between bond prices and interest rates means that debt holders realize gains in the value of their asset under periods of falling interest rates and decreases in the value of their asset when interest rates rise.

Pricing of a debt instrument that includes periodic interest payments involves two steps. The price of the debt instrument is the present value of the periodic interest payments plus the present value of the sum paid at maturity. Consider a two-year note with a promise to pay $1,000 at the end of two years. At the end of the first year and at the end of the second year, there are $100 interest payments. With an interest rate of 5 percent, the first interest payment has a present value of $95.23 (= $100 ÷ 1.05). The second interest payment has a present value of $90.70 (= $100 ÷ (1.05 × 1.05)). The $1,000 payment in two years has a present value of $907.03 (= $1,000 ÷ (1.05 × 1.05)). The bond sells for $1,092.96 (= $907.03 + $95.23 + $90.70).

---

### Exercise 3.1

(a) Calculate the price of a bond that promises to pay $1,000 in three years. There are annual (end-of-the-year) interest payments of $50. The interest rate on three-year debt instruments of comparable risk is 6 percent.

(b) Repeat the calculation assuming the interest rate is 8 percent.

(c) Calculate the price of a bond that promises to pay $1,000 in five years. There are annual (end-of-the-year) interest payments of $50. The interest rate on debt instruments of comparable risk is 6 percent.

(d) Repeat the calculation assuming the interest rate is 8 percent.

(e) Review the calculations. What is the relationship between bond prices and interest rates? How does the length of time to maturity affect the change in bond valuation given an interest rate change?

---

### Interest Rates: A First Look

Interest rates are the price of credit. Surplus units require a return to compensate for their sacrifice of liquidity and acceptance of risks. Deficit units make interest payments to use the surplus units' dollars to make purchases in excess of current income. The obligations of the deficit units are not troublesome

---

**Application Box 3.5**

Changes in the spread between interest rates are often interesting. For example, a widening spread between a high-risk bond and a low-risk one is a signal that investors expect the economy to grow weaker. In a weakening economy, the risk of default posed by the higher-risk borrower increases and the yield spread widens.

---

if their future earnings are sufficient to cover the obligations. Further, if deficit units acquire debt funds at one interest rate and earn a higher percentage on the use of these monies, equity holders reap the benefits of *financial leverage.*

At any point in time there are many interest rates, and each reflects a different risk level, maturity, liquidity, or earnings tax status. For example, the interest rate on a twenty-year Treasury bond is generally higher than the rate on a three-month Treasury bill because of the time to maturity of the financial instrument. A three-month commercial loan paid by a retailer to restock inventory carries a premium over the three-month Treasury bill rate because of risk and liquidity differences. The prime rate, the interest rate paid by a bank's biggest and most secure borrowers, is generally lower than the rate paid by an individual on a new-car loan.

Though interest rates on debt instruments differ, rates tend to move in the same direction. The forces that determine the supply and demand are common across the different debt instruments. In a strong macroeconomy, the demand for credit is high to finance plant and equipment expansions, the acquisition of inventory, and the purchase of homes and cars. During economic expansions, interest rates tend to rise. During periods of weak economic activity, the demand for credit softens, and interest rates tend to decline. However, the market for each debt instrument has unique supply and demand conditions, and all rates do not change at the same time or by the same amount. The factors affecting interest rate differentials are explored more thoroughly later in this chapter.

## The Money Supply

Defining the nation's money supply and understanding how the Federal Reserve manages the quantity of money highlight vital elements of the money and financial environments within which business and household decisions are made.

### Definition of the Money Supply

Economists do not agree upon the definition of the nation's *money supply.* However, the details of the debate are beyond the scope of this book. To proceed under simplifying assumptions, the definition of the nation's money supply is derived from two functions of money. Money is *a unit of account* and *a medium of exchange.* The unit of account function means that goods and services are priced in money terms. The medium of exchange function means that goods and services are exchanged for money.

### Application Box 3.6

The nation's money supply (M1) in November 2005 was $1,372 billion.

*Source:* www.economagic.com.

Therefore, one component of the money supply is currency and coins. However, many purchases are completed by writing checks, and dollar balances in checking accounts (demand deposits) are the largest part of the money supply. Checking deposits and currency and coin are the largest components of the M1 definition of money.

### The Equation of Exchange

One way to examine the relationship between the money supply and gross domestic product is through the equation of exchange (see Table 3.1).

The equation of exchange is an identity. On the left side of the equation, the supply of money ($M$) is multiplied by the *velocity* of money ($V$). The velocity of money is the average number of times a dollar or deposit is used to complete transactions during a year. For example, assume individuals are paid weekly and spend the full amount before their next pay period. Under these restrictive assumptions, the velocity of money is 52. If individuals are paid monthly and spend the full amount on goods and services prior to the next pay period, the velocity is 12.

*Table 3.1*
### Equation of Exchange

$$MV = PT$$

Where:

$M =$ money supply
$V =$ velocity of money
$P =$ price level
$T =$ number of transactions

The left side of the equation of exchange is *total expenditures.* It is the money supply multiplied by the velocity. The right side of the equation is *total receipts,* which are the average price of goods and services ($P$) multiplied by the number of transactions ($T$). The equation is an identity because total receipts must equal total expenditures.

The equation of exchange organizes and explains several important points. If the money supply changes, one or more of the other variables must change. If an increase in the money supply is simply held by individuals and institutions, velocity declines and the right side of the

## Application Box 3.7

The velocity of money depends upon more than the frequency of payroll. For example, businesses and households accumulate purchasing power over time. During periods of low interest rates, the opportunity cost of holding assets in the form of money is low, and the velocity of money declines. When interest rates are high, the opportunity cost of holding money is high, and the velocity rises.

equation remains unchanged. If some or all of the increase in the money supply is spent, the number of transactions and or the price level must change in response. Second, given the velocity of money, the effect of the increase in the money supply depends upon the slope of the aggregate supply curve (see page 64). At full employment, the aggregate supply curve is vertical

## Application Box 3.8

The equation of exchange was derived by Yale University professor Irving Fisher in 1911. Fisher wrote the famous $MV = PT$ equation based on a verbal explanation of the phenomenon in John Stuart Mill's 1848 book, *Principles of Political Economy*. Fisher used the equation to assert that there was a proportional relationship between increases in $M$ and increases in $P$. He believed that $V$ and $T$ changed independently of $M$, so the proportional relationship between $M$ and $P$ was a long-run condition.

*Source:* Robert Ekelund and Robert Hebert, *A History of Economic Theory and Method* (New York: McGraw-Hill Publishers, 1997).

(see page 64) and an increase in the supply of money leads to higher prices. This phenomenon is demand-pull inflation, the result of too much money chasing too few goods. At less than full employment, an increase in the money supply (assuming the velocity of money is constant) leads to some combination of more output and higher prices depending upon the slope of the aggregate supply curve (see page 64).

### *The Federal Reserve: A First Look*

The Federal Reserve System (Fed) is the primary regulator of the nation's banking and monetary system and manages the nation's money supply. The Fed was created by congressional act in 1913. Prior to the establishment of the Federal Reserve, central banking in the United States had a long and uneven record of success. Three important points are cited regarding the creation and structure of the Federal Reserve System. (1) The U.S. Constitution assigns the responsibility to coin and regulate money to Congress, and Congress reassigned this responsibility to the Federal Reserve. This reassignment properly separates Congress' authority to tax and spend from its ability to create money. The separation of authority prevents elected officials from passing spending legislation and printing new money to pay for these expenditures. (2) The Board of Governors, the most important of the Fed's management committees, is chaired by a presidential appointee (approved by Congress) and the membership of the committee is structured to ensure that no two-term president can appoint a majority. This structure builds political independence. (3) The Federal Reserve is an independent authority. Federal Reserve actions that affect the money supply, interest rates, and the macroeconomy do not require congressional or presidential approval. The chairman of the Federal Reserve, however, makes periodic reports to Congress.

### Application Box 3.9

Dr. Alan Greenspan served five terms as chairman of the Board of Governors of the Federal Reserve System, from August 11, 1987, until January 31, 2006. He was originally appointed by President Ronald Reagan and was reappointed by Presidents George H.W. Bush, Bill Clinton, and George W. Bush. Greenspan also served as the chairman of the Federal Open Market Committee, the Fed's principal body for making monetary policy. His tenure was marked by an unprecedented span of economic stability and confidence in the Federal Reserve's ability to effectively administer monetary policy.

### The Banking System and the Money Supply

To explain the critical role of the Fed and the commercial banking system in the nation's monetary system, Table 3.2 shows the balance sheet for a new bank. In Table 3.2 Bank A receives its first deposit ($100) in cash. The deposit is recorded as a liability because the bank owes these funds to the depositor. The corresponding asset is the cash, and these funds are *reserves*. Table 3.2 is the bank's balance sheet at the time the cash deposit is accepted and the money placed in the vault.

*Table 3.2*
**New Bank**

| Bank A | |
|---|---|
| Assets | Liabilities |
| Reserve = $100 | Deposit = $100 |
| Required = $10 | |
| Excess = $90 | |

### Application Box 3.10

For national banks, the Federal Reserve System sets reserve requirements. Required reserves are held as vault cash or on deposit with the Federal Reserve. The required reserve varies from none to 10 percent based upon the level of transaction. Though not precise, transactions can be thought of as deposits.

*Source:* Federal Reserve Board, "Reserve Requirements," www.federalreserve.gov/monetarypolicy/reservereq.htm.

A bank that holds 100 percent of its deposits in reserve in the vault maximizes safety. It can meet all withdrawals. However, a bank that holds 100 percent of deposits in the vault has no earnings unless it charges a safekeeping fee. Instead, banks operate under a *fractional reserve system,* believing depositors are unlikely to withdraw all of their deposits at the same time. Fractional reserve banking allows savings to be used by deficit units to purchase new equipment, inventory, or homes.

To ensure minimum liquidity, national banks are obligated to hold a percentage of their deposits in *reserves.* This percentage is the *reserve requirement,* and the requirement is imposed by the central banking authority (Federal Reserve). Referring to Table 3.2, the $100 in reserves comprises $10 in required reserves and $90 in *excess reserves.*

Banks use their excess reserves to acquire earning assets, and in Table 3.3 the bank makes a loan of $90 to a retail store owner who needs credit to purchase inventory for the upcoming selling season. Table 3.3 shows the bank's balance sheet after the loan has been made but before the borrower uses the credit to make purchases.

*Table 3.3*
## Deposit Expansion

| Bank A | |
|---|---|
| Assets | Liabilities |
| Reserves = $100 | Deposits = $190 |
| Required = $19 | |
| Excess = $81 | |
| | |
| Loans = $90 | |

The loan is granted in the form of a deposit, and the bank's liabilities rise to $190. Therefore, required reserves rise to $19, and excess reserves fall to $81. The original $100 deposit is still in the bank's vault.

The balance sheet in Table 3.3 exists only temporarily. The borrower uses the $90 loan to purchase inventory by writing a check to the manufacturer of the merchandise. The manufacturer deposits the check in Bank B (see Table 3.4). It is assumed that the manufacturer does not keep any additional currency or increase savings account balances. Table 3.4 shows that Bank B has recorded a $90 deposit. Bank B has an increase in excess reserves of $81 and is able to make a loan of that amount.

Table 3.5 shows Bank A's balance sheet after the check is cleared and payment is made to Bank B. Bank A has $100 in deposits and $10 in reserves, all of which are required. The loan, not

*Table 3.4*
## Multiple Deposit Creation

| Bank B | | |
|---|---|---|
| Assets | | Liabilities |
| Reserves = +$90 | | Deposits = +$90 |
| | Required = +$9 | |
| | Excess = +$81 | |

*Table 3.5*
## Balance Sheet

| Bank A | | |
|---|---|---|
| Assets | | Liabilities |
| Reserves = $10 | | Deposits = $100 |
| | Required = $10 | |
| | Excess = $0 | |
| Loans = $90 | | |

yet repaid, remains on the asset side of Bank A's balance sheet.

In Table 3.5, Bank A's reserves decline by $90 upon it sending that sum to Bank B to cover the check. At this time, Bank A is loaned up and cannot acquire any additional earning assets until the loan is repaid or the bank receives new deposits. The deposit creation process continues because Bank B has $81 in excess reserves and makes a loan (see Table 3.4).

The sequential loans lead to *multiple creations of deposits* that occur because of the fractional reserve banking system. The magnitude of the deposit creation is determined by the size of the reserve requirement. A 10 percent reserve requirement leads to a tenfold increase of the original deposit ($1 \div 0.1 = 10$). With a 5 percent reserve requirement, the original deposit increases twentyfold ($1 \div .05 = 20$). The deposit creation process appears to create money out of thin air; however, the borrower receives a deposit (an asset) and the corresponding liability is the borrower's debt. Neither the borrower nor the economy is wealthier. There is, however, an increase in the supply of money that can be used to purchase goods and services.

### Check Clearing

Historically, many checks were processed through local clearinghouses, where banks exchange

*Table 3.6*
## The Federal Reserve and Check Clearing

| The Federal Reserve | |
|---|---|
| Assets | Liabilities |
| | Deposits of Bank A = -$90 |
| | Deposits of Bank B = +$90 |

checks written against another's deposits. Where wide geographic separation exists between banks, local clearinghouses were ineffective, so the Federal Reserve facilitated the process by holding banks' interest-bearing deposits (see Table 3.6). Bank B deposited the check at the Fed. The Fed, in turn, debited the account of Bank A and returned the check to Bank A for the proper individual account to be debited.

The check-clearing process was streamlined in 2004 with "Check 21."[1] With the Check 21 process, banks create an electronic copy of each check. The check clears electronically, which negates the need to return the paper check to the bank upon which the check was written.

## Monetary Policy, Credit Availability, and Interest Rates

### Reserve Requirements

The Fed sets the required reserve percentage for nationally chartered banks to ensure a minimum level of liquidity and safety. A reduction in the reserve requirements creates excess reserves, allows additional loans to be made, and increases the deposit creation multiplier. Increases in the ratio compel banks to hold more reserves, allow fewer loans to be made, and decrease the deposit creation multiplier. Changes in reserve requirements are a monetary policy option for the Fed,

but it is a crude and infrequently used policy instrument.

### The Discount Rate and the Federal Funds Rate

Banks are obligated to meet the minimum reserve requirements over a reporting period, and the management task is not simple. Banks are unable to predict the precise inflows and outflows of their deposits. Unexpected withdrawals drain reserves, whereas unexpected inflows increase reserves. Neither a shortage nor an abundance of reserves is desirable. A deficiency in reserves violates regulations, and penalties ensue. An abundance of reserves carries an opportunity cost of lost interest income. Therefore, bank managers are challenged by a trade-off between liquidity and income. Large reserves make the bank liquid and ensure a bank's ability to meet depositors' withdrawals but also sacrifice interest income. Smaller quantities of reserves lead to higher bank earnings but also to a greater risk of failing to meet minimum reserve requirements.

Managing a bank's reserve position is an ongoing task, and the financial management decisions are made within the macroeconomic environment. During periods of economic weakness, the demand for credit is low, borrowers appear less creditworthy, and the opportunity cost of holding excess reserves is low. Under these macroeconomic conditions banks are less aggressive lenders and more liquid. In contrast, during periods of strong economic growth, the demand for loans is high, lending rates are high, and borrowers appear creditworthy. These circumstances encourage banks to be aggressive lenders. By minimizing reserves to make loans, banks are more vulnerable to unexpected withdrawals and shortfalls in their required reserves.

What happens if a bank falls short of meeting

*Table 3.7*
## Cash Management

| Bank A | |
|---|---|
| Assets | Liabilities |
| Reserves = $10 | Deposits = $100 |
|     Required = $10 | |
|     Excess = $0 | |
| Loans = $70 | |
| T-bills = $20 | |

| Bank A | |
|---|---|
| Assets | Liabilities |
| Reserves = $0 | Deposits = $90 |
|     Required = –$9 | |
|     Excess = –$9 | |
| Loans = $70 | |
| T-bills = $20 | |

its liquidity obligations? Refer to Table 3.7, which assumes a 10 percent reserve requirement. In the upper panel, Bank A is meeting its requirements, has no excess reserves, and holds $70 in loans and $20 in Treasury bills. Treasury bills are a short-term obligation of the U.S. government, a safe investment, and liquid (readily turned into cash without loss of value), but earn a lower interest rate than loans. Despite the earnings differential between Treasury bills and loans, banks hold some Treasury bills as *secondary reserves,* which generate interest income and are easily converted to cash to cover unanticipated cash withdrawals.

In the lower panel of Table 3.7, Bank A experiences an unexpected withdrawal of $10. The bank's payment reduces deposits and its reserves. After payment, Bank A no longer meets the reserve requirement. Four ways for the bank to respond are examined: buy deposits, sell the Treasury bills, borrow from the Federal Reserve discount window,

or purchase federal funds. The first two options involve managing the bank's assets, and the other two involve liability management.

### Asset Management

Many business units, domestic and foreign, frequently have large sums to invest for short periods of time. To attract new deposits, a bank offers an attractive interest rate on a large certificate of deposit. The new deposits allow the bank to meet its reserve requirement. A second asset management practice refers to the bank's $20 in Treasury bills. The market for Treasury bills is large, and selling $9 of Treasury bills enables the bank to meet its reserve requirements. This sale of Treasury bills highlights the distinction between primary and secondary markets. The bank purchased the Treasury bills at the original issue in the primary market. The Treasury was the seller and exchanged its obligation for cash. The bank's resale of the bill prior to maturity occurs in the secondary market. The Treasury is not engaged in this transaction. For the bank to sell Treasury bills in a secondary market there must be a willing buyer. The buyer may be another bank that has experienced an unexpected deposit inflow.

### Liability Management

The Fed's primary responsibility is to create and sustain a safe and secure banking system, and this obligates the Fed to help banks that are deficient in their reserve position. In the lower panel of Table 3.7 the bank is not meeting its reserve requirement. At risk is the bank's ability to meet its obligations to depositors. Furthermore, the failure of a single bank threatens the integrity of the entire banking system. Therefore, the Fed is ready to help the bank meet its minimum liquid-

*Table 3.8*
**Discount Window Transaction**

| Bank A | |
|---|---|
| Assets | Liabilities |
| Reserves = $9 | Deposits = $90 |
|     Required = $9 | Loans from Fed = $9 |
|     Excess = $0 | |
| Loans = $70 | |
| T-bills = $20 | |
| Federal Reserve System | |
| Assets | Liabilities |
| Loan to bank = $9 | Deposits of bank = +$9 |

*Table 3.9*
**Federal Funds Transaction, Step I**

| Bank A | |
|---|---|
| Assets | Liabilities |
| Reserves = $0 | Deposits = $90 |
|     Required = $9 | |
|     Excess = –$9 | |
| Loans = $70 | |
| T-bills = $20 | |
| Bank B | |
| Assets | Liabilities |
| Reserves = $20 | Deposits = $110 |
|     Required = $11 | |
|     Excess = $9 | |
| Loans = $70 | |
| T-bills = $20 | |

ity requirements. The Fed's mechanism is the *discount window.*

In Table 3.8, Bank A takes a short-term loan of $9 from the Federal Reserve through its discount window and pays the discount rate. The loan from the Fed is a liability for the bank, and the borrowed funds are recorded as reserves. The loan to the bank is an asset for the Fed; the corresponding liability is the increase in the bank's deposits at the Fed.

The discount rate is not determined by the interaction of supply and demand; it is set administratively by the Fed. Changes in the discount rate are announced by the Federal Reserve. A reduction in the discount rate communicates a willingness to inject reserves into the banking system, lowers interest rates, stimulates borrowing, and stimulates the economy. An increase in the rate communicates a reluctance to add reserves to the banking system in order to curtail economic expansion and prevent inflation.

The interest rate differential between what a bank charges on a personal loan and the discount rate appears to be an opportunity for banks to profit. But the Fed protects the safety of the banking system and does not seek to boost the profits of individual banks. Therefore, a bank's repeated visits to the discount window signal two possibilities: either the borrowing bank is unable to manage its balance sheet and experiences recurring liquidity problems (which can result in the bank's charter to operate being revoked) or the bank is trying to profit on the yield spread. Both prompt the Fed to investigate. To avoid this scrutiny, banks often prefer to borrow in the *federal funds market,* discussed next.

In Table 3.9, Bank A experiences an unexpected cash withdrawal, and its reserve position is deficient by $9. At the same time, Bank B experiences an unexpected deposit of $10, which pushes its total deposits to $110. Bank B has excess reserves of $9. The situations at Banks A and B create an opportunity for both to benefit. Bank A needs reserves to meet its requirements. Bank B does not want to hold excess reserves because of the opportunity cost of lost interest income. Bank B seeks to buy an earning asset, if only for a short period of time.

*Table 3.10*
## Federal Funds Transaction, Step II

| Bank A | |
|---|---|
| Assets | Liabilities |
| Reserves = $9 | Deposits = $90 |
|    Required = $9 | Loans to Bank B = $9 |
|    Excess = $0 | |
| Loans = $70 | |
| T-bills = $20 | |
| Bank B | |
| Assets | Liabilities |
| Reserves = –$9 | No change |
| Loans to Bank A = +$9 | |

Table 3.9 shows a willing buyer (Bank A) and seller (Bank B). Bank A sees the opportunity to meet its reserve requirement, and Bank B sees an opportunity to acquire an earning asset. The loan exchange between the two banks is a federal funds transaction, and the balance sheet entries are shown in Table 3.10.

Table 3.10 records the federal funds transaction. At Bank B there are two entries on the asset side of its balance sheet: a reduction in reserves and a loan to Bank A. At Bank A, the federal funds borrowed are a liability, and the reserves are an asset. With the loan, Bank A meets its reserve requirements, and Bank B earns interest income.

There are several important aspects of this market. (1) Federal funds transactions are free and voluntary transactions. The Federal Reserve System is not involved. The federal funds market satisfies the needs of both lending and borrowing banks. (2) The *federal funds rate* is determined by supply and demand. The Fed does not administratively set this rate. As discussed in regard to *open market operations,* the Fed affects the availability of reserves, which influences the federal funds rate. (3) Directional changes in

the federal funds rate provide insight into the macroeconomy and the future direction of other interest rates. In the absence of Federal Reserve policy, increases in the federal funds rate reflect an expanding economy, and other interest rates are expected to rise. Decreases reflect a weakening economy, and other rates are expected to follow. (4) Interpreting changes in the federal funds rate is complicated by Federal Reserve policy. Some increases in the federal funds rate in an expanding economy are the result of the Fed restricting the growth in bank reserves. Some declines in the federal funds rate in a recessionary economy are the result of the Fed increasing reserves.

### Open Market Operations

The Fed's primary tool of monetary policy is open market operations, and this is the mechanism that affects the availability of reserves in the banking system, the federal funds rate, other interest rates, and the macroeconomy. Table 3.11 shows transactions for expansionary open market operations.

In Table 3.11, Bank A is meeting the 10 percent reserve requirements, holding loans and Treasury bills. With no excess reserves, Bank A cannot extend additional credit until a loan is repaid or a new deposit received. Assuming Bank A is typical of the entire banking system, macroeconomic expansion is in jeopardy. Credit is unavailable to purchase inventory for future sales or to purchase goods and services.

To provide liquidity to the banking system to sustain economic growth, the Fed engages in expansionary open market operations by purchasing Treasury bills from Bank A. This transaction occurs in a secondary market. Bank A voluntarily sells the Treasury bills if the Fed pays an attractive price.

*Table 3.11*
**Expansionary Open Market Operations**

| Bank A | | |
|---|---|---|
| Assets | Liabilities | |
| Reserves = $10 | Deposits = $100 | |
| Required reserves = $10 | | |
| Excess reserves = $0 | | |
| Loans = $70 | | |
| T-bills = $20 | | |

| Federal Reserve | | Bank A | |
|---|---|---|---|
| Assets | Liabilities | Assets | Liabilities |
| T-bills = +$20 | Deposit Bank A = +$20 | Reserves = $30 | Deposits = $100 |
| | | | Required = $10 |
| | | | Excess = $20 |
| | | Loans = $70 | |
| | | T-bills = $ 0 | |

The transaction is recorded in Table 3.11. The Fed acquires the Treasury bills from Bank A, an asset for the Fed. The Fed pays for the purchase by crediting Bank A's deposits, and the deposit is a liability for the Federal Reserve. Bank A's balance sheet shows the sale of the Treasury bills and the increase in reserves.

The increase in excess reserves at Bank A (see Table 3.1) alters the supply and demand balance in the federal funds market and pushes the federal funds rate lower. Other interest rates fall, reflecting the new conditions of supply and demand in the credit markets. The macro-economy is stimulated because lower interest rates encourage credit-based spending. Correspondingly, the deposit expansion multiplier supports multiple deposits, loan creation, and an expanding economy.

Expansionary open market operations are appropriate when unemployment is high and economic expansion does not lead to demand-pull inflation. It is vital, however, to differentiate between the Fed prompting an increase in the money supply and Congress printing currency. Congressional spending bills are politically popular. If Congress persistently prints money to pay for spending projects, demand-pull inflation occurs. The politically independent Federal Reserve System rightly separates Congress' authority to spend from money creation. The Fed purchases Treasury debt if appropriate but does not do so for political expediency.

Contractionary open market operations operate in reverse. In Table 3.12, Bank A holds $10 in excess reserves and is able to make a loan. If the Federal Reserve perceives a threat of inflation, it sells Treasury bills from its portfolio, thereby limiting the banking system's ability to extend credit.

In Table 3.12, Bank A willingly buys the Treasury bills because the Fed makes an attractive price offer. For Bank A, the purchase is the acquisition of an asset and the purchase occurs in a secondary market. The Federal Reserve debits the deposits of

*Table 3.12*
**Contractionary Open Market Operations**

| Bank A | | Bank A | |
|---|---|---|---|
| Assets | Liabilities | Assets | Liabilities |
| Reserves = $20 | Deposits = $100 | Reserves = $10 | Deposits = $100 |
|    Required = $10 | |    Required = $10 | |
|    Excess = $10 | |    Excess = $0 | |
| Loans = $70 | | Loans = $70 | |
| T-bills = $10 | | T-bills = $20 | |
| Federal Reserve | | | |
| Assets | | Liabilities | |
| | | Deposits of Bank A = -$10 | |
| T- bills = -$10 | | | |

Bank A and reduces its holding of Treasury bills. The purchase of Treasury bills by Bank A increases its holdings of government debt and eliminates the excess reserves. Contractionary open market operations reduce the amount of excess reserves in the banking system. The federal funds rate is pushed higher, and other interest rates follow as supply and demand change. The higher cost and decreased availability of credit slow aggregate demand and reduce inflationary pressures in the economy.

*The Lagged Effect of Monetary Policy*

The execution of monetary policy is hindered by lag effects.[2] A recognition lag occurs because it is difficult for policy makers to interpret volatile economic indicators. Once policy needs are recognized, the Federal Reserve can act quickly, as monetary policy actions do not require political approval. The action lag is short. Once the Federal Reserve acts through open market operations, there is an operational lag in the effect on the macroeconomy: it may take three to eighteen months before interest rate changes affect economic activity.

The operational lag occurs for many reasons. Consider the Fed trying to stimulate the economy by purchasing Treasury bills from banks. The purchase intends to add reserves, increase the banking system's ability to lend, and push interest rates lower. The impact of the lower interest rates occurs with some delay. Households and businesses must recognize that rates have fallen and decide to take

---

*Exercise 3.2*

Show the balance sheet transactions of the Federal Reserve purchasing Treasury bills from a bank that has no excess reserves. Next, show transactions that occur as the bank makes a loan to a retailer who seeks the credit to restock inventory for the next season.

  (a) Discuss the nature of the fractional reserve banking system.
  (b) Discuss the effect of the transactions on interest rates.
  (c) Discuss the linkage of the transactions to the macroeconomy.

advantage of the more favorable credit conditions. Lower mortgage rates may prompt a household to build a new home. The start of the construction does not begin immediately. Only after construction begins do employment and income grow. Further, if lower interest rates lead to expectations of even lower interest rates, the lag effect of monetary policy gets longer as buyers postpone purchases until the rates decline more.

The lag effect of monetary policy creates problems. Consider a period during which the economy is growing and unemployment is shrinking. Prices are not rising rapidly, but developing conditions are conducive to inflation. Because of the lag, the Federal Reserve acts in advance of inflation actually being observed. In the absence of overt signs of inflation, the Fed is exposed to criticism for slowing the economy.

## Cyclical Effectiveness of Monetary Policy

Monetary policy affects the macroeconomy by altering the availability of credit and interest rates. Because of the link between the price and availability of credit and aggregate demand, monetary policy may be more effective in slowing the economy to reduce inflationary pressures than in stimulating economic expansion. Contractionary open market operations reduce the availability of reserves and push interest rates higher. At higher interest rates the present value of business investment projects is lower. Further, new construction projects and the purchase of new or replacement machines are postponed. Similarly, home and vehicle purchases are discouraged when interest rates and periodic payments rise.

In contrast, expansionary open market operations occur when the economy needs stimulus. Under such conditions, plant and equipment utilization rates are low, and businesses do not need to expand productive capabilities. Hence, lower inter-est rates may be insufficient to start an investment spending boom. Similarly, with unemployment high and consumer confidence low, lower interest rates may be insufficient to boost residential construction and the purchase of consumer durables. In a weak economy, lower interest rates may be inadequate to stimulate aggregate demand. Fiscal policy may have a greater stimulating effect on the economy.

## Monetary Policy Versus Fiscal Policy and the Microeconomic Effects

Both monetary and fiscal policy actions affect aggregate demand and influence firms' selling environments. Government spending and taxation decisions directly affect aggregate demand, and monetary policy actions alter the availability of credit, interest rates, and aggregate demand. Importantly, monetary and fiscal policies have different microeconomic effects and differently affect the economic environments within which firms and households make decisions.

The details of a fiscal policy action are enormously important to a firm's microeconomic environment. An expansionary fiscal policy action that increases expenditures for highway construction has different microeconomic effects than an equivalent dollar spending increase on military hardware, health care, or defense. The production cost chain of each industry is different; therefore, different industries are affected. Additionally, as different industries are affected, the economic effects of fiscal policy actions differ by geographic region of the country. Similarly, the microeconomic effects of tax cuts differ from the effects of government spending increases. Households do not buy the same goods as the government; hence, different industries and regions are affected. Also, the details of a tax change are important. A tax cut for low-income households encourages consumption and improves the selling environment for some retailers. In turn, sales of consumer goods track through the production cost chain, and the macroeconomic effect of a tax cut depends upon whether the consumer products are manufactured domestically or overseas. An income tax for the wealthy stimulates the demand for different goods and services. In contrast, a tax incentive for business investment spending impacts the microeconomy differently and has different geographic implications.

Monetary policy actions have different microeconomic effects. Monetary policy affects the availability of credit and interest rates. Those industries whose sales are dependent upon borrowed funds are affected the most. Automobile manufacturers, the construction industry, and those who make industrial machines and tools are examples of the most heavily affected. The production cost chain of each industry affects suppliers, and different geographic areas are affected.

### Financing the Federal Budget Deficit

In Table 2.10 the increase in government spending sparks a multiplier process that leads to an increase in output and employment. The example in Table 2.10 is oversimplified, however. In reality, the macroeconomic effects of the fiscal policy action depend upon how the deficit is financed. This section raises the following questions: How are those additional government expenditures financed? Is there sufficient liquidity in the economy to support higher levels of aggregate demand without inhibiting spending elsewhere in the economy? How does the financing of the deficit affect spending across the economy?

When tax receipts are insufficient to cover outlays, the government's budget is in *deficit*. The accumulation of annual deficits comprises the *national debt*. Even when the budget is in deficit, however, the federal government must pay its bills.

---

**Application Box 3.11**

In December 2005, the U.S. national debt was approximately $8.2 trillion. Interpreting the consequences of the national debt is problematic, but two major issues emerge.

First, future generations inherit the debt and the financial obligations. At the same time, they also inherit what the debt financed. If future generations inherit an interstate highway system and some of the debt to pay for it, the question is simple: Is the roadway worth the cost to the next generation?

Second, if the deficit is financed domestically, future generations inherit both the interest costs and the interest income. If the future tax burden differs from the interest income earned, there is a redistribution of income. If, however, the debt is financed by foreign lenders, the interest payments are sent overseas.

The worst case for future generations is to inherit financial obligations payable to foreigners for deficits that were accrued to finance the current consumption of a prior generation.

*Source:* For debt figure: Ed Hall, "U.S. National Debt Clock FAQ," www.brillig.com/debt_clock/faq.html.

---

Because Congress reassigned the regulation of the nation's money supply to the Federal Reserve System, Congress is not permitted to print money to cover the deficit. Where does the government get the money to pay its bills?

To cover its obligations, the government borrows. It offers promissory notes in the form of Treasury bonds, notes, and bills, and these debt instruments differ by time to maturity. Bonds mature in five years or longer; notes mature in more than one year and up to five years, and bills mature over periods from three months to one year. These Treasury debt instruments have two attractive characteristics. As full-faith obligations of the government, Treasury debt is low-risk. Also, established secondary markets make the debt instruments liquid. Buyers of U.S. Treasury debt include banks, other financial institutions, non-financial businesses, individuals, foreigners, and the Federal Reserve.

The macroeconomic effect of the government's deficit spending depends on two issues: How would the monies that purchase the government debt have been used otherwise? Who buys the government debt instruments?

How would the money have been used otherwise? This important question raises the issue of *crowding out*. Assume the government deficit occurs at a time when the private sector's demand for credit is strong. Businesses want credit to finance increases in inventory and to purchase new plant and equipment. Households seek credit to finance their purchases of homes and vehicles. Under these conditions government's acquisition of funds through its sale of debt instruments prevents a business or household from borrowing and making a purchase. One component of aggregate demand (government spending) crowds out another (business or consumer spending). Deficit spending by the government occurs, but there is no net increase in aggregate demand. The macroeconomy is not stimulated.

The crowding out occurs as government (a not-for-profit entity) increases borrowing, which (all else equal) leads to higher interest rates. At higher interest rates, private sector borrowers withdraw from the credit markets and postpone purchases. Crowding out is characterized by rising interest rates and the diversion of scarce productive resources from private sector use to public sector use. In contrast, during a period of economic weakness, businesses and households do not seek credit to make purchases, and government borrowing does

## Application Box 3.12

In simple terms, a country must pay for its purchases. If consumers do not spend all of their income, they save. If government does not spend all of its tax revenues, it ends up with a surplus (savings). Savings are useful for an economy, allowing the purchase of equipment to permit more production in the future.

A problem arises when individuals and government do not save. In the United States today, consumers save very little and the federal government has a propensity for budgetary deficits. The problem is how to pay for everything purchased and finance the purchase of new equipment for future production.

One resolution occurs on an international basis. Many U.S. purchases are imports, and the trade deficit results in transfers of funds to foreigners. Foreigners have the ability to invest those funds in the United States for nongovernmental uses. Thus a budget deficit reduces the funds available in the United States. The gap can be filled by a trade deficit, contingent upon foreigners returning funds to the United States through financial investments. This connection between the budget deficit and the trade deficit is known as the "twin deficits."

not crowd out private sector spending. Under such conditions, the government's deficit spending has an expansionary effect.

If the financing of a government deficit crowds out private sector spending, the deficit does not have a short-term macroeconomic effect. However, there are potentially serious long-term economic consequences. If financing the deficit prevents businesses from expanding plant and equipment, the economy's long-run growth potential is reduced, as new technology and new machines are the foundation of long-term economic expansion. At the microeconomic level, firms (and employees) that produce and sell the products purchased by the government differ from those that provide goods to the private sector. Industry and geographic effects are different, and decision makers in business units and households must understand the microeconomic implications.

Who buys the debt? This question is important because the source of the funds used to purchases Treasury debt affects the macro consequences of deficit financing. The issue is simple: does the purchaser of the Treasury debt introduce new funds into the credit market?

Assume a U.S. resident or domestic business purchases Treasury debt. If these funds would have been available in the financial markets, there is no increase in the funds in the financial markets. In contrast, the Fed's purchase of newly issued Treasury debt is similar to printing new money. To complete the purchase, the Fed credits the Treasury's accounts. These Treasury deposits are subject to the deposit expansion multiplier. The nation's money supply rises, and the increase in government spending sets off a multiplier process that pushes income, output, and employment higher. Potential crowding out is reduced or eliminated because the financial system has additional liquidity to meet private and public needs. However, the Fed is not obligated to buy new Treasury debt. If the Fed decides not to buy additional Treasury debt (fearing multiple deposit creation and inflation), the Treasury competes with the private sector for the available credit. Interest rates rise and crowding out occurs.

International businesses, individuals, and governments lend to finance the U.S. government. If foreign financial capital purchases government debt (and would not have been used for any other financial investment in the United States), potential crowding out is reduced by the inflow of new money. International purchases of government debt are recorded in the balance of payments (see pages 68–69), and these purchases affect currency exchange rates and, in turn, imports and exports. The effect of international investments in U.S. financial markets is examined in the appendix to Chapter 4.

## Interest Rates

Interest rates are the price of credit, and changes in interest rates have a substantial effect on the macroeconomy. Interest rates affect businesses' and households' willingness to make purchases on credit. For example, consider an individual planning to purchase a new $25,000 vehicle. For purposes of the example, the full amount of the purchase price is financed over five years. For simplicity, one payment is made at the end of each year. At 5 percent interest on the loan, the annual cost of the vehicle is $5,774; at 8 percent, the annual cost is $6,261. Higher interest rates raise the cost of purchases and reduce aggregate demand.

A second example of the effect of interest rate changes refers to business investment spending.

**Application Box 3.14**

Loan amortization payments are determined through the use of present value calculations. Assume a $25,000 loan for five years at 8 percent. The present value of the series of payments must equal the loan amount. To solve for the payment:

$$\$25,000 = \text{annual payment} \times \text{PVIFA}$$

where PVIFA = present value interest factor of an annuity (in this case, five years at 8 percent) (see the present value tables at the end of the book)

$$\$25,000 = \text{annual payment} \times 3.9927$$

$$\text{Annual payment} = \$6,261$$

Consider a firm examining the purchase of a machine that increases output by 100 units per year (see Table 3.13). It is expected that each additional unit of output is sold at $2. The life expectancy of the new machine is five years, and it has no salvage value or disposal cost. The purchase price of the machine is $200. The example is simplified by ignoring the tax consequences of the loan and the annual depreciation of the machine. At 5 percent, the present value of the increased profits from the increased sales ($216.46) exceeds the cost of the new machine ($200). The machine should be purchased. At 10 percent, the present value of the increased profits ($189.52) is less than the price of the machine ($200). The machine should not be purchased.

The numeric example is important. It shows that the change in interest rates has a significant impact on a firm's decision to purchase the new equipment. First, changes in investment spending are subject to the multiplier. Hence, the magnitude of the impact of the interest rate change increases and the effects of the interest rate change spread across the economy. Second, the interest rate change affects the selling environment for the firm that produces the equipment, the firms that supply material inputs, the workers, and the firms that sell consumer goods to those workers. Investors' returns are correspondingly affected. Third, the impact of interest rate changes on investment decisions exemplifies the importance of monitor-

*Table 3.13*
**Business Investment Analysis**

|  | Period 1 | Period 2 | Period 3 | Period 4 | Period 5 |
|---|---|---|---|---|---|
| Additional income | $200 | $200 | $200 | $200 | $200 |
| Variable costs | $150 | $150 | $150 | $150 | $150 |
| Net income | $50 | $50 | $50 | $50 | $50 |
| Present value at 5 percent | $47.62 | $45.35 | $43.19 | $41.13 | $39.17 |
| Present value at 10 percent | $45.45 | $41.32 | $37.56 | $34.15 | $31.04 |
| Present value of income at 5 percent = $216.46 | | | | | |
| Present value of income at 10 percent = $189.52 | | | | | |

ing interest rates as part of the environment within which decisions are made. Further, interest rate changes affect the demand for homes and durable consumer products such as automobiles and appliances, and changes in aggregate demand spark the multiplier process.

---

### Exercise 3.3

Consider the purchase of a new home involving a $100,000 mortgage.

(a) Calculate the annual payments assuming the mortgage rate is 5 percent.

(b) Calculate the annual payments assuming the mortgage rate is 7 percent.

(c) Assuming annual mortgage payments cannot exceed 30 percent of the borrower's gross pay, determine the minimum income that qualifies for a loan at 5 percent and the minimum income that qualifies for the same loan at 7 percent.

---

## Components of Interest Rates

The discussion so far has simply referred to interest rates. However, there are many different rates, and it is useful to examine why interest rates differ. Five components of interest rates are considered: risk, tax treatment, inflation expectations, liquidity, and maturity.

### Risk

Different debt instruments carry different degrees of default risk, and all else being equal, the greater the risk, the higher the interest rate. Lending to the federal government is relatively low risk, and the government's borrowing costs for comparable maturities are generally lower. Similarly, a bank

---

### Application Box 3.15

December 21, 2005
Ten-year corporate bond interest rates

High quality = 5.72 percent
Medium quality = 6.04 percent

*Source: Wall Street Journal,* December 21, 2005.

---

charges its biggest and best customers their *prime rate,* and other borrowers pay premiums over prime based on their risk level.

The risk premium in a debt instrument is not constant over the business cycle. In a weakening economy, the risk of default rises and the risk premium rises. In a strengthening economy, risk premiums decline because even relatively weak borrowers have a better chance to repay on time. The change in the differential between a higher-risk corporate bond and a lower-risk one is a leading economic indicator. When the differential shrinks, it reflects investor expectations of a strengthening economy and a reduction in default risk. When the differential increases, the message is reversed. Investors expect a weakening economy and an increase in default risk.

### Tax Treatment

The tax status of the interest earned on a debt instrument affects interest rates. For example, the interest income on municipal bonds is exempt from federal income tax. For an individual in a 33 percent tax bracket, earning 9 percent on an investment subject to income tax is equivalent to 6 percent interest on income-tax-free municipal bonds. Given comparable risk and maturity, income-tax-free municipal bonds or notes carry lower interest rates.

## Inflation Expectations

Assume an individual purchases a five-year note that promises to repay $100. At the point of purchase, the market rate of interest on five-year notes is 5 percent. The buyer pays $78.35 (the present value of $100 in five years at 5 percent) for the promissory note. The *nominal interest rate* is 5 percent. To the buyer's dismay, inflation turns out to be 3 percent each year over the five years. This reduces the purchasing power of the $100 bond, and the *real interest rate* is 2 percent (the nominal interest rate minus the rate of inflation).

A lender who requires a 5 percent real rate of interest and who expects 3 percent annual inflation insists on an 8 percent nominal interest rate. For a five-year promissory note, a purchaser with the same inflation expectation willingly pays $68.06 (the present value of $100 in five years at 8 percent). If the 3 percent expected annual inflation actually occurs, there is no implicit transfer of income from borrower to lender. If the rate of inflation is more than 3 percent, the borrower wins because the $100 will be repaid with cheaper dollars. If the actual inflation is less than 3 percent, the lender earns a real rate of return that is greater than 5 percent.

The sensitivity of interest rates to expected inflation affects the outcome of the Federal Reserve System's open market operations. When the Fed conducts expansionary policy, it buys Treasury bills from the banking system. This increases the supply of reserves and ordinarily lowers interest rates. If, however, the monetary policy action raises the threat of inflation, interest rates may rise. Similarly, if the Fed reduces reserves, interest rates increase unless offset by the effect of borrowers and lenders, who revise downward their expectations of inflation.

## Liquidity

The liquidity of a debt instrument refers to the ease of converting it back into cash without loss of value. Investors require compensation to surrender liquidity. All else being equal, the greater the liquidity the lower the interest rate. The liquidity of an asset is affected by many variables, including the breadth of a secondary market and the time to maturity.

To examine the relationship between interest and the time to maturity of a debt instrument, it is necessary to establish the inverse relationship between the price of a bond and the interest rate. Consider a note that matures in one year and promises to pay $100. This note, at 5 percent interest, sells for $95.24 (= $100 ÷ 1.05). At 10 percent, the same promise to pay the $100 in a year sells for $90.91 (= $100 ÷ 1.10). The price of the debt instrument is inversely related to the interest rate.

Consider a one-year debt instrument. At the point of purchase, the interest rate is 5 percent, and the purchase price is $95.24. Immediately

---

**Application Box 3.16**

Treasury Inflation-Protected Securities (TIPS) are marketable securities whose principal adjusts in response to changes in the Consumer Price Index. When the Consumer Price Index rises, the principal increases at the same rate.

TIPS pay interest at a fixed rate that is determined at auction. Because the rate is applied to the principal and the principal changes with inflation, interest payments also vary with the Consumer Price Index.

At the maturity of a TIPS, the investor receives the greater of the adjusted principal or the original investment. This provision protects the investor from deflation.

following the purchase, the market rate of interest rises to 6 percent, and the resale value of the note falls to $94.34 (= $100 ÷ 1.06). In contrast, consider a two-year debt instrument. At the point of purchase, the interest rate is 5 percent and the purchase price is $90.70 (= $100 ÷ (1.05 ×1.05)). After the purchase, the interest rate rises to 6 percent. The price of the two-year note declines to $89.00 (= $100 ÷ (1.06 ×1.06)). The one-year debt instrument declines in value by $0.90, whereas the two-year debt instrument declines in value by $1.70. The price of the longer-term debt instrument is more sensitive to the interest rate change, thereby making long-term debt less liquid because of the threat of the loss of market value. In turn, short-term interest rates are generally lower than long-term rates.

## Maturity

The *yield curve* examines the relationship between interest rates and the time to maturity of a debt instrument. Figure 3.2 plots actual interest rates at a point in time for debt instruments that are alike in all respects except for time to maturity. In Figure 3.2 the vertical axis is the interest rate, and the horizontal axis is the time to maturity. The pattern of interest rates relative to the time to maturity is the yield curve.

The yield curve in Figure 3.2 is upward-sloping. Because long-term debt is less liquid, long-term rates are generally higher than short-term rates and the yield curve is usually upward-sloping. However, the following discussion of the *expectations theory* of the yield curve examines changes in the relationship between long-term and short-term interest rates.

To examine the expectations theory two assumptions are made: that the analysis ignores the liquidity premium in long-term interest rates, and that a short-term debt instrument has a one-year

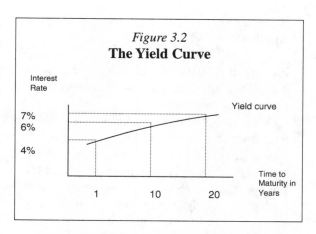

*Figure 3.2*
**The Yield Curve**

maturity and a long-term debt instrument has a two-year maturity.

At a given point in time, an investor sees that the interest rate on a one-year debt instrument is 5 percent and the two-year rate on an instrument of comparable risk is 6 percent. What choice is proper for the investor? These observed interest rates are insufficient to make an investment decision. Because the investor can make successive one-year investments or a two year investment, the investor anticipates the one-year interest rate one year in the future.

If the investor believes the one-year interest rate one year from now will rise to 8 percent, two consecutive one-year investments offer a higher return than a two-year investment. Consecutive one-year investments at 5 percent and 8 percent offer a higher return than 6 percent for each of two years. Investors direct money to the one-year market. In turn, short-term rates fall and long-term rates rise.

The investor is indifferent between the one- and two-year investments when there is no earning differential. Assume the investor sees a 6 percent per year return on a two-year debt instrument and a 5 percent return for a one-year instrument. If the investor expects a one-year rate of 7 percent one year from now, there is no earning advantage in

## Application Box 3.17

Examination of the financial futures market also provides insight into investor expectations of future interest rates.

Often, financial market participants are able to predict needs to raise funds or invest funds at a certain time. For example, a residential real estate developer anticipates the need for funds in a certain month to begin a construction project. Similarly, a manufacturer anticipates in the same month the inflow of cash based on a contractual agreement with a buyer.

The developer's and the manufacturer's needs complement each other. Both have incentives to agree today to deliver and accept funds at a predetermined time in the future and at an interest rate agreed upon today. This transaction is a *financial futures* transaction.

Financial futures transactions are recorded in the major daily newspapers. While borrowers and lenders may have expectations that prove to be wrong, monitoring the futures interest rates provides a summary of the expectations of financial market participants.

rates. This occurs if investors expect more rapid macroeconomic growth or an increase in inflation. An inverted yield curve occurs when long-term interest rates are lower than short-term interest rates. This interest rate structure means investors expect short-term rates to be lower in the future. An inverted yield curve is a predictor of recession. Investors anticipate a weaker macroeconomy in which the demand for credit is low and where the Fed is likely to engage in expansionary open market operations.

### Exercise 3.4

Using the *Wall Street Journal,* construct the government securities yield curve.

(a) Comment on the shape.

(b) What does the shape imply about expectations for future short-term interest rates?

(c) Why is an inverted yield curve a leading indicator of a business slowdown?

(d) If a yield curve grows increasingly steep, does it signify expectations of rising inflation?

## The Debt and Equity Markets

either market. Ignoring the mathematics of compounding interest and the risks associated with not knowing the one-year interest next year, the critical conclusion is that the long-term rate is equal to the average of the current one-year rate plus the expected one-year rate. Therefore, investors examine the yield curve and interpret expectations of future short-term interest rates to make decisions accordingly.

Changes in the slope of the yield curve reflect revised investor expectations. For example, the yield curve becomes steeper if investors revise upward their expectations of future short-term interest

The equity valuation formula was introduced in the prior chapter with the assumption that 100 percent of the firm's earnings are paid as dividends. No earnings are retained. Table 3.14 restates the formula, and the emphasis in this chapter is on investors' required rate of return and the role of interest rates in determining equity values.

The numerator is investors' expectations of the firm's dividends per share per period. The denominator discounts those dividends to present value, and the interest rate used for discounting to present value is investors' required rate of return. The re-

*Table 3.14*
## Equity Valuation

$$\text{Price} = \frac{D_1}{(1+r)} + \frac{D_2}{(1+r)^2} + \frac{D_3}{(1+r)^3} + \frac{D_n}{(1+r)^n}$$

where:

$D$ = earnings and dividend by time period

$r$ = investors' required rate of return

quired rate of return comprises three components: the risk-free interest rate, seen as the rate on three-month Treasury bills; a risk premium for entering the equity market, where the size of the premium depends upon the individual investor's aversion to risk; and a premium for company-specific risk. The company-specific risk reflects a firm's vulnerabilities to competition, changes in technology, exposure to the business cycle, and buyer tastes. All else equal, higher risks lead to a higher required rate of return and a lower share price.

Monetary policy affects the risk-free rate, which is a component of the required rate of return. Assume expansionary open market operations by the Federal Reserve. The monetary policy action af-

---

## Application Box 3.18

A firm's beta coefficient measures the volatility of its stock price relative to an average stock. By definition, an average-risk stock has a beta coefficient of 1.0, so a firm with a beta coefficient of 2.0 is twice as risky as the average stock. A firm's sensitivity to the business cycle is one determinant of its beta coefficient.

Investors' required rate of return on a particular investment varies with the degree of risk. All else equal, a higher beta coefficient translates into a lower price for a share.

---

fects the value of a share in two ways. First, expansionary open market operations increase reserves in the banking system and push short-term interest rates lower. As Treasury bills and other short-term interest rates fall, investors' required rate of return falls. The present value of the expected stream of earnings and dividends rises. Stock prices increase. Second, for some businesses lower interest rates increase the demand for their products and increase profitability. For interest-rate-sensitive firms, the decrease in interest rates has a double-barreled effect on their stock price: a smaller denominator (lower required rate of return) and larger numerator (higher dividends) push the stock price higher.

Contractionary monetary policy affects equity values in the opposite direction. Higher Treasury bill interest rates raise the risk-free rate, raise investors' required rate of return, and reduce the present value of the stream of income. Also, higher interest rates reduce the expected earnings of interest-rate-sensitive firms. Both forces push equity prices lower.

The effect of interest rate changes and economic fundamentals on equity values is complicated at turning points in the business cycle. Consider the following example. An economic expansion has been under way, perhaps induced by expansionary monetary policy. The Fed's expansionary action pushes the investors' required rate of return lower (the denominator) and raises expected earnings (the numerator). Equity values soar as the economy expands. However, continued good economic news raises the threat of inflation, and so interest rates rise. Which force is greater: the expected increase in earnings in the numerator or higher interest rates in the denominator? The stage of the business cycle determines if good economic news is good or bad for the equity market.

The same uncertainty occurs on the other side of the business cycle. During a business downturn, investors lower their expectations of future corporate earnings. As the numerator shrinks, the value of shares declines. At some point, incessant bad news on the economy leads investors to believe that the Federal Reserve will take aggressive action to push interest rates lower to stimulate the economy. Lower interest rates, at some point, offset the deteriorating profit performance, and stock prices rise.

## Summary

This chapter's focus on the money and financial system further defines environmental conditions within which firms and individuals make decisions and which affect the outcomes of those choices.

## Review Terms

| | |
|---|---|
| Asset and liability management | Fractional reserve banking |
| Beta coefficient | Futures market |
| Bond valuation | Indirect finance |
| Crowding out | Interest rate differentials |
| Deficit units | Liquidity |
| Demand-pull inflation | Open market operations |
| Direct finance | Primary and secondary markets |
| Discount rate | Real and nominal interest rates |
| Equation of exchange | Required reserves |
| Excess reserves | Stock value calculations |
| Federal funds rate | Surplus units |
| Federal Reserve System | Time value of money |
| Financial intermediaries | Velocity of money |
| Financing the debt | Yield curve |

## Discussion Questions

1. Show the balance sheet entries of a Federal Reserve purchase of securities from a bank. What are the interest rate and macroeconomic consequences?

2. Explain why changes in the federal funds rate tend to precede changes in all other interest rates.

3. Why is the federal funds rate typically a little higher than the Federal Reserve's discount rate?

4. What are the advantages of monetary policy relative to fiscal policy? What are the disadvantages?

5. Assume your organization is considering the purchase of a new machine that is expected to lower materials costs by $500 over each of the next five years. The machine costs $2,000 and has no salvage value at the end of the fifth year. Is it wise to buy the machine if the cost of funds is 5 percent? Is it wise to buy the machine if the cost of funds is 10 percent?

6. Assume reserve requirements are 5 percent and that a bank receives a new deposit of $100. What is the maximum possible deposit expansion?

7. Explain the following: inflation is the result of too much money chasing too few goods.

8. Assume an advisory role in your firm. Explain why monitoring the Federal Reserve can help the firm make better decisions.

9. Assume a stock pays a $1 dividend in the current period. Investors expect the earnings and dividends to grow by 5 percent per year, and investors' required rate of return is 9 percent. Calculate the stock price and the price-to-earnings ratio. Repeat the calculations assuming an interest rate increase leading to a 6 percent investors' required rate of return.

10. Assume an investment advisory role. Explain why monitoring the Federal Reserve

helps provide better investment advice.

11. Using the *Wall Street Journal,* examine the yield curve and the financial futures tables. Based upon this data, what is the three-month Treasury bill rate expected six months in the future? Is the rate higher or lower than today? What might be the cause of any expected change in the rate?

12. Using the Federal Reserve's Web site (www.federalreserve.gov/FOMC), find the minutes of the most recent meeting of the Federal Reserve's Open Market Committee. Summarize the committee's actions and discuss the implications for the economy.

**Notes**

1. Federal Reserve Financial Services, "Check 21 Services," www.frbservices.org/Retail/Check21.html.

2. Bob Woodward, *Maestro: Greenspan's Fed and the American Boom* (New York: Simon and Schuster, 2000), pp. 134–35.

# Case Study 3.1

# Economic Scorecard

Assume you are a corporate economist for a large U.S.-based heavy manufacturing firm and that the firm competes against European rivals at home and abroad. Use Internet data sources to develop a management briefing. The briefing should include the following: (1) a review of the current state of the U.S. economy based on a presentation of key economic and financial indicators, (2) expected U.S. economic conditions over the next twelve months and the forces predicted to drive the economy, (3) issues of economic and financial uncertainty in the economy, and (4) the effects of the economic outlook on the firm.

# 4

# Supply and Demand and
# Market Processes

The first three chapters focus on the firm's macroeconomic and financial environments. The final four chapters examine the firm's microeconomic environment and provide decision makers with additional tools for making business and personal decisions.

**Learning Objectives**

The successful reader understands:

- How markets work and how firms allocate resources internally
- The role of price and the allocation of resources
- The interplay between the goods and the resource market
- The concepts of demand and supply elasticity

## The Circular Flow and Markets

Figure 4.1 shows the two-sector circular flow model seen previously in Chapter 2. The two participants are households and businesses. In the goods market, households express a force of demand, and businesses express a force of supply. There is a separate market for each good or service and grade of product. In the resource market,

households express a force of supply, and businesses express a force of demand. Demand in the resource market is a *derived demand*. Businesses purchase factors of production based on their expected contribution to the production of goods and services salable for profit. There is a separate resource market for each grade of resource input. Both individual goods and resource markets are defined geographically, and the geographic scope of a market determines the number of competitors and the number of buyers.

Referring to Figure 4.1, each transaction in the goods market and in the resource market involves two flows. Real goods and services or resource inputs are exchanged for money. Transactions are defined by the quantity exchanged over a fixed period of time and the price. In everyday life, the money price of a product is the number of dollars required to make a purchase. The money price of one product relative to another defines the opportunity cost. For example, the money price of a cup of coffee is $1 and the money price of a doughnut is $0.50. The opportunity cost of one cup of coffee is two doughnuts. The distinction between the money price and relative price (or opportunity cost) is important. If the money price of a cup of coffee increases to $1.50, the opportunity cost of one cup of coffee rises to three doughnuts. Buyers and sellers respond to the change in the relative prices. In the pages that follow, references to a rise

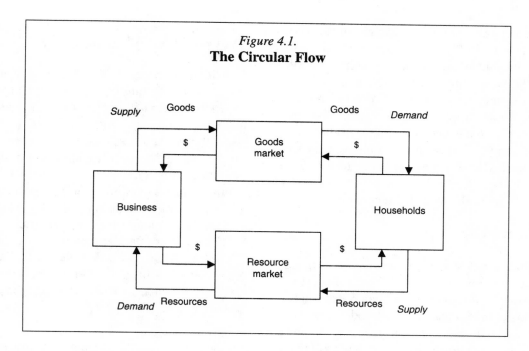

*Figure 4.1.*
**The Circular Flow**

or fall in the price of a product assume other prices remain unchanged.

In a free market economy resource inputs are privately owned by households, and entrepreneurs are the catalysts in the creation of jobs, income, and production. Entrepreneurs incur business risks upon purchasing resource inputs in expectation of producing and selling a good or service for profit. Businesses pay for resource inputs based on the expected market value of the resource's contribution to the production of a good or service. The linkage between the dollar value of one's productivity and income is an incentive for individuals to acquire marketable skills and to work hard. This pursuit of self-interest leads to higher productivity and is advantageous for society as a whole. Also, those making the largest contribution to the production process earn the greatest ability to consume goods and services, and their willingness to make purchases affects the mix of goods produced.

Each transaction in a free economy is voluntary.

Buyers and sellers motivated by self-interest opt not to make a purchase or sale if the terms of a transaction are unsatisfactory. For example, in the goods market, a prospective buyer examines a sweater and its price on a retailer's shelf and decides not to buy it. Similarly, the seller of a house rejects a buyer's bid because the price is too low. In the resource market, an individual turns down a job offer because the wage is too low.

Buyers and sellers enter markets uncertain about others' intentions. Neither group knows the specific goals, preferences, and interests of the other. For example, a business produces and prices a product without knowing exactly how households will respond. Similarly, a job candidate files an application without full knowledge of what the employer is willing to pay. Market processes exchange information between buyers and sellers, and voluntary transactions occur if a mutually agreeable price is found.

Households and businesses enter markets with

competing self-interest objectives. In the goods market, households seek products at the lowest price, and businesses seek the highest possible price. In the resource market, divergent objectives involve wages and the prices of other resource inputs. Households want the highest payment (income) from businesses for their productive resources, and businesses prefer the lowest possible payments. Market processes mediate the differences in buyer and seller objectives and lead to voluntary and self-interest-directed transactions.

## Market Processes

Markets for goods, services, and resources operate as an auction process, though markets differ in terms of the pace at which buyers and sellers exchange information. For example, on a commodities exchange buyers and sellers meet face-to-face, exchanging at a rapid-fire rate information about their willingness to buy and sell at different prices. In the residential real estate market, similar information is exchanged, albeit more slowly. The efficiency of a market is defined by the speed and accuracy with which information is exchanged. More-efficient markets allow buyers to identify and assess buying options, and the increased competition in efficient markets forces lower prices for buyers.

Market processes provide an important *coordination function* across the economy. Consider the hamburger, fries, and beverage you had for lunch yesterday. How did the array of products needed to produce the meal get to the restaurant at the right time? Further, how are intermediate-stage products coordinated along the production cost chain? In a command economy, an economic czar or government bureaucracy anticipates your lunch needs and directs raising cattle, growing potatoes and grain, and transporting items at the appropriate time. In an economy characterized by changing buyer wants and complex input-output relationships, the challenge to

**Application Box 4.1**

Consider the process of purchasing a new car. Prior to the Internet, prospective buyers expended time visiting showrooms to gather price and product information. This information collection process was cumbersome and often unpleasant, and it required return trips to a dealership to negotiate.

When gathering information is difficult, buyers make choices with imperfect knowledge and are vulnerable to paying high prices and receiving lower-quality products.

The Internet facilitates the collection of price and product information. Sellers are thrust into more competitive markets, and buyers benefit.

coordinate production across the economy is overwhelming. The likely outcome is an overabundance of some items and not enough of others.

Markets replace the governmental bureaucracy, and voluntary decisions by entrepreneurs coordinate economic activity. An entrepreneur who anticipates your lunch needs purchases the necessary inputs. Profit incentives flow along the production cost chain (see page 31) and provide other entrepreneurs with incentives to produce beef, potatoes, and vegetables and to transport them at the appropriate time. If entrepreneurs erred in anticipating your lunch preferences, their pursuit of profit quickly and automatically redirects the use of scarce productive resources to meet buyer needs.

## Markets as Buying and Selling Environments

Households and businesses buy and sell goods and services and productive resources in markets, and markets are important environments within which decisions are made. Three considerations help decision makers define a market: What is the product? Who are the rival sellers? Who are the buyers?

Defining a market requires defining the product. Often, the definition of a product is slippery. In the goods market, consider a buyer of a new automobile. The buyer is unlikely to be choosing between a high-performance sports car and a compact, fuel-efficient vehicle. Though both are cars, the products do not compete and are not in the same market. Also, consider a buyer shopping for a birthday gift. Choices abound. Defining a market as flowers, dinner, or jewelry is inappropriate. A broader definition of the gift market is more useful to identify the competition. Further, the definition of a market is not static. Technology changes bring forth new goods, and changes in the use of existing products make the definition of a market and the scope of competition a dynamic process. Similarly, in the resource market, electricity, oil, natural gas, and coal compete as energy products and technologies change.

Once a product is defined, the next step identifies the rival sellers, and this requires specifying the geographic scope of the market. Consider grocery stores. There are many buyers (households) and many sellers (stores) nationwide, but the relevant market for a grocery is limited by the buyers' willingness to drive. Despite many grocery stores nationwide, a small town's market resembles a monopoly. However, the scope of grocery store rivalries extends to convenience stores, mini-marts, fast-food places, and home-delivery restaurants. Second, the geographic scope of a market is limited by transportation costs. For example, the weight of coated corrugated shipping containers limits the geographic scope an individual seller serves. Third, e-shopping eliminates geographic boundaries for some products and intensifies interfirm rivalries.

Identifying the buyers helps to direct marketing

## Application Box 4.2

*Product positioning* refers to activities that create and maintain a concept of the firm's product in the minds of customers. Marketers develop *perceptual maps* by asking consumers questions about their perceptions of products with respect to two or more product differentiators. For example, a perceptual map for breakfast cereals assesses competing products by price and by healthfulness. The map helps decision makers identify their most direct rivals and the closest substitute products.

## Exercise 4.1

Discuss each of the following:

(a) The market system relies upon self-interest to achieve maximum economic well-being of the community as a whole.

(b) No single individual or government bureaucracy decides effectively what, how, and for whom to produce. How do prices and the pursuit of profit coordinate independent units across the economy?

(c) Self-interest is the driving force that brings forth new goods and services and new methods of production.

(d) Entrepreneurs are the driving force in a market economy, but the consumer rules.

(e) Discuss the advantages and disadvantages of an economic system that rewards workers on the basis of the expected market value of their productivity.

### Exercise 4.2

For your employer:

(a) Define the product or service, geographic scope, manner in which it serves buyers, and the closest rivals.

(b) Who are the most preferred buyers?

(c) What new products or technologies make your firm vulnerable?

efforts. In the goods market, a business brings forth a good or service with a particular price and characteristics. It appeals to a subset of buyers defined by their use of the product, preference pattern, age, gender, and other variables. By defining the target buyer group, marketers can carefully craft and direct their messages. In the resource market, individuals who assess their skills and employment aspirations target potential employers and engage in a focused job search. By knowing how the seller seeks to meet buyer aspirations, employees choose their desired working environment.

## The Goods Market: Supply, Demand, and Equilibrium

### The Force of Demand

An individual enters the goods market with a willingness and ability to purchase a good or service. Table 4.1 shows an individual's *demand function* $(D_x)$. The number of units of the product the individual buyer is willing and able to purchase is the dependent variable $(D_x)$. The independent variables include the price of the product, the price of alternative products, the buyer's preference for the product, income, net wealth, interest rates, demographic factors, and the expectations of the future price of the product.

Figure 4.2 shows the buyer's demand curve. It

*Table 4.1*
### Individual's Demand Function

$$D_x = f(P, P_y, Y, T_p, W, E, A, S, E, O)$$

where:

$D_x$ is the individual's demand (in units) for the product

$P$ is the price of the product

$P_y$ is the price of substitute and complementary products

$Y$ is the buyer's income

$W$ is the buyer's wealth, net of debt

$T_p$ is the buyer's tastes and preferences

$E$ is the buyer expectations of product prices in the future

$A$ is the buyer's age

$S$ is the buyer's gender

$O$ is other variables that affect the buyer's demand

### Application Box 4.3

Marketing researchers quantify the demand relationship in Table 4.1. Their goal is to identify the income and demographics of the target buyers and to design and implement effective selling initiatives.

indicates the number of units of the product the buyer is willing and able to purchase at each price over a given period of time. The demand curve is based on an *all-else-equal assumption*. By referring to a buyer's willingness and ability to make a purchase, the demand curve reflects the effective demand for the product. The *law of demand* specifies an inverse relationship between the product's price and the quantity demanded, so the buyer's demand curve is downward-sloping.

In Figure 4.2, the buyer is willing and able to purchase thirty-five units at $5 per unit over

## Application Box 4.4

Many natural and physical scientists control variables in laboratory settings. For example, a chemist controls the temperature and humidity when testing a chemical reaction.

Business analysts and social scientists lack the ability to conduct controlled experiments. Economists develop theoretical models to run simulations in which the all-else-equal assumption is used.

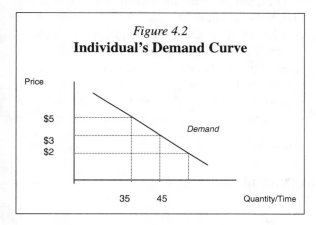

Figure 4.2
**Individual's Demand Curve**

## Exercise 4.3

Provide an example of the application of the all-else-equal assumption and discuss the analytical benefits of the assumption.

### Change in Demand Versus a Change in the Quantity Demanded

The all-else-equal assumption helps to differentiate between a *change in the quantity demanded* and a *change in demand* (see Figure 4.3).

A change in the quantity demanded occurs when the price of the product changes, all else equal. In Figure 4.3, begin with the demand curve $D_1$. The price of the product falls from $5 to $3; no other variables affecting the buyer's demand change. The buyer responds to the price decline and increases the quantity demanded from thirty-five to forty-five units. The buyer's response to the price change is depicted as a movement along the demand curve.

The change in the quantity demanded raises an important issue: how sensitive is the buyer's demand for the product to a change in the price? The *price elasticity of demand,* examined more carefully later in this chapter, measures the buyer's sensitivity to a change in the price of the product, all else equal.

A change in demand occurs when one of the variables held constant by the all-else-equal assumption is allowed to change. In Figure 4.3, $D_1$ indicates the number of units the buyer is willing and able to purchase while earning $50,000 per year. Assume the buyer's income rises to $75,000 per year, all else equal. At each price the buyer is willing and able

a given period of time. The all-else-equal methodology assumes that the buyer's income, age, gender, and tastes and the price of other goods remain unchanged. These assumptions isolate the effect of price on the number of units the buyer is willing and able to purchase. If any of the independent variables change, the demand curve shifts.

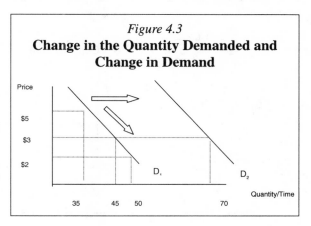

Figure 4.3
**Change in the Quantity Demanded and Change in Demand**

## Application Box 4.5

A tax on alcoholic beverages changes the price of the product for buyers and results in a change (decrease) in the quantity demanded. An advertising campaign discouraging alcohol consumption seeks a change in demand by reducing buyers' preferences and shifting the demand curve to the left.

*From Individual Demand to Market Demand*

Figure 4.4 extends the analysis from an *individual's demand curve* to a *market demand curve*. In Figure 4.4, there are only two buyers in this market, and the demand curves for persons A and B are shown. The market demand curve in the lower panel is the sum of the two consumers' willingness and ability to buy at each price. At $3, person A purchases forty-five units and person B purchases forty units. The market demand at a $3 price is eighty-five units.

to purchase more units. The demand curve shifts to the right from $D_1$ to $D_2$. At a price of $3, the buyer increases the amount purchased from forty-five to seventy units. The shift of the buyer's demand curve raises the question of the degree of sensitivity of demand to a change in income. The change in demand relative to a proportionate change in income is the *income elasticity of demand;* this concept is explored more carefully later in the chapter.

The addition of the individual demand curves in Figure 4.4 assumes that each buyer's preferences develop independently and that buyers do not adjust their purchases in response to the buying patterns of others. However, if person B's preference for the product increases because of purchases by person A, the market demand moves further to the right. Current style and snob appeal increase the

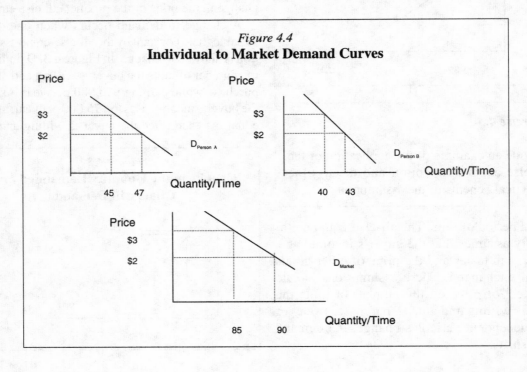

*Figure 4.4*
**Individual to Market Demand Curves**

## Application Box 4.6

Thorstein Veblen (1857–1929), the first economist of note to be born in the United States, was a critic of the capitalistic system. His 1899 book *The Theory of the Leisure Class* examined the practice of consumption and the formation of tastes. Economists during his time analyzed consumption by separating purchases and measuring the pleasure received from each purchase individually. Veblen argued that this theory was not completely correct, as people are guilty of *conspicuous consumption*—that is, purchases are not made independently of other purchases. People purchase goods to emulate their peers. The pleasure from purchasing a good comes not only from the good itself but also from the knowledge that the good is the same one others own.

*Source:* Robert Ekelund and Robert Hebert, *A History of Economic Theory and Method* (New York: McGraw-Hill, 1997).

*Table 4.2*
### Individual Seller's Supply Function

$$S_x = f(P_x, P_y, R, T, E, O)$$

where:

$S_x$ is the number of units the firm is willing and able to produce and sell
$P_x$ is the price of the product
$P_y$ is the price of other products the firm is able to produce
$R$ is the cost of resource inputs
$T$ is the technology utilized
$E$ is the expectation of the future price of the product
$O$ is the other variables that affect supply

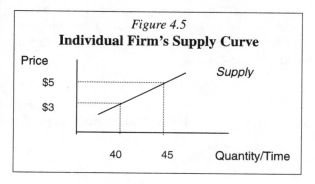

*Figure 4.5*
**Individual Firm's Supply Curve**

market demand for a product, and marketers seek to take advantage of fads.

### *The Force of Supply*

The supply side of the market is examined using the same methodology. Table 4.2 shows the generalized supply equation for an individual firm. The number of units willingly produced and sold by the firm is the dependent variable ($S_x$), and the independent variables are the price of the product, the price of other products the firm is able to produce, the price of resource inputs, the technology utilized (which defines the inputs needed), and the expected future price of the product.

Figure 4.5 shows the individual firm's supply curve. The *law of supply* states a positive relationship between the number of units of a product a firm is willing and able to sell and its price, all else equal, over a given period of time.

### *Change in Supply Versus a Change in the Quantity Supplied*

Analogous to the demand side of the marketplace, a distinction is made between a *change in the quantity supplied* and a *change in supply*. With reference to Figure 4.6, an increase in the price of the product from $3 to $5, all else equal, prompts businesses to increase the quantity supplied from

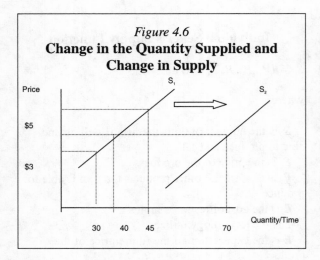

*Figure 4.6*
**Change in the Quantity Supplied and Change in Supply**

A change in supply occurs when a variable other than the price of the product changes. For example, in Figure 4.6, the price of a resource input declines, and the supply curve shifts to the right, from $S_1$ to $S_2$. At $3, with all of the other variables affecting supply remaining constant, the supply increases from forty units to seventy units.

*From a Firm's Supply to Market Supply*

The market supply is determined by adding the number of units willingly sold at each price by each firm in the market. Figure 4.7 assumes the market consists of only two firms.

In Figure 4.7, at a price of $3, firm A willingly produces and sells forty units and firm B willingly produces and sells forty-five units. The market supply is eighty-five units. The market supply curve in Figure 4.7 represents a menu of price and quantity combinations acceptable to the sellers of

forty to forty-five units over a fixed time period. The change in the quantity supplied leads to consideration of producers' sensitivity to change in the price of the product; this discussion is deferred until later in the chapter.

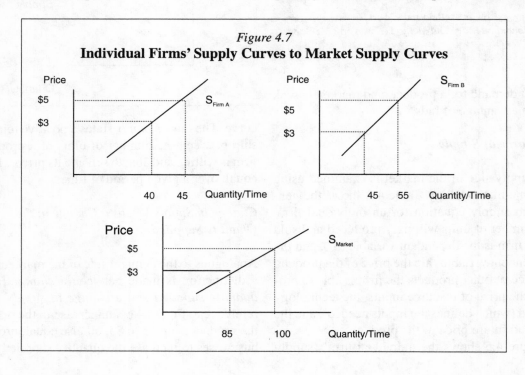

*Figure 4.7*
**Individual Firms' Supply Curves to Market Supply Curves**

the product. The following section brings market supply and demand together to explain the role and functions of markets and prices.

### Supply, Demand, and Market Equilibrium

Figure 4.8 shows market supply (Figure 4.7) and demand (Figure 4.4) on the same set of axes. It is important to remember that buyers and sellers enter markets with their own preferences. Showing supply and demand on the same diagram is a useful simplification to explain market processes, but initially buyers do not know the sellers' supply curve and sellers do not know the buyers' demand curve. A market's auction-like processes allow buyers and sellers to exchange information and come to a mutually acceptable agreement.

To initiate the exchange of information between buyers and sellers, assume an initial price of $5. Suppliers want to sell one hundred units at this price, but buyers are willing and able to purchase only seventy-five units. There is a *surplus* of twenty-five units when the price is $5. Importantly, the size of the surplus depends upon the price of the product. The sellers recognize the unsold goods as the surplus. The surplus creates an incentive for sellers to lower their price to sell their unwanted inventory.

In contrast, at a price of $2, sellers offer eighty units, but buyers want ninety units. There is a *shortage* of ten units at a price of $2. The shortage is recognizable: shelves are emptied quickly, and some buyers are unable to purchase the product. Sellers have an incentive to raise their price.

Conditions of surplus or shortage are unstable. At $5 the surplus encourages sellers to lower their price to reduce their inventory. At $2, the shortage encourages sellers to raise their price. As buyers and sellers interact and respond to a surplus or shortage, the market finds the *equilibrium price,*

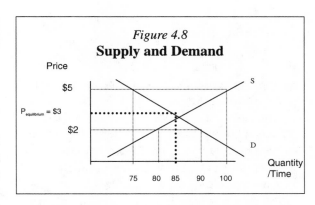

*Figure 4.8*
**Supply and Demand**

where the quantity supplied and the quantity demanded are equal. At the equilibrium price of $3 the *equilibrium quantity exchanged* is eighty-five units. At a price of $3, all buyers who are willing and able to purchase the product are satisfied, and all sellers who are willing and able to sell are simultaneously satisfied. In equilibrium, there is no incentive for the price to move upward or downward unless there is a change in demand or supply.

### Changes in Supply, Demand, and Equilibrium

To examine the functions of price, consider a $5 price (see Figure 4.8). A surplus exists, and sellers have an incentive to lower their price. However, assume a legally imposed *price floor,* which prohibits sellers from reducing the price. The surplus persists as producers respond to the price of $5. However, the price floor is sustainable only if the government purchases the surplus at the legal price. Furthermore, the government cannot resell its purchases or reintroduce the surplus into the market and still sustain the controlled price. The surplus is stored or destroyed, or producers are paid not to produce the product.

The price floor example demonstrates the *incentive effect of price.* The controlled price of $5, a floor price, encourages production, and at that

## Application Box 4.7

The government supports the prices of many agricultural products. Two justifications of this policy are as follows. (1) Agriculture is a way of life fundamental to the U.S. character, and price supports preserve family farms. (2) Price supports protect farmland from being lost to residential and commercial development.

An example of a price control below the equilibrium price occurred in New York City during World War II. To encourage in-migration to build war materials, rental prices were controlled and a shortage developed.

Prices set below the equilibrium level occur in other settings. Consider a vacation resort whose primary revenue source is nightly lodging fees. This resort offers recreational opportunities including golf, tennis, and water sports. Tee times at the attractive hours are finite, and the quantity demanded exceeds the quantity supplied at the current price. In response to the shortage, the resort could raise the price at the peak load periods. It chooses not to raise the price, concerned about guest relations. In turn, the most attractive tee times are rationed by reservation.

price businesses overproduce relative to market demand. The controlled price inaccurately reflects buyers' willingness and ability to purchase that product, sending a misleading signal and incentive to producers. In turn, too many resources are allocated to produce this item. The resultant surplus reflects a misallocation of scarce resources. The economy fails to meet the constrained maximum (see page 9).

At a price of $2 (see Figure 4.8), a shortage

occurs. Assume the price is controlled by the government and it is illegal to raise it. This circumstance is a *price ceiling*. A *rationing* problem arises. Who gets the scarce products? Sellers cannot legally ration the product by raising the price, so they rely upon *non-price rationing mechanisms,* including a first-come-first-served system, favoritism, or graft.

### Coordination, Market Efficiencies, and Internal Transfers

In free markets prices move up and down in response to supply and demand conditions, and production responds to buyer preferences. Consider the upper panel of Figure 4.9. Buyers willingly substitute products A and B based on their relative prices. The market for each product is in equilibrium. In the lower left panel, the demand for product A rises, and households expend more of their income on this product. In turn, the demand for product B declines, reflecting the fact that buyers have finite income. The increase in the demand for product A creates a shortage at the original price. The shortage leads to a higher price and to an increase in the quantity supplied. How are the producers of product A able to get the additional resources?

In industry B, the decline in the demand for the product results in a surplus at the original price. The surplus leads to a decline in the price of the product and to a reduction in quantity supplied. Resources are released from the production of product B and migrate to the production of product A. Profit-seeking entrepreneurs respond to the price and profit signals and produce the mix of goods desired by those who have the willingness and ability to spend. Inefficient producers who cannot earn a profit at the market price of the product are driven out of business.

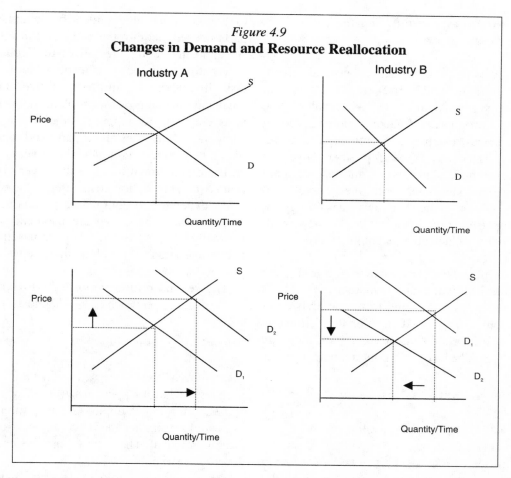

*Figure 4.9*
**Changes in Demand and Resource Reallocation**

The change in buyer preferences (see Figure 4.9) extends across many industries. The increase in demand for product A and the decrease in demand for product B impact suppliers and geographic regions through the products' respective production cost chains. The shift in buyer preferences alters prices. In turn, profit-seeking entrepreneurs respond to the price signals and alter the mix of goods produced. More of product A is produced and less of product B is produced. The self-interest motivation of entrepreneurs directs the use of resources and serves the well-being of those who are willing and able to pay.

**Exercise 4.4**

Show the direction of change in price and quantity under each of the following conditions:

(a) Resource prices decline.
(b) Buyers' preference for the product increases.
(c) Resource input prices fall and the price of a substitute good for buyers falls.

*Controlled Prices: Surplus, Shortage, and the Role of Price*

Free markets foster competition between sellers, and buyers benefit. Rival sellers are exposed to self-interest-motivated buyers who evaluate the alternative products and make a choice based on relative prices and product features. Therefore, sellers who meet buyers' needs prosper; those who do not meet buyers' needs fail, and resources are released to produce other goods. Free markets lead to production efficiency and low prices for buyers, and competition creates incentives for new products, product enhancements, and new production technologies.

These important benefits of free markets are lost inside firms when intermediate-stage products and services are transferred from one division or department to another. Consider the following. When an individual's car needs repair, there are two choices. The buyer can contract with a garage to diagnose the problem, identify the replacement parts needed, acquire the parts, and install them. A single firm completes all of the repair tasks. Alternatively, the buyer is responsible for all the tasks involved: soliciting competitive bids from mechanics to diagnose the problem and specify the parts, comparison-shopping for the parts, accepting competitive bids to install the parts, and contracting with a mechanic to complete the repairs.

The first option minimizes the buyer's *transaction costs*. Transaction costs refer to the time and effort expended to complete a purchase. In this case, the buyer is spared inconveniences by the vertically integrated garage. High transaction costs encourage firms to complete multiple tasks in the production cost chain.

The second option imposes high transaction costs on the buyer. Each task—diagnosis, parts ac-

---

**Application Box 4.8**

Increases in the price of gasoline create hardships. Immediately following a price increase, it is difficult for consumers to conserve very much. The price increase acts as a tax, and households and businesses reduce other purchases. These reductions trace through the production cost chain and adversely affect many firms.

While the short-term effects of the price increase are unsettling, the price increase alters incentives. Consumers learn to use mass transit and insulate their homes. Producers learn to conserve and switch to alternative types of fuel. Most importantly, entrepreneurs respond to the change in the price of gasoline and seek new technologies and energy sources.

---

**Application Box 4.9**

Outsourcing is a process through which a firm chooses to hire a supplier in lieu of self-providing the service. For example, a manufacturer hires an outdoor maintenance firm for lawn care and snow removal. The contract process calls for competitive bids.

Before deciding to outsource, the manufacturer learns how much it spends to self-perform the service. This permits comparison and a decision.

The maintenance firm has some cost advantages. It maximizes staff and asset use rates by selling to multiple buyers.

While the buyer may realize savings, the buyer also loses some control over the maintenance process. For example, lawn care or snow removal is completed as specified in the contract. A buyer's special needs are difficult, and perhaps costly, to accommodate.

quisition, and installation—is a distinct transaction requiring time, effort, and coordination. But there are compensating advantages. The buyer chooses among competing sellers for each separate activity and negotiates the most favorable price. The buyer will select the second option if the expected savings are valued more highly than the transaction costs.

The integration of distinct activities into a firm generates management problems. Consider your university. Its product is education. However, support activities, including administrative and secretarial services, food service, and janitorial services, are essential ingredients. By employing staff to provide these services, the university surrenders the opportunity to solicit competitive bids. For example, janitorial services can be self-provided by the university or contracted to another firm.

When the janitorial services are self-provided, problems arise. Without examining competitive bids, how does the university determine if the services are efficiently provided? Also, those employed in janitorial services are sheltered from competition. Does the loss of market incentives reduce work effort and innovation? Without measures of the profitability of support services, how does the university allocate resources among competing uses?

Choosing to self-provide a service or an intermediate-stage product has some benefits. The self-producer retains control of the process. The university's self-provided janitorial services may respond more effectively to unplanned events, which do not require renegotiation of a contract. A manufacturer self-producing parts controls the quality and the delivery times.

### Cost Centers and Profit Centers

Integrated firms raise the question of *cost and profit centers*. In a profit center, the manager maximizes the center's net revenue. A firm with multiple profit centers allocates resources on the basis of expected

---

**Application Box 4.10**

Cost accountants spend a lot of time estimating the cost of individual activities and distributing common costs across a firm. Effective cost accounting is an essential step in properly assigning costs and, in turn, measuring the profitability of individual units within the firm. In the absence of effective cost accounting, the profitability of individual departments, divisions, or tasks is not properly determined. The firm thus lacks market-like profit signals to allocate scarce resources among competing uses.

---

rates of return. For example, assume a firm produces several different products or operates in several different geographic regions. If each functions as a profit center, the firm completes the resource allocation process in a way comparable to free market processes. Expected profits direct the allocation of resources among competing demands.

The calculation of a profit center's net revenue is complicated if support services are common and shared by several profit centers. For example, a firm organized by geographic territory relies upon centralized accounting, finance, research and development, and human resources functions. To calculate the profitability of the profit centers, centralized costs are apportioned by activity or location. Cost drivers such as percentage of the firm's employees, time spent, revenue, and square footage are often used for allocating common costs. If, however, costs are misallocated, false profit signals result, and the firm misallocates resources.

In a cost center, managers are evaluated on the basis of controlling costs. Cost centers commonly include service and administrative departments, and revenues may not exist. Cost centers are problematic. The firm lacks market signals to allocate resources. Therefore,

## Exercise 4.5

Discuss the nature of market-oriented econo-mies and command economies. Consider how these economic systems differ by the following:

(a) Decisions what to produce
(b) Decisions how to produce
(c) Decisions how much to produce
(d) Decisions to accommodate change

## Exercise 4.6

How does your employer allocate finite orga-nizational resources among competing uses? Are market allocation principles applied? If not, what are the possible consequences?

## Exercise 4.7

How has the Internet changed the way buyers shop for new cars? How does the Internet make the new car market more efficient, and how do consumers benefit? What are the consequences for sellers?

many firms establish *internal transfer prices,* which create an accounting charge on the receiving depart-ment and a revenue credit to the selling department. Appropriate transfer prices create an internal market and provide the firm with a market-like mechanism to allocate resources inside the firm.

## Supply and Demand: Elasticity Measurements

The concept of demand elasticity refers to the respon-siveness of buyers to changes in the variables that affect demand. The following section examines the price elasticity of demand, the income elasticity of demand, and the cross-price elasticity of demand.

## Exercise 4.8

A firm is able to borrow at 7 percent and invests in capital projects that offer a 4 per-cent return above the cost of funds. With management's requirement to earn at least 11 percent (a hurdle rate), should the following automation project be funded?

| Capital Cost and Projected Labor Savings | | | | | |
|---|---|---|---|---|---|
| | Year 1 | Year 2 | Year 3 | Year 4 | Year 5 |
| Capital cost | $1,000,000 | | | | |
| Projected labor savings | | $275,000 | $300,000 | $325,000 | $350,000 |

Assume the new equipment has a five-year life with no salvage value, and ignore the tax consequences of the interest payments and income.

## Price Elasticity of Demand

Figure 4.10 displays two market demand curves. How sensitive are buyers to a change in the price of the product, all else being equal? A change in the price prompts buyers to alter the quantity demanded, and the buyers' response to the price change is reflected by their movement from one point on the demand curve to another.

In Figure 4.10, the two demand curves reflect different degrees of buyer responsiveness to a price change. In the diagram to the left, the price of the product falls from $10 to $8, a 20 percent reduction. Buyers increase the quantity demanded from ten to eleven units, a 10 percent change. The price decline prompts a proportionately smaller change in the quantity demanded. This situation is described as *price-inelastic,* because buyers are relatively insensitive to the change in the price. In the right-hand diagram, the same 20 percent price decline prompts a 50 percent increase (from ten to fifteen units) in the quantity demanded. Buyers are highly responsive to the change in the price of a product. The situation is described as *price-elastic.*

### Table 4.3
### Price Elasticity of Demand

Price Elasticity of Demand =

$$\frac{\% \text{ Change in Quantity Demanded}}{\% \text{ Change in Price of Product}}$$

The formula to calculate the price elasticity of demand is shown in Table 4.3. It is the ratio of the percentage change in the quantity demanded to the percentage change in the price of the product. The reader is reminded of the all-else-equal assumption: all other factors that affect demand are held constant.

Applying the formula to the left-hand diagram of Figure 4.10, the price decrease from $10 to $8 prompts an increase in the quantity demanded from ten to eleven units. The price elasticity of demand over that section of the demand curve is –0.5 (= 10% ÷ –20%). The negative sign on the resulting figure reflects the law of demand, which refers to an inverse relationship between price and quantity demanded. The absolute value of the result signals the degree of buyer sensitivity to the price change.

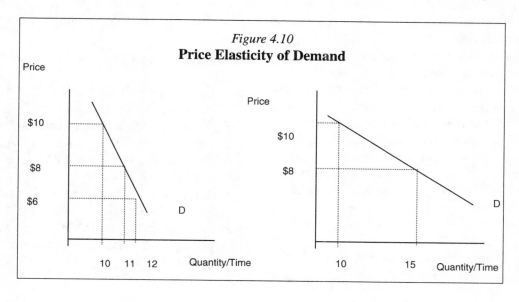

### Figure 4.10
### Price Elasticity of Demand

With the price elasticity of demand less than 1, the demand is price-inelastic. The buyer is relatively insensitive to the price change from $10 to $8.

In the right-hand panel of Figure 4.10, the same 20 percent change in the price (from $10 to $8) prompts a 50 percent increase in the quantity demanded (from ten units to fifteen units). The price elasticity of demand is –2.5 (= 50% ÷ –20%). The absolute value of the resulting figure is greater than 1, indicating that the demand is price-elastic. Over the segment of the demand curve from $10 to $8, the percentage change in the quantity demanded exceeds the percentage change in price.

The price elasticity of demand is different over different sections of the demand curve. Refer to the left panel of Figure 4.10. The price elasticity of demand is –.0.5 over the price range from $10 to $8. Assuming a straight-line demand curve, a further $2 price decline to $6 (a 25 percent reduction) prompts an increase in the quantity demanded from eleven to twelve units (a 9 percent increase). The price elasticity of demand over the segment of the demand curve from $8 to $6 is –0.36 (= 9% ÷ 25%). Similarly, the price elasticity of demand is different if the analysis examines a price increase or a price decrease. Simply, a decline in price from $10 to $8 is a 20 percent change; however, an increase in price from $8 to $10 is a 25 percent change. The direction of change affects the elasticity calculation.

Trying to calculate the price elasticity of demand in the real world is filled with methodological problems. To isolate the effects of a price change from $10 to $8, all other variables must be held constant. However, over the period in which the price changes, the analyst is unable to control all of the other variables. The all-else-equal assumption is violated.

### Determinants of the Price Elasticity of Demand

Despite the problems measuring the price elasticity of demand, several determinants of the degree of buyer sensitivity to a price change have been identified, including luxuries versus necessities, the availability of substitutes, the price as a proportion of one's budget, and time.

Buyers are relatively insensitive to changes in the price of necessities. An insulin-dependent diabetic requires a fixed daily dose of medication and does not vary the quantity consumed in response to a price change. The diabetic's demand for insulin is highly price-inelastic. In contrast, the purchase of a luxury (inessential) product is readily forgone, and buyers are more sensitive to changes in the price, thereby making the demand price-elastic.

Distinguishing between luxuries and necessities is complicated by time and place. For example, a restaurant meal may be a luxury; however, it becomes a necessity for travelers. Similarly, a round of golf is a luxury; however, for an individual on a golfing vacation, the product is a necessity. Sellers who recognize the conditions under which the good or service is sold price accordingly.

The availability of attractive substitutes increases the price elasticity of demand. If buyers readily substitute bananas for apples, a small increase in the price of apples leads to a proportionately larger reduction in the quantity de-

### Application Box 4.11

Airlines use the concept of price elasticity of demand to set prices. Ticket requests for flights the next day are interpreted as necessities and are priced high. Reservations made weeks in advance are considered luxuries and are priced lower.

Business-oriented hotels charge high prices midweek. On weekends, the same hotel room may be many dollars cheaper. Business travel is necessity-like, whereas weekend trips are luxury-like.

manded. Buyers display a price-elastic demand by rearranging their consumption and substituting bananas for apples. To prevent product substitutions, marketers attempt to build brand loyalty to make other products less attractive substitutes. Similarly, companies try to prevent rivals from securing shelf space, and producers attempt to link sales of related products. For example, sellers of manufactured products seek tie-in sales of repair and maintenance to reduce substitution among service providers.

The availability of substitutes forces individual firms to make careful distinctions between the price elasticity of demand for their industry's product in general and the price elasticity of demand for their own product specifically. For example, the price elasticity of the demand for cereal is affected by buyer preferences and the degree to which alternatives are perceived as good substitutes. Whatever the price elasticity of the demand for cereal, the demand for any individual brand of cereal is likely to be more price-elastic, as there is a wider range of substitutes.

Buyers are insensitive to changes in the price of items that account for a small percentage of their total budget. For example, a few cents' increase in the price of chewing gum draws little notice. Similarly, an individual vacationing at a costly beach resort vacation is (relatively) insensitive to the price of a cold beverage. The price of the beverage is a small percentage of the total cost of the trip, thereby making the demand price-inelastic.

When confronted with a rise in the price of gasoline, buyers initially have only a few options to reduce the quantity demanded. Over time, more substitutes arise. Buyers can purchase a more fuel-efficient vehicle, join a car pool, move closer to work, or choose improved mass transit options. The longer the time period, the more price-elastic the demand for the product, all else equal.

## The Price Elasticity of Demand and the Total Revenue Test

When the demand for a product is price-elastic, a price decrease lowers the gross revenue per unit. However, the proportionate increase in the quantity demanded is larger than the proportionate change in price of the product. The gross revenue rises. But nothing is known about the change in profit until the costs of producing the additional units are determined. Where the demand is price-elastic, a higher price yields more revenue per unit, but a proportionately larger decline in the quantity demanded results in a lower gross revenue. Again, nothing is known about the change in profit until the cost savings from lower production are determined. In sum, when the demand for a product is price-elastic, changes in price and gross revenue vary inversely.

If the demand for a product is price-inelastic, a price increase only slightly discourages the quantity demanded. The decline in the quantity demanded is proportionately smaller than the increase in price. Total revenue rises. With a price decrease, the increase in the quantity demanded is

**Application Box 4.12**

The *total revenue test* provides some guidance for pricing decisions. For example, consider a movie theater that experiences many unsold seats during weekday showings. The incremental cost to the theater of another viewer is very low. If owners believe the price elasticity of demand is greater than 1, cutting the price of a ticket raises revenue and profit. Thus, the ticket price for a matinee showing is lower than that for a prime-time showing. This conclusion assumes the matinee price does not lead to fewer sales at prime-time hours.

insufficient to offset the decline in revenue per unit, and total revenue declines. Where the demand for a product is price-inelastic, total revenue and the price of the product vary directly.

### The Price Elasticity of Demand, the Economic Environment, and Management Decisions

The microeconomic environment within which a firm operates affects buyer sensitivity to a change in the price. For example, in a market characterized by commodity-like products, the demand for each firm's product is price-elastic because of the availability of substitutes. For these firms, improved profit margins occur through reduced costs and not through higher prices. Alternatively, a small-town grocery store is aware that buyers must travel to a neighboring town to shop at another store. Assuming convenience stores and mini-marts are poor substitutes, the small-town grocery takes advantage of the price-inelastic demand and charges somewhat higher prices.

Operating in a price-sensitive environment challenges managers. Firms in such environments must operate efficiently, and they study why buyers are sensitive to changes in their prices. One frequent explanation is that the firm has not distinguished its product or service from that of rivals. Awareness of buyer price sensitivity forces firms to consider ways to distinguish themselves more effectively from competitors, perhaps by trying to build brand loyalty.

### Income Elasticity of Demand

The *income elasticity of demand* measures buyer sensitivity to a change in income, all else equal. In Figure 4.11, $D_1$ is a buyer's demand curve for a product given an income of $75,000 per year. If the buyer's income rises to $100,000 per year, all else being equal, the buyer is willing and able to

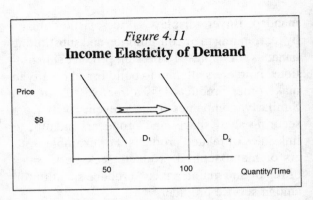

*Figure 4.11*
**Income Elasticity of Demand**

purchase more units of the product at each price. The buyer's demand curve shifts to $D_2$.

In Figure 4.11 the buyer, earning $75,000 per year, purchases fifty units at a price of $8. When the buyer's income increases to $100,000 per year (a 33 percent increase), one hundred units are purchased at a price of $8 (a 50 percent increase). The formula to calculate the income elasticity of demand is shown in Table 4.4.

*Table 4.4*
**Income Elasticity of Demand**

$$\text{Income Elasticity of Demand} = \frac{\%\ \text{Change in Demand}}{\%\ \text{Change in Income}}$$

The calculation of the buyer's income elasticity of demand occurs at a given price. Refer to Figure 4.11. At a price of $8, the buyer purchases fifty units while earning $75,000 per year. When earning $100,000 per year the same buyer purchases one hundred units, all else equal. The income elasticity of demand is 1.5 (= 50% ÷ 33%).

In the example, the buyer's demand for this product is income-elastic. The proportionate increase in the units purchased exceeds the proportionate change in income. The result of the calculation is greater than 1. The demand for luxury

**Application Box 4.13**

Firms that sell a product for which the demand is income-elastic are vulnerable to the business cycle. These firms monitor economic conditions carefully and engage in macroeconomic forecasting. These firms are at risk of over- or underproduction if their macroeconomic and sales forecasts are incorrect. These firms prefer production systems that quickly accelerate or decelerate production.

Employees and investors in these companies must be similarly astute. For employees, raises and job security vary over the business cycle. For investors, earnings and dividends vary over the business cycle.

**Application Box 4.14**

The successful use of financial leverage occurs when a firm uses borrowed monies (debt) to increase the returns to the equity holder. By earning more with the use of the borrowed funds than it pays in interest, the firm boosts earnings and the value of its stock.

Financial leverage raises the firm's debt-to-equity ratio and is risky. Debt represents fixed interest obligations. Firms that operate in a business-cycle-sensitive industry are particularly sensitive to this risk. Firms with sales that are relatively insensitive to the business cycle have a greater opportunity to pursue financial leverage.

and high-priced goods tends to be more income-sensitive than the demand for essential and routine purchases. For routine and necessary purchases, the buyer's demand tends to be income-inelastic.

The example in Figure 4.11 refers to a single buyer. However, the analysis readily adapts to the market demand for a product. In the equation in Table 4.4, the change in income refers to aggregate, economy-wide income and the change in demand refers to the market as a whole. The condition of an income-elastic demand defines a business-cycle-sensitive industry; firms in these industries reduce their vulnerability to swings in the business cycle by preferring equity to debt financing, preferring long-term contracts to short-term ones, and seeking flexible production and inventory systems. Further, employees of firms subject to an income-elastic demand face pressures similar to those their employers must deal with. These workers are vulnerable to being laid off during periods of economic weakness and are advised to hold relatively low levels of personal debt. Further, investors in these firms experience volatility in the price of a share

of stock over the business cycle. In advance of an economic recovery and expansion, expected earnings are adjusted upward and push the stock price higher. In anticipation of a recession, expected earnings are revised downward.

In contrast, where the market demand for a product is income-inelastic, sellers are relatively insensitive to the business cycle. The proportionate change in demand for their product is smaller than the proportionate change in national income. These firms offer secure employment over the business cycle and less volatile stock prices. These firms are more likely to rely upon debt financing and longer-term contracts for materials, equipment, labor, and facilities.

Generally, the income elasticity of demand is a positive number. Income and demand vary directly. However, the demand for an *inferior good* varies inversely with income. The term "inferior good" does not imply a lesser-quality good or service. The term indicates that the demand goes down when incomes rise, and it goes up when incomes fall. Sellers of inferior goods are countercyclical to the macroeconomy. Consider a firm engaged in mortgage foreclosures. A weaker economy causes the number of defaults on payments to rise, so this company does better when income declines. Similarly, consider a generic-brand beverage. When the economy is strong and incomes are rising, buyers purchase a branded label. When the economy is weak and incomes are falling, buyers shift to the lower-priced generic. The generic product is an inferior good, and the firm's financial performance is countercyclical to the macroeconomy. These businesses realize higher sales and profits when the economy weakens.

### Cross-Price Elasticity of Demand

The *cross-price elasticity of demand* refers to the percentage change in the demand for a product relative to a percentage change in the price of another product. Table 4.5 shows the formula to calculate the cross-price elasticity of demand.

Assume good X is pizza. How sensitive are buyers of pizza to a change in the price of good Y, hamburgers? A second and different example assumes good X is golf balls and good Y is the price of a round of golf. How sensitive is the demand for golf balls to a change in the price of playing golf?

Examples indicate the two possibilities. A reduction in the price of hamburgers prompts buyers to purchase fewer pizzas. Buyers substitute relatively lower-priced hamburgers. The cross-price elasticity of demand is a positive number, and the two products are *substitutes*. The greater the absolute value of the cross-price elasticity of demand, the more readily buyers substitute the products in response to a change in their relative prices. Sellers who are vulnerable to a high cross-price elasticity of demand with another product are exposed to intense price competition, focus on reducing their costs of production, and care-

*Table 4.5*
**Cross-Price Elasticity of Demand**

Cross-Price Elasticity of Demand =

$$\frac{\text{\% Change in Demand for Good X}}{\text{\% Change in Price of Good Y}}$$

fully monitor prices of substitute products. These sellers lack brand identity and may seek product differentiation strategies to reduce the cross-price elasticity of demand.

In contrast, an increase in the price of a round of golf leads to a decline in the demand for playing golf, and in turn to a drop in the demand for golf balls. The cross-price elasticity of demand between a round of golf and golf balls is a negative value, indicating that the two goods are *complementary products* that are jointly consumed. Sellers who make a product that is in a close complementary relationship with another item must carefully monitor the price of the other product to anticipate changes in the demand for their own product.

### Other Demand Elasticity Concepts

The demand for products is sensitive to changes in many variables, and each leads to a different elasticity measurement. The demand for new and previously owned homes and automobiles is inversely related to changes in interest rates; this demonstrates the *interest rate elasticity of demand*. Similarly, the demand for fuel-efficient automobiles (or fuel-inefficient automobiles) is sensitive to the price of a gallon of gasoline; this defines the *fuel price elasticity of demand* for automobiles.

Decision makers who understand demand elasticity identify the variables to which sales are the most sensitive (highly elastic), monitor those environmental conditions to which their firm is most vulnerable, and make decisions aligned with the realities of their marketplace.

## Exercise 4.9

The following table shows buyers' (economy-wide) willingness and ability to purchase movie tickets over one year.

| Price | Quantity | Quantity/Income | Quantity/Price of Y | Quantity/Interest Rate |
|-------|----------|-----------------|---------------------|------------------------|
| $12 | 10 | 16 | 11 | 10 |
| $10 | 14 | 21 | 15 | 14 |
| $8 | 19 | 27 | 20 | 19 |
| $6 | 24 | 33 | 25 | 24 |
| $4 | 28 | 35 | 29 | 28 |

**Notes:**

The column headed Price shows different prices of movie tickets.

The next column, headed Quantity, shows the number of units (in millions) purchased at each price, given that the national income is $1.5 billion, the average price of a concert ticket is $25, and the prime interest rate is 6 percent.

The column headed Quantity/Income shows the number of units (in millions) purchased, given that the national income is $2.0 billion; the average price of a concert ticket is $25, and the prime interest rate is 6 percent.

The column headed Quantity/Price of Y shows the number of units (in millions) purchased, given that the national income is $1.5 billion; the average price of a concert ticket rises to $30, and the prime interest rate is 6 percent.

The column headed Quantity/Interest Rate shows the number of units (in millions) of purchases, given that the national income is $1.5 billion; the average price of a concert ticket is $25, and the prime interest rate is 5 percent.

Do the following:

(a) Calculate the price elasticity of demand, assuming a price change from $10 to $8. Assume that the national income is $1.5 billion, the price of a concert ticket is $25, and the prime rate is 6 percent.

(b) Calculate the income elasticity of demand, assuming that the price is $8 and national income rises from $1.5 billion to $2.0 billion, the average price of a concert ticket is $25, and the prime interest rate is 6 percent.

(c) Calculate the cross-price elasticity of demand, assuming that the price of the product is $8 and the average price of a concert ticket rises to $30. National income is $1.5 billion, and the prime interest rate is 6 percent.

(d) Calculate the interest rate elasticity of demand at a price of $8. Assume that the national income is $1.5 billion; the average price of a concert ticket is $25, and the prime rate decreases from 6 percent to 5 percent.

(e) Prepare a memo to the management of this firm, report your findings, and comment on the management implications.

## Supply Elasticity

### The Price Elasticity of Supply

The *price elasticity of supply* measures the responsiveness of the quantity supplied to a change in price, all else equal. Table 4.6 indicates the formula.

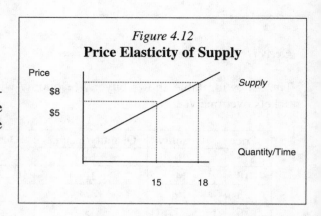

Figure 4.12
**Price Elasticity of Supply**

*Table 4.6*
**Price Elasticity of Supply**

Price Elasticity of Supply =

$$\frac{\text{\% Change in the Quantity Supplied of Good X}}{\text{\% Change in the Price of Good X}}$$

The law of supply cites a direct relationship between the price of a product and the quantity supplied. The all-else-equal assumption includes the cost of resources, the technology employed, and the prices of other goods. The positive relationship between the price of the product and the quantity supplied means the price elasticity of supply is a positive number. A figure greater than 1 indicates that the percentage change in the quantity supplied is greater than the percentage change in the price. This reflects a *price-elastic supply* over the particular range of the supply curve. A figure less than 1 indicates a price-inelastic supply, in which the percentage change in the quantity supplied is smaller than the percentage change in the price. Figure 4.12 provides an example.

Referring to Figure 4.12, assume the price rises from $5 to $8. This increase is 60 percent. In response, the quantity supplied increases from fifteen to eighteen units, a 20 percent change. The price elasticity of supply over the range from $5 to $8 is 0.33 (= 20% ÷ 60%). The result of the calculation is a positive number, reflecting the direct relationship between price and the quantity supplied. The value is less than 1, so supply is price-inelastic over the given range of

the supply curve. As with price elasticity of demand, the calculation of the price elasticity of supply relies upon the all-else-equal assumption.

### Determinants of the Price Elasticity of Supply

The price elasticity of supply depends upon four factors: substitutability, capacity, marginal cost, and time.

The more readily productive resources shift from one good to another, the greater the supply elasticity. For example, a farmer planted a field of corn. If the price of corn rises, the farmer cannot increase production until the following growing season, when acreage can be shifted from the production of soybeans to corn.

A firm operating at 100 percent capacity is unable to increase the quantity supplied in response to a price increase. The supply is price-inelastic. Similarly, where a good or service is unique (such as an original painting by Picasso), the quantity supplied is insensitive to the price.

The more costly it is to produce the next unit of output, the more price-inelastic the supply. For example, if to increase production a manufacturer needs a second and more costly second shift of workers, this increase in the cost of producing the next unit discourages additional production. The supply is price-inelastic.

## Application Box 4.15

The price elasticity of supply has important macro- and microeconomic consequences.

In macroeconomics, consider the aggregate supply curve (see page 64). Assume an increase in aggregate demand. The more price-elastic the aggregate supply curve, the greater the increase in real output and the smaller the impact on inflation. If the aggregate supply curve is price-inelastic, the increase in aggregate demand has a larger effect on the price level and a smaller effect on real output.

In microeconomics, consider a firm in a growing market. If its production capacity and production process yield a price-elastic supply curve, the firm grows sales as the market expands. A rival whose supply curve is price-inelastic is unable to grow with the market. Market share shifts in favor of the firm able to expand production.

Time affects the price elasticity of supply. Longer time periods allow for resources to flow from one use to another and increase the price elasticity of supply. Consider, for example, an accounting firm. Its staff size limits the number of tax returns it is able to complete. With time to add staff, more returns are completed in response to the price change.

### Other Supply Elasticity Measurements

On the demand side of the market, a distinction is made between a change in the quantity demanded and a change in demand (see page 107). A similar distinction is important on the supply side of the market. A change in the quantity supplied refers to the supplier's response to a change in the price of the product, all else equal. In Figure 4.13, the price increases from $8 to $10. Referring to $S_1$, the quantity supplied

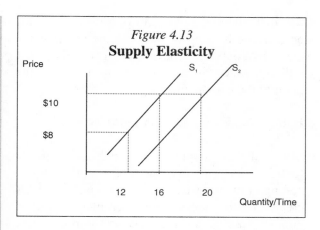

Figure 4.13
**Supply Elasticity**

increases from twelve to sixteen units. The price elasticity of supply is 1.32 (= .33 ÷ .25). The supply is price-elastic.

A change in supply occurs when one of the variables affecting supply (other than the price of the product) changes. In Figure 4.13, assume the price of a resource input declines. The supply curve shifts to the right. This increase in supply from $S_1$ to $S_2$ leads to an elasticity measurement: the *resource cost elasticity of supply* (see Table 4.7).

Table 4.7
**Resource Price Elasticity of Supply**

Resource Price Elasticity of Supply =

$$\frac{\% \text{ Change in Supply}}{\% \text{ Change in Resource Cost}}$$

Assume the price of a resource input declines from $100 per ton to $90 per ton, a 10 percent decline. Referring to Figure 4.13, the supply curve shifts to the right, which indicates an increase in supply. At a product price of $10, the firm willingly produces and offers for sale twenty units. In response to the 10 percent decline in the price of the resource input, there is a 25 percent increase in the supply of product. The resource price elasticity of supply is –2.5. The negative sign reflects the fact that a decline in the cost of a resource yields an increase in supply. The absolute value of the elasticity coefficient indicates that the producer's willingness to produce and sell is sensitive to the price of the resource input.

## Public Goods and Market Failures

Much of this chapter has emphasized the effectiveness of free markets to allocate resources among competing uses. However, *public goods* create circumstances where free markets fail to allocate resources effectively and public sector involvement is necessary to correct for market failures.

Public goods are, by definition, products or services that are consumed jointly by members of a community. This characteristic of a public good violates market principles and necessitates a public sector response. For example, a loaf of bread is a *private good*. A buyer purchases and consumes the bread, and no one else can consume the same loaf of bread. However, a landowner who sprays private wetlands to control mosquito infestations provides benefits to others. The presence of fewer mosquitoes is simultaneously enjoyed by all members of the community, and so spraying for mosquitoes is a public good. All members of the community enjoy the benefits at the same time even without paying for it. No one can be excluded from the benefit, and each member of the community has an incentive to be a *free rider*. Free riders enjoy the benefits of a public good without paying for the good or service.

The free rider problem distorts consumer choices and leads to an underallocation of resources to the production of public goods. With incentives to conceal one's preferences for a public good and be a free rider, the expressed dollar demand for the product is less than the

**Application Box 4.16**

Excludable public goods are goods that are available to anyone, but their use can be monitored and restricted. Examples are community swimming pools, church classrooms, and toll roads. Even though a payment mechanism can be set up to charge those who use the good, the initial decision to construct the good can be problematic. Potential consumers have the incentive to exaggerate their planned use of the good to convince administrators to build it. Administrators must do careful research (for example, traffic studies for a toll road) and solicit long-term contracts (pool memberships and church pledges) to ensure the project will be paid for.

true preference for the good. Because for-profit businesses respond to actual expenditures, free markets underallocate resources to the production of public goods. The free rider problem necessitates that government provide the public good and pay for it through the collection of mandatory taxes.

The same joint consumption issue arises with regard to *spillover costs*. Consider a paper plant. The production process requires clean water and causes water pollution. The incentive for the producer is to keep production costs low by releasing effluents into the stream. In turn, those living downstream incur the costs. Because there is no market mechanism for those downstream to be compensated by the upstream paper mill, a public sector response is needed. The government can impose rules and regulations that prohibit the discharge of pollutants, or it can assess fees for pollution discharges to discourage the release of effluents.

## Summary

This chapter explains the interactions of supply and demand in the marketplace and develops concepts of elasticity. Markets are developed as environments within which business and personal decisions are made and which affect the outcomes of the decisions. The advantages of free and un-obstructed markets are extended to the transfer of intermediate-stage goods and services inside the firm.

## Review Terms

| | |
|---|---|
| All-else-equal assumption | Inferior goods |
| Circular flow of income | Non-price rationing |
| Cross-price elasticity of demand | Price elasticity of demand |
| Equilibrium price and quantity | Price elasticity of supply |
| Externalities | Price floor and ceiling |
| Financial leverage | Public goods |
| Free rider | Resource market |
| Goods market | Substitute goods |
| Incentive function of price | Supply and demand |
| Income elasticity of demand | Transfer prices |

## Discussion Questions

1. Indicate the direction of change in the equilibrium price and quantity demanded under each of the following circumstances.

   (a) Households' preferences change in favor of the good.
   (b) The price of a substitute good rises.
   (c) Income rises.
   (d) The price of a critical natural resource input falls.

2. Use the following data and complete the calculations indicated below.

*Table D4.1*

| Price and Quantity Data | | | | |
|---|---|---|---|---|
| Price of Product X | Quantity if Income = $50,000 $P_y = \$9$ Interest Rate = 6% | Quantity if Income = $60,000 $P_y = \$9$ Interest Rate = 6% | Quantity if Income = $50,000 $P_y = \$10$ Interest Rate = 6% | Quantity if Income = $50,000 $P_y = \$9$ Interest Rate = 4% |
| $12 | 25 | 30 | 30 | 26 |
| $10 | 35 | 40 | 42 | 36 |
| $8 | 42 | 50 | 50 | 43 |
| $6 | 45 | 55 | 53 | 46 |

   (a) Calculate the price elasticity of demand, assuming a price decrease from $12 to $10 and assuming income is $50,000. The price of the substitute product is $9 and the interest rate is 6 percent.
   (b) Calculate the income elasticity of demand, assuming the price of the product is $8 and income rises from $50,000 to $60,000 while the price of the substitute product is $9 and the interest rate is 6 percent.
   (c) Calculate the cross-price elasticity of demand, assuming the price of the product is $8, the price of the substitute product changes from $9 to $10, income is $50,000, and the interest rate is 6 percent. Are the two products substitutes or complements?

(d) Calculate the interest rate elasticity of demand, assuming the price of the product is $12, the price of the substitute product is $9, income is $50,000, and the interest rate falls from 6 percent to 4 percent.

(e) Using this data from a single buyer, prepare a memo to the management of this firm and comment on the calculations.

3. Explain why free markets underproduce public goods. Explain why the government plays an important role in protecting the environment.

4. Discuss how tax policies can be structured as incentives to reduce pollution. Evaluate tax policies as an alternative to regulations.

5. Indicate the direction of change (up or down) of the equilibrium price and quantity given the following conditions.

Consumers' preference for the product rises.
The cost of a material input falls.
The price of a substitute product falls.
The price of a complementary product falls.

6. Assume an automobile manufacturer self-produces a part and transfers the part from one division to another. The same part is available from an independent producer at a price of $10. The auto manufacturer has a cost of capital of 10 percent. Given the data below, should the part be made or purchased?

(a) Invested capital = $1,000,000
(b) Fixed costs = $100,000 per year

(c) Variable costs = $1.50 per unit
(d) Units produced = 100,000 per year

7. Referring to question 6, under what conditions should the auto manufacturer continue to produce the part? If the parts manufacturer charges an internal transfer price of $12, what distortions occur?

8. The following data show the price and quantity demanded for business and vacation airline travelers from New York City to Miami.

*Table D4.2*

| Business and Vacation Travelers | | |
|---|---|---|
| Price | Quantity Demanded by Vacationers | Quantity Demanded by Business Travelers |
| $200 | 1,000 | 3,000 |
| $250 | 700 | 2,550 |
| $300 | 560 | 2,220 |
| $350 | 460 | 2,000 |
| $400 | 390 | 1,900 |

(a) Calculate the price elasticity of demand for the business traveler and for the vacation traveler, assuming a price increase from $250 to $300 per ticker.

(b) Why do you think these travelers are differently sensitive to price?

(c) How can the airlines identify the different travelers and legally price the tickets differently?

(d) Does the same analysis apply to the pricing of theater tickets, movie tickets, and tee times? Explain.

9. Lakefront properties have a price-inelastic supply and personal computers have a price-elastic supply. Assume the population doubles and the demand for each product doubles at each price.

(a) What happens to the equilibrium price and quantity in each market?
(b) Which market has the larger change in price? Which has the larger change in the quantity exchanged?

# Appendix 4.1

# The Market for Foreign Currency Exchange

## Exchange Rates

The manager of any firm in today's globally interconnected economy must be concerned with the risk of fluctuating currency exchange rates. For example, suppose a U.S. manufacturing firm builds a product that uses a component made by a Japanese firm. In order to purchase the Japanese part, the U.S. firm must pay in the Japanese currency, the yen. The U.S. firm converts its U.S. dollars to Japanese yen to facilitate the transaction with the Japanese firm. Not only does the U.S. firm have to worry about changes in the Japanese firm's price, but it also must be concerned with changes in the currency exchange rate between the dollar and the yen.

The *exchange rate* between two currencies is the quantity of one currency that can be exchanged for one unit of the other currency. In August 2005, one U.S. dollar could be exchanged for 109 yen, and by December 2005 one U.S. dollar could be exchanged for 117 Japanese yen.[1] Over this period the U.S. dollar *appreciated* relative to the Japanese yen, as more yen could be exchanged for one U.S. dollar in December. The Japanese yen *depreciated* relative to the U.S. dollar over this period. This result is good news for the U.S. manufacturing firm buying a Japanese part, as the stronger U.S. dollar makes the part less expensive.

The price of a U.S. dollar is expressed in the quantity of another currency that is exchanged for it. Chapter 4 describes how the prices of goods and services are determined by the forces of supply and demand. The price of a U.S. dollar, its currency exchange rate, is explained using the principles of supply and demand. Figure A4.1 displays the supply and demand for dollars in the currency exchange market between the dollar and the yen. The demand curve represents the amount of dollars demanded by people who want to exchange yen for dollars at various prices of a dollar. The supply

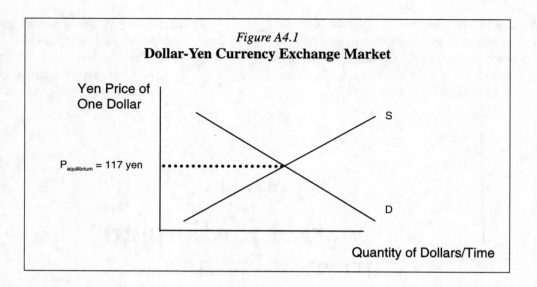

*Figure A4.1*
**Dollar-Yen Currency Exchange Market**

curve represents the amount of dollars supplied by people who want to exchange dollars for yen at various prices of a dollar. The intersection of supply and demand is the December 2005 exchange rate: 117 yen per dollar.

To understand how the exchange rate between the yen and the dollar changes, the factors that affect the supply and demand of U.S. dollars in the exchange market with the yen are examined. Suppose Japanese consumers increase their demand for goods and services from the United States. This causes more dollars to be demanded in the dollar-yen exchange market, as there is an increase in the demand for exchanges from yen to dollars. The demand curve in Figure A4.1 shifts to the right, the yen price of a dollar increases, and the dollar appreciates. Conversely, suppose U.S. consumers demand more Japanese goods and services. This causes more dollars to be supplied in the dollar-yen exchange market, as there is an increase in the supply of dollars for exchanges from dollars to yen. The supply curve in Figure A4.1 shifts to the right, the yen price of a dollar decreases, and the dollar depreciates.

## Exchange Rate Determination

There are numerous factors that affect exchange rates. Understanding how each factor specifically affects the rate of exchange essentially boils down to what ultimately happens to the supply and demand of currency in the exchange market. In addition to changes in consumer preferences for domestic or foreign products, relative changes in the following market fundamentals affect the exchange rate between two currencies: inflation, real income, real interest rates, productivity, profitability and risk of investments, government policy, and future expectations. Each market fundamental is discussed in turn.

As the rate of *inflation* increases in the United States relative to Japan, all else equal, the U.S. dollar depreciates relative to the yen. As prices of U.S. goods and services rise, two things occur relative to the dollar-yen exchange market. First, U.S. consumers demand more of the relatively cheaper Japanese goods and services, so the supply of dollars in the exchange market increases. Second, Japanese consumers demand less of the relatively expensive U.S. goods and services, so the demand for dollars decreases as well. Both of these effects result in a decrease in the yen price of the dollar.

As the *level of real income* increases in the United States relative to Japan, all else equal, the U.S. dollar depreciates relative to the yen. With a booming U.S. economy, consumers in the U.S. are more likely to increase their importing of Japanese goods and services. The supply of dollars in the dollar-yen exchange market increases, and the yen price of the dollar decreases.

As *real interest rates* increase in the United States relative to Japan, all else equal, the U.S. dollar appreciates relative to the yen. The rise in interest rates could be a result of market conditions or action taken by the Federal Reserve to curb inflation and slow down the economy. The increase in real interest rates has two effects on the dollar-yen exchange market. First, U.S. consumers begin to spend less as their cost of borrowing increases. Japanese imports decrease, and the supply of dollars in the dollar-yen exchange market also decreases. Second, with higher U.S. interest rates Japanese investors increase their demand for the U.S. dollar, as U.S. investments are more attractive. Both of these effects result in an increase in the yen price of the dollar.

As the *level of productivity* increases in the United States relative to Japan, all else equal, the U.S. dollar appreciates relative to the yen. With greater productivity, U.S. firms manufacture products more efficiently than firms in Japan and charge lower prices. U.S. exports to Japan increase, and the Japanese increase their demand for the U.S. dollar. The yen price of the dollar increases as a result.

Changes in the *level of risk and profitability associated with U.S. investments* relative to Japan also affect the dollar-yen exchange rate. If investors perceive that the U.S. equity market is riskier

without a related increase in potential profit, then the U.S. dollar depreciates. Investors in Japan move out of their U.S. investments and demand less dollars in the dollar-yen exchange market. The yen price of the dollar decreases.

Changes in *government policy* have a significant impact on exchange rates. Often countries such as Japan that are heavily dependent on exports promote a weak currency to make their products and services more attractive on the global market. The Japanese government accomplishes this through various combinations of monetary, fiscal, and trade policies. Using monetary policy, the Japanese lower interest rates and make Japanese investments relatively unattractive to U.S. investors. The supply of dollars on the dollar-yen exchange market decreases, and the yen price of the dollar rises. The dollar appreciates while the yen depreciates. The Japanese could use fiscal policy via tax incentives and increased government spending to increase imports from the United States. This increases the demand for dollars on the dollar-yen exchange market, and the yen price of the dollar rises. Again, the dollar appreciates while the yen depreciates. Certainly, the Japanese could also use specific trade policies (tariffs and quotas) to promote their exports and also influence the yen-dollar exchange rate.

It is essential for the global manager to understand how market fundamentals affect currency exchange rates, but understanding how *future expectations* affect exchange rates is probably the most important lesson of all. Currency traders, investors, and global managers all watch market fundamentals very closely. If they expect a change in the market environment to cause the yen to depreciate relative to the dollar in the near future, they make necessary adjustments. Currency traders sell their yen for dollars, investors pull out of Japanese investments and move into U.S. investments, and global managers in the United States put off purchasing Japanese parts until they become cheaper. All three of these reactions cause the yen to depreciate. Often expectations about a change in a currency exchange rate become a self-fulfilling prophecy. To make the best decisions for their organization, managers must be aware of how potential changes in the economy affect currency exchange rates.

**Note**

1. OANDA Corporation, "FXHistory: Historical Currency Exchange Rates," www.oanda.com/convert/fxhistory.

# Case Study 4.1

# Homes at Barry's Woods

## Introduction

Homes at Barry's Woods, Inc., an active-living retirement community in south-central Pennsylvania, are priced from $250,000 to $400,000, and the community offers many lifestyle amenities.[1] The developer and principal investor, Ryan Thomas, believes that the homes are appealing to buyers because of these amenities, which include community security services, manicured lawns and gardens, outside home and grounds maintenance, golf, tennis, swimming, lawn bowling, and an active clubhouse program.

Residents must be fifty-five years of age or older. Children are not permitted to live permanently in the community, although adult children are permitted to visit overnight and participate in recreational activities with their parents. Surveys of the residents indicate that the recreational facilities are an important reason for their purchase of a home at Barry's Woods. Approximately 60 percent of the residents are fully retired, 30 percent continue to

work or are active volunteers in the nearby town of Gettysburg, and 10 percent are modestly active.

South-central Pennsylvania attracts many retirees from the Philadelphia, Baltimore, and Washington, D.C., metropolitan areas. Ryan Thomas is committed to a four-stage expansion of the community from its current 300 homes (2006) to 450 homes by 2010. Thomas is confident in the success of the planned expansion. He cites the rapid sale of previous homes, an attractive location, mild weather, favorable state tax treatment of retirement income, cultural opportunities, and proximity to historic Gettysburg.

## Don Tubbs

Don Tubbs is the resident golf professional and director of golf operations. Don sees his responsibility as going beyond simply managing the golf operations. He knows that many residents are avid golfers. Their games and camaraderie are a big portion of their lives and significant contributors to the success of Barry's Woods.

Learning of Ryan Thomas' plan to increase the number of homes over the next four years, Don is studying the implications of the growth on demands on the golf program.

## Are Nine Additional Golf Holes Needed?

When Don accepted the position at Barry's Woods he was aware of the possible need to expand the golf course. Barry's Woods owns several hundred acres of currently unutilized land. Wetland restrictions prohibit the use of this land for new homes; however, an additional nine holes can be carefully built and maintained without violating environmental restrictions. In considering the costs and benefits of expanding the golf course, Don is permitted to treat the acquisition price of the land as a sunk cost and exclude it from the analysis.

Don knows corporate policy. A proposed capital project, such as an addition to the golf course, must show a minimum 8 percent after-tax rate of return before being approved and funded by the board of directors.

To begin his analysis Don gathers information to make three crucial estimates. Note that except for the construction costs associated with the nine holes, all amounts are considered end-of-year cash flows.

- The construction of the new holes can be completed for $1.8 million. For purposes of his analysis, this is treated as an up-front commitment of funds and a time period zero expenditure (beginning of 2007). Of the construction cost, $1.2 million of the cost is not depreciable, while the other $0.6 million is depreciable equipment and specialized construction (irrigation and drainage systems). For ease of analysis, Don has been advised that an average depreciable life of ten years

for tax purposes is reasonable. This ten-year depreciation life begins when the nine holes are placed into service in year three (2009).
- The construction period lasts twelve months, and an additional twelve months are needed to "season" the course prior to the start of play (2007–2008). This means that revenues are generated from the new nine holes beginning in year three (2009).
- Annual maintenance expenses for the additional nine holes are estimated to be $125,000. For purposes of his analysis, this expenditure commences in year three (2009).

## Historical Data

Don has gathered the following data to consider the implications of the residential growth on the golf operations:

- Golf season begins on April 1 and runs through September 30. While play occurs throughout the year, from October through March play is minimal, and so it is excluded from Don's analysis. On average twenty-seven days per month are playable from April through September. Over the peak play period, play does not vary by day of the week.
- Golfers are asked to reserve tee times, and 90 percent of the requests are for tee times between 9:00 A.M. and 2:00 P.M. Tee times are separated by fifteen-minute intervals to allow players to walk the course rather than use carts. Groups of two, three, or four are accommodated between 9:00 A.M. and 2:00 P.M. On average, each tee time serves three players.
- Residents of Barry's Woods pay a $20 fee for eighteen holes. Guests and non-residents pay $40. Golf carts are $10 for eighteen holes.

Approximately one-half of the golf groups use carts and the others walk the course.

- In 2006, on average each home site generated four rounds of golf by a resident and two rounds by a non-resident per month. This ratio of rounds per resident has grown by about one-half of a round per year and is expected to top out at six rounds per resident per month. No change in non-resident play is expected.
- Historical and forecasted data for April through September for the years 2003–2010 are shown in Table C4.1. These data reflect the continuous increase in the number of homes. The table also shows the number of homes to be built. It is believed the same 97 percent occupancy rate will be sustained. By 2010 Barry's Woods will be fully developed.
- For simplicity, assume that over the analysis period there are no increases in annual fees for golf or for maintenance costs.

**Questions to Consider**

1. Based on the historical data, what is the annual increase in golf play per home site?
2. Using this rate of increase in play per home site, estimate the desired number of rounds during the April-to-September period for each forecasted year.
3. Calculate the number of rounds of play per month that can be provided assuming (a) the current pattern of three players per round and then (b) a rules change that allows only groups of four during the peak period of 9:00 A.M. to 2:00 P.M.
4. Assuming three players per tee time, when does the desired play within the preferential time period exceed the capacity of the course? Remember that each month has twenty-seven playable days.

5. Is it proper for Don Tubbs to seek to meet 100 percent of the demand at the most desired time periods with an average of three players and at the current price?
6. Assume the price elasticity of demand for golf at Barry's Woods over the relevant price range is 0.75.

   (a) What does this indicate about buyers' sensitivity to the price of a round of golf?
   (b) For 2007, by what percentage should the price of a round of golf increase to fully price-ration the available tee times? Redo the calculation for 2010.
   (c) Will these price increases disturb the residents of the community?
   (d) Are these new prices a deterrent to potential purchasers of new homes in Barry's Woods?

7. As Tubbs, would you prefer to hold the price constant?
8. What non-price rationing procedures could Tubbs employ? As Tubbs, are you comfortable using non-price rationing techniques to distribute the preferred tee times?
9. Assuming the after-tax weighted average cost of capital to Barry's Woods is 8 percent, can you justify the construction of a new nine holes? Use a net present value approach to arrive at your answer. You may assume that the useful life of the new holes is twenty years from original construction. Be careful to consider the timing of the after-tax cash flows, including tax savings from depreciation.
10. If the 8 percent after-tax rate is not met, can golf make a justifiable claim to being a cost center?

*Table C4.1*
**Historical and Forecast Data: Homes and Rounds of Golf**

| Historical Data | | | Forecast Period | | |
|---|---|---|---|---|---|
| 2003 | Number of Homes | Rounds of Golf | 2007 | Number of Homes | Rounds of Golf |
| April | 225 | 982 | April | 325 | |
| May | 225 | 982 | May | 325 | |
| June | 225 | 982 | June | 325 | |
| July | 225 | 982 | July | 325 | |
| August | 225 | 982 | August | 325 | |
| September | 225 | 982 | September | 325 | |
| 2004 | | | 2008 | | |
| April | 250 | 1,212 | April | 375 | |
| May | 250 | 1,212 | May | 375 | |
| June | 250 | 1,212 | June | 375 | |
| July | 250 | 1,212 | July | 375 | |
| August | 250 | 1,212 | August | 375 | |
| September | 250 | 1,212 | September | 375 | |
| 2005 | | | 2009 | | |
| April | 275 | 1,467 | April | 400 | |
| May | 275 | 1,467 | May | 400 | |
| June | 275 | 1,467 | June | 400 | |
| July | 275 | 1,467 | July | 400 | |
| August | 275 | 1,467 | August | 400 | |
| September | 275 | 1,467 | September | 400 | |
| 2006 (current year) | | | 2010 | | |
| April | 300 | 1,746 | April | 450 | |
| May | 300 | 1,746 | May | 450 | |
| June | 300 | 1,746 | June | 450 | |
| July | 300 | 1,746 | July | 450 | |
| August | 300 | 1,746 | August | 450 | |
| September | 300 | 1,746 | September | 450 | |

11. Given that non-residents pay $40 per eighteen holes and residents pay only $20, can golf claim the price differential adds to the value of the real estate? If a transfer price (equal to the spread between non-residents and residents) from real estate to golf is assessed per round of resident golf beginning in 2009, does the golf course expansion meet the 8 percent rate of return?

12. How does the seasonal use of the golf course affect the rate of return? What other industries have similar seasonal patterns? What industries have day-of-week cycles and which have time-of-day cycles? What are the peak load planning problems?

13. Does the golf course add to the value of the real estate? If comparable homes in the area in communities without a golf course sell for $25,000 less, recalculate the rate of return on the nine-hole expansion.

14. Which variables in your net present value analysis have values that are subject to the greatest deviation from your estimates?

15. Tubbs made a variety of simplifying assumptions to facilitate his analysis. Which of these assumptions might have the greatest impact on the results obtained from the analysis?

16. Finally, as Tubbs, write a memo to Ryan Thomas in which you present your recommendation.

## Note

1. This case was prepared by Donald Butt, Assistant Professor of Accounting at Mount Saint Mary's University.

# 5

# The Costs of Production

This chapter examines the relationship between costs and output and discusses how a firm's costs of production influence production, pricing, and competitive strategy decisions.

## Learning Objectives

The successful reader understands:

- The relationship between costs and output
- How costs affect production and pricing decisions
- How costs affect the number and relative size of competitors in a market
- How the structure of costs helps to define a firm's competitive strategy

The primary question in this chapter is how costs vary with output. The answer depends upon the *economic time period*. Economists recognize four distinct time periods: the market period, the short run, the long run, and the very long run. The time period distinctions do not coincide with calendar time. Rather, the time periods refer to degrees of flexibility in the production process. Other topics in this chapter include the relationship between the costs of production and the number and relative size of firms in an industry as well as the business strategy implications of a firm's costs of production.

## Accounting and Economic Costs

Before examining the economic time periods, it is necessary to establish that economists view costs differently than accountants do. Economists include opportunity costs, which affect the allocation of finite resources among competing uses.

Consider the video rental store in Table 5.1. This store's gross sales revenue is $100,000. The direct payments for rent, videos, utilities, and labor total $80,000.

*Table 5.1*
### Explicit Costs and Accounting Profit

| Income Statement | |
|---|---|
| Item | $ |
| Gross sales revenue | $100,000 |
| • Rent, materials, labor, and utilities | $80,000 |
| Accounting profit | $20,000 |

Table 5.1 shows the video store's profit is $20,000. This calculation is the accountant's definition of profit. Accountants consider only direct payments. In Table 5.1, the direct payments are made to employees and suppliers. The opportunity costs of the resources employed are not included in the profit calculation.

Table 5.2 calculates the video store's *economic profit* by including the two opportunity costs. First, to open the store the owner invests $10,000.

Assuming an interest rate of 5 percent, the owner forgoes $500 in interest income per year. Second, the owner devotes forty hours of week to work in the store and forgoes the best alternative job, which pays $35,000 per year.

*Table 5.2*
**Accounting and Economic Profits**

| Item | $ |
|------|------|
| Accounting profit | $20,000 |
| • Forgone interest | −$500 |
| • Forgone wage | −$35,000 |
| Economic profit | −$15,500 |

Table 5.2 indicates that the owner of the video store realizes an *economic loss* of $15,500 over the period. The economic loss means the owner's opportunity cost is not met, and the resources are more highly valued in another use. The owner responds to this signal and directs capital and time to a more highly valued use. This decision by the

**Application Box 5.1**

A corporation's equity holders have a risk-adjusted opportunity cost of capital of 13 percent. The risk-free long-term interest rate on bonds is 10 percent, and the investors require an additional 3 percentage points for the risk of equity ownership.

To maximize the equity holders' wealth, the firm establishes a *hurdle rate* of 13 percent. Before financial capital is allocated to any investment project, it must show at least a 13 percent rate of return.

Projects with an expected rate of return in excess of 13 percent pass the hurdle. These projects satisfy the opportunity cost and are funded by the firm.

owner of the video store reflects an important aspect of a free market economy: that individuals' self-interest-oriented decisions contribute to the well-being of the community. The owner's decision to close the store releases scarce resources to produce other goods and services that are more highly valued in the marketplace.

In contrast, if the owner of the video store earned an economic profit, resources in other industries would recognize their opportunity costs and migrate into the video store industry. Decision makers respond to economic profits or losses and direct resources to the highest-valued use.

**Exercise 5.1**

Stacey resigns from her job, at which she was earning $50,000 per year. To open a new retail shop, she uses $75,000 of her savings, which had been invested in a certificate of deposit earning 4 percent per year. In the first year, the business generates $125,000 in gross revenue, and her costs were as follows: rent is $30,000, utilities are $11,000, wages are $38,000, and materials are $17,000.

(a) Calculate the accounting profit or loss.
(b) Calculate the economic profit or loss.
(c) Discuss the implications for the use of resources.
(d) What other variables should Stacey consider before opening a new retail shop?

**Costs and Output**

As noted, the relationship between costs of production and output varies according to the economic time period studied. Below, the periods are examined in sequence from the least to the greatest amount of flexibility in the production process.

## The Market Period

The market period is the shortest of the economic periods. The question of how costs vary with output is not relevant in this period, for production has already taken place. The firm cannot vary the rate of production, and the operative question is whether to hold products in inventory or sell. Consider a local cash crop farmer who brings freshly picked tomatoes to a regional market. Early in the day, the farmer adheres to the stated price. As the day passes, the farmer is faced with a problem: should the price of the tomatoes be reduced for quick sale or can the same tomatoes be brought to market the next day?

The market period decision for the seller is dictated by storage costs. What does it cost to hold products in inventory for future sale? Higher storage costs, all else equal, increase the pressure to discount the price to make an immediate sale. The costs of storage include the physical deterioration of the product, the loss of market value because of anticipated style or fashion changes, the physical costs of storage, the implicit interest costs, and the opportunity costs of projects funded with the cash receipts from immediate sale.

The cash crop farmer recognizes that the shelf life of a fresh tomato is limited, so late in the day the farmer cuts the price. Any income from the sale of the product is better than disposing of the product. Similarly, a retailer discounts winter merchandise at the end of the selling season, noting that unsold goods must be hauled to storage and that styles change every season.

Buyers and sellers who recognize the market period benefit. Consider the potential purchaser of a new car. A buyer who wants the reliability and freshness of a new vehicle but is unconcerned about driving the latest model knows that sellers discount unsold vehicles at the end of the model year. By waiting until then, the buyer can purchase the vehicle at discount. By discounting the price, the seller moves a vehicle out of inventory. Similarly, airlines respond to market period pressures, knowing the value of an unsold seat is lost once the plane departs. An air traveler who is unconcerned about the certainty of the departure time flies standby to take advantage of the market period opportunity.

## The Short Run

In the short run, firms have the flexibility to change the rate of production. However, the short run constrains the way in which the firm alters its rate of production. In the short run, a distinction is made between *fixed* and *variable* factors of production. For example, a manufacturer operates in the short run with its factory space and machinery. These are the fixed factors of production because of the difficulty and time involved in changing the size of the factory and the technology employed. In the short run, the manufacturer varies its rate of production only by altering the utilization of variable factors of production, including labor and materials.

### The Fixed Factor and the Variable Factor

In the short run one or more factors of production cannot be changed, and these fixed factors of production create fixed costs. For example, an airline's fleet of planes, defined by their number and technology, cannot be changed quickly. The aircraft are a fixed factor of production. The associated loan or bond payment is a fixed cost. Similarly, a retailer leases space in a mall. For the duration of the lease, the space is a fixed factor of production, and the contractual monthly rental payment is a fixed cost.

Variable factors of production work with the fixed factors to produce output. For example, the

## Application Box 5.2

A fixed cost does not rise or fall as the firm's rate of production changes. Once incurred, a firm is obligated for these costs even if no production occurs. The fixed costs are *sunk costs.*

A firm properly produces in the short run if sales revenues exceed the variable costs. Revenues in excess of variable costs cover at least some of the fixed costs and reduce the loss. Therefore, short-run production decisions are made on the basis of variable costs and not fixed costs.

airline needs fuel and personnel to complete a flight. The retailer hires hourly workers based upon the volume of business. The requisite fuel, number of hourly employees, and materials used vary with the rate of production. These inputs are variable factors of production and lead to variable costs.

## *Exercise 5.2*

For your firm, provide examples of fixed factors of production and fixed costs as well as variable factors of production and variable costs. For a typical rate of output, are fixed costs larger or smaller than variable costs?

### The Short Run: Costs and Output

The relationship between costs and output in the short run is examined in two steps. The first step examines the relationship between the units of the variable factor employed and the units produced over a fixed time period. The second step translates the linkage between physical units of

input and output to the relationships between costs and output.

Table 5.3 shows the variable input and output relationship for a manufacturing firm. Three points are noted. First, the output data are for a specific duration and are based on the results of engineering studies; second, only one variable factor of production is used in the production process; third, the input and output data are specific to the size of the fixed factor and the technology.

*Table 5.3*
**Total, Average, and Marginal Product**

| Total Product Output | Units of Variable Factor | Average Product | Marginal Product |
|---|---|---|---|
| 0 | 0 | 0 | — |
| 10 | 1 | 10 | 10 |
| 25 | 2 | 12.5 | 15 |
| 34 | 3 | 11.3 | 9 |
| 42 | 4 | 10.5 | 8 |
| 46 | 5 | 9.2 | 4 |
| 48 | 6 | 8.0 | 2 |
| 47 | 7 | 6.8 | -1 |

Referring to Table 5.3, the *average product* is output divided by the number of units of the variable factor employed. The *marginal product* is the change in output divided by the change in the number of units of the variable factor. For example, the fifth worker raises output from forty-two to forty-six units and has a marginal product of four units.

The marginal product of incremental workers is characterized by three distinct stages of production. Importantly, the analysis is unrelated to the skills of the workers; each worker is equally proficient and dedicated. The three stages of production result from the gains from specialization and the division of the variable factor (labor) employed.

## Application Box 5.3

Marginal product analysis affects a student's study habits. The marginal product is the increase in the student's grade on an exam divided by an incremental hour of study, and the number of hours of study is the variable factor. Initial increases in study time raise the student's grade by an increasing amount (increasing returns). In turn, additional hours of study yield successively smaller increases in the test score (diminishing returns to the variable factor). The student determines the appropriate amount of study time by comparing the value of the gain in the test score to the opportunity cost of the additional time studying.

A marketing manager expects increasing returns as initial advertising dollars build customer awareness and sales. After some level of advertising, the gain in sales from even more advertising diminishes. Using cost-benefit analysis, the manager determines the appropriate level of advertising.

## Application Box 5.4

The example in Table 5.3 assumes production requires only one variable input. Where two or more variable inputs are employed with the fixed factor, managers must find the best combination of variable resources.

The methodology for finding the best combination of resources is an instructive application of marginal analysis. The optimal use of resources occurs when the ratio of the marginal product to the price of each input is equal.

A landscaper studies the marginal product of an additional dollar spent on fertilizer and an additional dollar spent on labor. Resources are allocated to the use with the higher marginal product relative to its price. Reallocation continues until the marginal product of each use relative to its price is the same.

The first stage of production is characterized by *increasing marginal product*. In this stage, the incremental worker increases output at an increasing rate. In Table 5.3 the first worker produces ten units of output, and the second worker adds fifteen more. There are no skill differentials between the workers; rather, the second worker permits specialization and the division of labor. Each worker builds task-specific skills, and the team of two workers reduces the time expended in moving from task to task.

The second stage of production involves *diminishing marginal product*. In Table 5.3 workers three through six have a positive marginal product. In this stage of production, output rises as additional workers are employed, albeit at a diminishing rate. For example, the third worker's marginal product is nine units, whereas the fourth worker produces eight additional units of output. These workers are no less skillful than those previously hired. Rather, the diminishing marginal product occurs because the best opportunities for specialization and the division of labor have already been addressed.

The third stage involves *negative returns to the variable factor* and refers to worker seven. This incremental worker is no less skillful. Rather, there are no opportunities to further divide tasks. Worker seven has nothing to do but create distractions that reduce output.

To examine the implications of this input and output analysis, four assumptions are made: workers are paid in terms of physical units of output, the current wage is seven units, goods and services are bartered, and products are traded at a fixed rate. Given the wage of seven units per period, the firm hires the first worker who contributes ten units of output; the difference of three units is claimed by the owner. The second worker generates increasing returns. If it makes sense to hire the first worker, it makes sense to hire the second worker. This worker adds fifteen units to output and is paid seven units; the eight additional units are claimed by the owner.

The marginal product of incremental workers declines with the third worker. How many units of labor should the profit-maximizing firm employ? In turn, how many units of output should the profit-maximizing firm produce? The decision rule is to hire additional workers whose marginal product exceeds the wage. The firm hires worker three (whose marginal product is nine units and is paid seven units) and worker four (whose marginal product is eight units and is paid seven units) but not worker number five, who contributes only four units of output—an amount lower than the wage. In total, the firm produces forty-two units of output. One important lesson emerges: diminishing marginal product limits the size of the firm in the short run.

Money is introduced into the analysis in Table 5.4 with the assumption that each unit of output sells for $2. With this assumption, the worker's marginal product is expressed in dollars per unit produced, which is referred to as the *value of the marginal product*. For example, worker four has a marginal product of eight units. At $2 each, the value of the marginal product of the fifth worker is $16.

Assuming the market wage is $16, this firm hires worker three but not worker four (whose value of the marginal product is less than the wage). Several implications emerge. (1) If these workers threaten a strike and successfully push the wage to $20, worker three is dismissed. (2) Worker three remains employed if the firm sells the same number of units at $2.50 (= $20 ÷ 8). This outcome is unlikely; it

*Table 5.4*
**Value of the Marginal Product**

| Output | Units of Variable Input | Average Product | Marginal Product | Value of Marginal Product |
|---|---|---|---|---|
| 0 | 0 | 0 | — | — |
| 10 | 1 | 10 | 10 | $20 |
| 25 | 2 | 12.5 | 15 | $30 |
| 34 | 3 | 11.3 | 9 | $18 |
| 42 | 4 | 10.5 | 8 | $16 |
| 46 | 5 | 9.2 | 4 | $8 |
| 48 | 6 | 8.0 | 2 | $4 |
| 47 | 7 | 6.8 | −1 | −$2 |

assumes the demand for the product is perfectly price-inelastic and that the seller passes the full amount of the wage increase forward to the buyer in the form of higher prices. (3) Alternatively, if all workers successfully negotiate wage increases of the same percentage and if all firms raise their prices by that same percentage, no workers are dismissed. At the same time, no one realizes any real gain in purchasing power. (4) Given worker productivity, one worker group achieves real wage gains at the expense of some other group. The most likely to gain are those who produce a good or service for which buyers exhibit a price-inelastic demand. Also, worker three remains employed at a wage of $20 if productivity gains lift this worker's marginal product from eight units to ten units (and the value of the marginal product rises to $20). The critical conclusion is that productivity gains across the economy are the source of real wage increases and improvements in the standard of living.

*Inputs, Output, and Cost*

The physical input and output relationship in Table 5.4 extends to the relationship between short-run

*Table 5.5*
## Short-Run Costs and Output

| Output | Fixed Cost | Units of Variable Factor | Unit Cost Variable Factor | Total Variable Cost | Total Cost | Average Cost | Marginal Cost |
|---|---|---|---|---|---|---|---|
| 0 | $100 | 0 | $10 | $0 | $100 | – | – |
| 10 | $100 | 1 | $10 | $10 | $110 | $11.00 | $1 |
| 25 | $100 | 2 | $10 | $20 | $120 | $4.80 | $.66 |
| 34 | $100 | 3 | $10 | $30 | $130 | $3.80 | $1.11 |
| 42 | $100 | 4 | $10 | $40 | $140 | $3.33 | $1.25 |
| 46 | $100 | 5 | $10 | $50 | $150 | $3.26 | $2.50 |
| 48 | $100 | 6 | $10 | $60 | $160 | $3.33 | $5.00 |

costs and output. In Table 5.5, there are two as-sumptions: the firm's fixed costs are $100, and each unit of the variable factor is employed at $10 per period.

In Table 5.5, the output and units of the variable factor columns are repeated from the prior table. The seventh worker is not included because this worker has a negative marginal product and is never employed. Fixed costs are $100 and do not vary with the rate of production. Even if the firm does not produce, it incurs the fixed cost. The cost per unit of the variable factor is $10, and it is as-sumed more workers are hired at the same price. Therefore, the total variable cost is the number of units of the variable factor multiplied by the cost per unit. Total cost is the sum of the fixed cost plus variable costs. Short-run average costs are total costs divided by output. The marginal cost is the change in total cost divided by the change in output. For example, increasing output from thirty-four to forty-two units (a change of eight units) raises total costs from $130 to $140 (a $10 change), and the incremental cost of each these units is $1.25 (= $10 ÷ 8).

The graphics of the short-run cost curves are displayed in Figure 5.1. The vertical axis plots

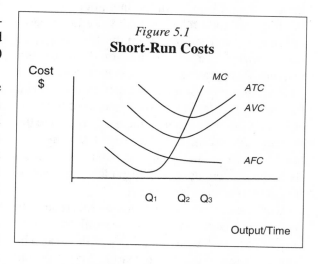

*Figure 5.1*
**Short-Run Costs**

the costs in dollars corresponding with the rate of output per time period on the horizontal axis.

From Figure 5.1, the average fixed cost (AFC) declines as output rises and the short-run average total costs (ATC) and average variable costs (AVC) and the marginal cost (MC) are U-shaped. The downward-sloping portion of the cost curves co-incides with the increasing marginal product of the variable factor, and the upward-sloping portion of the curves reflects the diminishing marginal prod-uct of the variable factor. The average total cost and the average variable cost converge as output rises. The marginal cost curve passes through the minimum point of both the average variable cost curve and the average total cost curve.

## Costs and Output and Management Decisions

In the short run, the firm pays its fixed costs even if the firm does not produce. For example, a bond payment is owed by an indoor sports complex even if it chooses not to operate. One implication is that firms determine their rate of production without regard to fixed costs. Consider the indoor sports complex. During the winter months its courts and fields are used heavily in the late afternoons and evenings and on weekends. In the mornings, early afternoons, and summer months the facility is underutilized. The underutilization of the facility results in an operating loss for the year. Though the business is not profitable, revenues earned exceed the variable costs. Revenues in excess of the variable costs cover a portion of the fixed costs, and the business operates in the short run. The firm loses less by operating in the short run than by shutting its doors immediately. The firm closes as soon as it is able to sell its fixed assets.

The management of the indoor sports facility recognizes that the facility is underutilized during certain parts of the day and times of the year. The firm also recognizes that its marginal costs during these low-use periods are minimal: a single low-wage worker and utilities. Therefore, the indoor sports facility allows senior citizens to use the facility in the morning and early afternoon at a deep discount off the regular retail price. As long as the firm earns revenues in excess of its marginal cost, the price discount improves the firm's profits (or minimizes its losses).

Consider a firm in a growing market. How much should it produce? The tempting answer is "as much as possible," but that is wrong. A firm

---

### Exercise 5.3

(a) Discuss the following: in order to ensure competitiveness, laws are needed to prevent firms from pricing products below the full cost of production.

(b) What problems do you foresee if such a proposal is adopted nationally? How do the problems escalate when considering international trade?

---

produces and sells another unit if the marginal revenue exceeds the incremental cost. Refer to Table 5.5, and assume the firm can increase sales from thirty-four to forty-two units and sell each unit at $1.30. These units of output should be produced and sold because the incremental revenue ($1.30 per unit) exceeds the incremental costs ($1.25 per unit). However, the firm should not produce and sell units forty-two to forty-six because the incremental cost ($2.50 per unit) exceeds the incremental revenue ($1.30 per unit). The firm finds the profit-maximizing rate of production when the incremental cost (marginal cost) is equal to the incremental revenue (marginal revenue).

Two conclusions are important. First, diminishing marginal product causes the increase in short-run marginal costs, and the increasing marginal costs constrain the size of the firm in the short run. Second, the production decision is made using marginal analysis. The decision to produce is made by comparing the incremental revenue to the incremental cost.

## The Degree of Operating Leverage

Table 5.6 refers to a firm's short-run production costs at different rates of output. The firm's total costs of production at each rate of output are the sum of fixed plus variable costs. Table 5.6 analyzes

*Table 5.6*
## Operating Leverage

| Units | Gross Revenue | Fixed Costs | Variable Costs | Profit |
|-------|---------------|-------------|----------------|--------|
| 25 | $125 | $100 | $20 | $5 |
| 34 | $170 | $100 | $30 | $40 |
| 42 | $210 | $100 | $40 | $70 |
| 46 | $230 | $100 | $50 | $80 |

the effects of the relative sizes of fixed and variable costs. In Table 5.6 it is assumed the firm sells additional units of output for $5. Gross revenue is the number of units sold multiplied by the price. The firm's profits are gross revenue minus fixed costs and minus variable costs.

In Table 5.6 the firm's fixed costs are much larger than its variable costs at all rates of output. The relationship between fixed costs and variable costs determines the degree of operating leverage, a measure of the sensitivity of profits to changes in sales (see Table 5.6).

Table 5.7 shows that the degree of operating leverage is the ratio of the percentage change in profits to the percentage change in sales. Assume the firm increases sales from twenty-five to thirty-four units (a 36 percent increase). Given this change in sales, profits rise from $40 to $70 (a 75 percent increase). The degree of operating leverage is 2.08 (see Table 5.7). Correspondingly, if sales decline from thirty-four units to twenty-

*Table 5.7*
## Degree of Operating Leverage

$$\text{Degree of Operating Leverage} = \frac{\%\text{ Change in Profits}}{\%\text{ Change in Sales}}$$

$$= \frac{75\%}{36\%}$$

$$= 2.08$$

### Application Box 5.5

Some industries utilize technologies that require substantial investments in fixed assets, including electric utilities, telephone companies, steel mills, airlines, and chemical producers. The technology and associated fixed costs result in a high degree of operating leverage. Grocery stores experience relatively fewer fixed costs. They also have relatively higher variable costs and a lower degree of operating leverage.

five units (a 26 percent decline) and profits fall from $40 to $5 (an 87 percent decline), the degree of operating leverage is 3.3. The proportionate decline in profit is larger than the proportionate decline in sales.

A firm's degree of operating leverage is an important environmental condition within which management decisions are made. An operating leverage ratio greater than 1 indicates that profits rise (or fall) proportionately faster than sales. Therefore, a firm with a degree of operating leverage greater than 1 prospers as sales rise and is financially vulnerable when its sales slump.

All else equal, the greater a firm's degree of operating leverage, the greater its vulnerability to downswings in the business cycle. To reduce this financial vulnerability, firms with a high degree of operating leverage prefer equity financing over debt financing, reduce fixed costs by choosing (when possible) short-term leases over purchases and part-time workers over full-time workers, and are quick to offer discounts and rebates when sales weaken. Low variable costs permit these firms to make sales at discounted prices. Equity investors take advantage of operating leverage by purchasing shares of high-operating-leverage firms at the start of a

### Exercise 5.4

(a) A personal service firm has a fixed cost of $1,000. The variable costs per unit output are $50 and constant. Services sell at $100 per unit.

(b) Calculate the degree of operating leverage, assuming sales rise from 100 to 110 units.

(c) Discuss the management implications of the calculation.

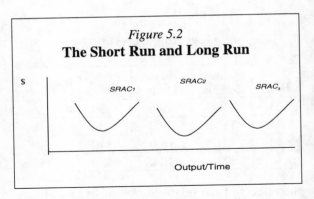

*Figure 5.2*
**The Short Run and Long Run**

business cycle expansion and selling those shares before a business cycle downturn.

### The Long Run

In the long run, firms enjoy greater production flexibility. All factors of production are variable. The long run is a period of transition, in which a firm increases or decreases its rate of production by adding or subtracting units of all factors of production and changing the technology. Once the transition is complete, production occurs in a new short-run situation.

Figure 5.2 displays a firm's *long-run average and marginal cost curves*. The starting point is the firm operating with a fixed factor (a factory of 10,000 square feet), and the corresponding short-run average cost curve, designated as $SRAC_1$. In the short run, the firm increases its rate of production by employing more units of the variable factor, but it is subject to the diminishing marginal product of the variable factor, which constrains its size.

Following Figure 5.2, the manufacturer has the option to remain in its current plant or move to a new facility with 200,000 square feet and technology suited for the more rapid rates of production. The cost curve associated with the new plant and technology is designated as $SRAC_2$. The short-run average costs when operating a larger, 220,000-square-foot facility with different technology

is designated as $SRAC_3$. If the firm decides to purchase a new plant and equipment, it makes a long-run adjustment. Once the move to the new facility is complete, the firm produces in its new short-run circumstance.

Referring to Table 5.3, the firm has many short-run production alternatives, and each option is distinguished by the particular size and technology of the fixed factor. The firm's production options are designated by subscripted short-run average cost curves. The decision to move into a larger production facility or office is risky, costly, and difficult to reverse. The appropriateness of the investment in new plant and equipment (and technology) is determined through *capital budget analysis*.

### The Capital Budget Decision

The decision to commit to a costly expansion of plant and equipment is complex. Analytical difficulties arise because new plant and equipment have a multiyear life. Costs are incurred today, but the expected increases in sales attributable to the new plant and equipment occur over time and are forecast values.

Table 5.8 refers to a manufacturing firm considering the purchase of a machine that costs $125,000 net of the sale of the old machine. The cost occurs in year zero. The new machine has a five-year life with no salvage value at the end of the period. The

**Application Box 5.6**

The capital budget in Table 5.8 highlights the distinction between profit and cash flow.

Income statements are generally expressed on an accrual method of accounting, in which revenues and expenses are recognized as they occur rather than when the cash actually changes hands. For example, a $5,000 sale of an item on credit in December 2005 is recorded in that year. In March 2006, the cash is collected and no revenue is recorded. The primary advantage of the accrual accounting method is that it matches revenues and expenses in the period in which they occur, thereby providing an appropriate measure of profit.

The annual depreciation expense reflects "using up the capital good." The depreciation charge properly reduces net income and taxes each period. When the depreciation is recorded, no cash changes hands, and the firm has cash available for other uses. Therefore, to monitor the net cash flow from the acquisition of a piece of capital equipment, the depreciation is added to the after-tax profit each period.

purchase of the new machinery allows the firm to increase output by 1,000 units per year, and Table 5.8 indicates that unit sales attributable to the new machine are 500 units in year one, 750 units in year two, and 1,000 units in years three through five. All sales are made at a price of $200. The variable cost to produce each additional unit is $100. The firm's cost of capital is 10 percent. For simplicity, the analysis assumes a straight-line depreciation schedule over five years, so the annual depreciation charge is $25,000 (= $125,000 ÷ 5).

Referring to Table 5.8, two items are noted.

*Table 5.8*
**Capital Budget Decision**

|  | Year 0 | Year 1 | Year 2 | Year 3 | Year 4 | Year 5 |
|---|---|---|---|---|---|---|
| Capital cost | $125,000 | $0 | $0 | $0 | $0 | $0 |
| Unit sales increase | 0 | 500 | 750 | 1,000 | 1,000 | 1,000 |
| Revenue increase | $0 | $100,000 | $150,000 | $200,000 | $200,000 | $200,000 |
| Variable cost | $0 | ($50,000) | ($75,000) | ($100,000) | ($100,000) | ($100,000) |
| Depreciation | $0 | ($25,000) | ($25,000) | ($25,000) | ($25,000) | ($25,000) |
| Pre-tax profit | $0 | $25,000 | $50,000 | $75,000 | $75,000 | $75,000 |
| Tax (25%) | $0 | $6,250 | $12,500 | $18,750 | $18,750 | $18,750 |
| After-tax profit | $0 | $18,750 | $37,500 | $56,250 | $56,250 | $56,250 |
| Depreciation add-back | $0 | $25,000 | $25,000 | $25,000 | $25,000 | $25,000 |
| Cash flow | $0 | $43,750 | $62,500 | $81,250 | $81,250 | $81,250 |
| PV factor (at 10%) | 0 | 0.9091 | 0.8264 | 0.7513 | 0.683 | 0.6209 |
| PV of cash flow | $0 | $39,773 | $51,650 | $61,043 | $55,494 | $50,448 |
| Present value of net cash flow = $258,408 | | | | | | |

First, the firm pays tax on its profits at a rate of 25 percent. Second, the annual depreciation of the new machine is treated as a cost, which reduces the net income for each period. However, depreciation is a non-cash expense, and the depreciation is added to the after-tax profits to calculate the cash flow from the investment in the new machine.

Table 5.8 indicates that the present value of the cash flow from the investment in the machine ($258,408) exceeds the purchase price of the machine ($125,000). Based on the projected sales and projected costs, this investment is appropriate given the firm's cost of capital.

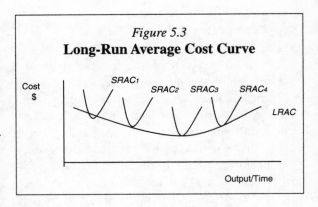

Figure 5.3
**Long-Run Average Cost Curve**

---

### Exercise 5.5

(a) Assume your firm is considering an automation project that costs $1,000,000. The project has a life expectancy of seven years, and the equipment has no salvage value. It is expected to reduce labor costs by $200,000 beginning in the following year. The labor savings are expected to grow by 5 percent per year for each of the next seven years.

(b) Should the investment be made if the firm's cost of capital is 10 percent?

---

*Economies and Diseconomies of Scale*

Figure 5.3 displays a series of short-run average cost curves, each referring to different sizes and technologies of the fixed factors of production. Here the focus is on the relationship between costs and output in the long run.

Figure 5.3 shows *the long-run average cost curve,* which is drawn by connecting the outside edges of the short-run average cost curves. The long-run average cost curve indicates the lowest possible average cost for each rate of output. Because production occurs only in the short run,

each point on the long-run average cost curve corresponds with a point on a short-run average cost curve. The minimum point on the long-run average cost curve represents the point of maximum production efficiency. It is the rate of output at which the average cost is minimized.

The long-run average cost curve is U-shaped, reflecting *economies* and *diseconomies of scale.* The downward-sloping portion of the long-run average cost curve reflects economies of scale. Over this section of the long-run average cost curve the average cost of production declines as the rate of output increases. The primary cause of economies of scale is technology. As a firm increases its rate of production in the long run, it adopts automated production processes and technologies suitable for faster rates of production. In addition, new production processes and technologies yield new opportunities for specialization and the division of labor, and the expanded size of the firm generates opportunities for volume purchases and to spread advertising expenses over a larger output.

The upward-sloping portion of the long-run average cost curve reflects diseconomies of scale. Over this section of the long-run average cost curve the average cost of production rises. The primary causes of diseconomies of scale are management issues. As the firm grows, layers of bureaucracy multiply. Decision making slows, coordination between operating areas in the firm is more difficult, and individual initiative and creativity are stifled.

The lowest point on the long-run average cost curve is the *minimum efficient scale (MES)*. The MES is the scale of operations at which all of the available economies of scale have been achieved. Under known technologies, the MES shows the rate of production at which the average cost is the lowest.

---

### Exercise 5.6

Consider a lemonade stand.

(a) In the short run, as more labor is hired, how can tasks be divided? How does the division of labor lead to increasing and then diminishing returns to the labor, a variable factor?

(b) How do diminishing returns limit the sales of the lemonade stand in the short run?

(c) Describe a possible long-run adjustment for the lemonade stand. Why do you think this proposal leads to economies of scale?

(d) What circumstances lead to diseconomies of scale in the lemonade stand's operations?

---

*Scale Economies and Industry Structure*

The shape of the long-run average cost curve influences the structure of an industry and competitive strategies of individual firms. The structure of an industry refers to the number and relative size of firms. Consider industry A and industry B in Figure 5.4. Both industries have sales of 1 million units. For industry A, maximum production efficiency for a single firm is achieved at a rate of production of 25,000 units; for industry B, maximum production efficiency occurs with a rate of production of 100,000 units. Industry A is likely characterized by a large number of relatively small firms, whereas industry B is characterized by a smaller number of relatively larger firms.

A measure of an industry's structure is its *concentration ratio*. Table 5.9 shows the four-firm concentration ratio, which is the percentage of total industry output produced by the four largest firms in the industry. The higher the four-firm concentration ratio, the greater the dominance of the largest firms in the market.

An industry's concentration ratio is affected by the definition of the geographic scope of a market.

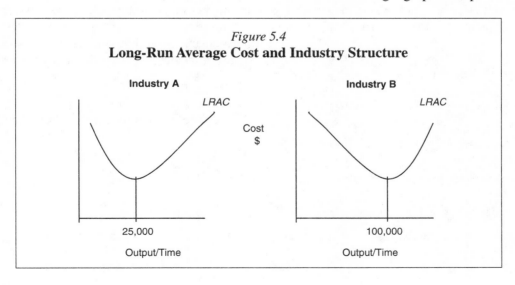

*Figure 5.4*
**Long-Run Average Cost and Industry Structure**

*Table 5.9*
## Four-Firm Concentration Ratio

$$CR_4 = \frac{\text{Output of the Four Largest Firms}}{\text{Industry Output}}$$

*Table 5.10*
## Justifiable Concentration Ratio

$$\text{Justifiable } CR_4 = \frac{4 \text{ (Output at Maximum Efficiency)}}{\text{Industry Output}}$$

For example, nationwide there are many gasoline stations, and the concentration ratio at the national level suggests the market is highly competitive. Yet national economic data often poorly reflect local conditions. In a regional marketplace, there may be only one or two sellers, thereby making the local market more monopoly-like.

In contrast, the *justifiable concentration ratio* (see Table 5.10) calculates the percentage of the market held by four firms that are producing at maximum efficiency. In Table 5.10, the denominator is industry output. The numerator, based on engineering estimates, is four times the rate of output of a firm producing at the minimum point of the long-run average cost curve. A justifiable concentration ratio of 75 percent means that four firms operating at maximum production efficiency should hold three-fourths of the industry's sales.

Comparing the concentration ratio to the justifiable concentration ratio provides managers with an important picture of their industry environment.

For example, assume the concentration ratio is 30 percent and the justifiable ratio is 60 percent. The industry consists of too many small firms relative to the requisites of production efficiency. Decision makers who recognize the microeconomic environment anticipate a wave of mergers and consolidations. In contrast, if the justifiable ratio is 60 percent and the actual ratio is 70 percent, the largest firms in the industry are too big relative to the requisites of production efficiency. The microeconomic environment leads to spin-offs that shrink the size of the larger firms in the industry.

The justifiable concentration ratio is based on engineering estimates given known technologies. Technology changes lead to changes in the justifiable concentration ratio. In Figure 5.5, the industry experiences a change in technology that shifts the long-run average cost curve downward and to the right. The new point of maximum efficiency occurs at a higher rate of output and a lower average cost.

Figure 5.5 indicates conditions that destabilize an industry. In an environment of technological change that increases the minimum efficient scale,

## Application Box 5.7

| Four-Firm Concentration Ratios, 1997 | |
|---|---|
| Industry | % of Shipments |
| Major appliances | 66.6% |
| Breakfast cereal | 86.7% |
| Furniture and related products | 11.2% |
| Food manufacturing | 10.9% |

*Source:* Census of Manufacturers, www.census.gov/prod/ec97/m31s-cr.pdf.

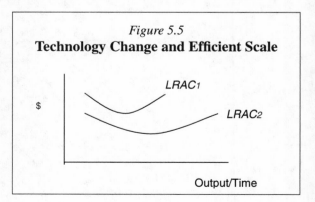

*Figure 5.5*
**Technology Change and Efficient Scale**

the justifiable concentration ratio increases. If the actual concentration ratio is lower, the technology change sets off mergers and acquisitions.

Figure 5.5 reflects an industry in which the technology advance necessitates a greater rate of production to achieve efficient scale, evidenced by the shift of the minimum point of the long-run average cost curve downward and to the right. Following the technological change, the minimum efficient scale is achieved at a more rapid rate of production. However, some technological advances create efficiencies at lower rates of production. Two examples are steel mills and publishing. In publishing, old typesetting technologies required long production runs. Large volume and mass market periodicals dominated. With desktop publishing, small-circulation journals compete for consumer dollars. The technology change alters the microeconomic environment to which managers respond.

*Economies of Scale and Competitive Strategy:*

Competitive strategy refers to the specific way in which a firm tries to differentiate itself from rivals. The intentions of the strategy are to become a preferred seller and to realize above-average returns in the industry. The two generic strategic options are product differentiation and price. A firm's choice is affected by its size relative to the minimum efficient scale (see Figure 5.6).

In Figure 5.6 a cost advantage accrues to the larger firm through economies of scale. A larger firm chooses to compete on price. The smaller-scale firm, with higher unit costs, is unable to compete on price and instead seeks a valued niche status. For example, a mass retailer sells men's suits based on price. A specialty shop competes successfully if the customized service and selection of designer labels and tailoring warrant a premium price. If the niche seller does not distinguish itself

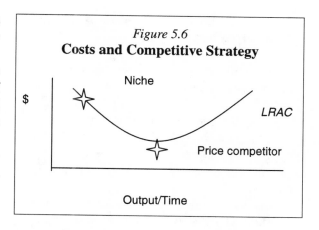

*Figure 5.6*
**Costs and Competitive Strategy**

in a manner important to buyers, it is unable to charge a premium price and will ultimately go out of business. It is the victim of inefficiencies attributable to its small scale relative to the MES.

*X-Inefficiency*

The long-run average cost curve shows the lowest possible average costs for each alternative rate of output, assuming the firm uses the most efficient technology. The firm in Figure 5.7 displays *X-inefficiency*: it is producing at a rate consistent with achieving maximum production efficiency, but its actual costs are higher than the minimum possible, as shown by the gap between the long-run average cost curve and the firm's actual unit cost.

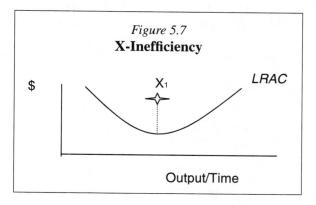

*Figure 5.7*
**X-Inefficiency**

## Application Box 5.8

Firms experience cost differences relative to rivals for many reasons. Two are worth noting. First, U.S. firms tend to have substantially higher health care benefits than international rivals, and the U.S. health care system is part of the reason. This difference provides a selling advantage for some international rivals.

Second, established firms are sometimes challenged by previously agreed-upon labor contracts, giving new entrants into the industry an advantage. This difference offers an advantage to new entrants into the industry.

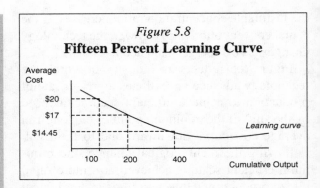

*Figure 5.8*
### Fifteen Percent Learning Curve

X-inefficiency occurs for several reasons. One possibility is that workers are poorly selected, trained, motivated, or supervised. Personnel may be lazy or unaware of cost-saving opportunities. Alternatively, sales may have grown rapidly, and the firm did not have sufficient time to install the appropriate technologies or risk-averse decision makers were reluctant to incur the expense of new technologies. X-inefficiency is less likely to exist in markets characterized by a large number of sellers who compete on the basis of price. Under these market conditions, X-inefficient firms are driven out of the marketplace by more efficient rivals.

### Learning Curve Economies

Another factor that affects costs is learning by doing. Whereas economies of scale lead to lower average costs as the rate of production rises, *learning curve economies* are derived from cumulative experience.

Figure 5.8 provides an example of learning curve economies. Typically, learning curves are defined by the percentage that unit costs tend to decline each time cumulative output doubles. Figure 5.8 shows a 15 percent learning curve. At a cumulative output of 100 units, the average cost was $20. Over time cumulative output grows to 200 units, and the average cost declines by 15 percent ($3 per unit) to $17. After cumulative output doubles again, to 400 units, the average cost declines to $14.45.

Learning curve economies are not realized automatically. Rather, the potential advantages of cumulative experience must be carefully nurtured because the benefits of the cumulative experiences reside in the firm's human resources. Two significant management lessons are noted. First, it is individual employees who, by virtue of experience, acquire know-how and uncover ways to increase efficiency. In environments where learning curve opportunities exist, compensation systems reward seniority. Second, an environment conducive to learning curve efficiencies requires managers to be good listeners. Ideas come from individuals, and ideas affect efficiency only if the creative ideas are heard, examined, and implemented.

### Economies of Scope

Economies of scope affect a firm's costs of production in another way. Economies and diseconomies of scale alter average costs based upon changes in

*Table 5.11*
**Economies of Scope**

| Units of Food | Units of Clothing | | | | |
|---|---|---|---|---|---|
| | 0 Clothing | 1 Clothing | 2 Clothing | 4 Clothing | 8 Clothing |
| 0 Food | $0 | $4 | $7 | $13 | $24 |
| 1 Food | $3 | $7 | $7 | | |
| 2 Food | $7 | | $12 | | |
| 4 Food | $15 | | | $20 | |
| 8 Food | $25 | | | | $36 |

the rate of production of a product. Learning curve economies affect costs of production based upon the cumulative production of a product. Scope economies affect costs based upon the production of multiple goods. For example, a lawn and garden firm sells landscaping and lawn maintenance services during the summer months. By diversifying into snow removal in the winter months, the firm's fixed-asset use rate rises. Further, by serving the same clients over twelve months, the firm's advertising and promotion costs relative to sales decline.

The firm in Table 5.11 sells two products: food and clothing. The table shows different rates of sale of each product, and the dollar values in the body of the table refer to the firm's total costs. If neither food nor clothing is sold, the firm's total cost is zero. If the firm sells one unit of food and no clothing, its total cost is $3. If the firm sells one unit of each product, the total cost is $7.

Table 5.11 displays both economies of scale and economies of scope. Economies of scale refer to declining average costs as the firm increases the rate of production (or sale) of a single product. As the retailer sells double the amount of clothing (while selling no food), total costs do not double. For example, when sales double from two units to four units, total costs rise from $7 to $13. Scale economies are similarly achieved as the firm increases its sales of food. While not selling clothing, increasing the sales of food from four units to eight units increases costs from $15 to $25. Economies of scope are seen reading diagonally down and to the right on Table 5.11. Begin from the sale of one unit of clothing and one unit of food. If sales double to two units of both products, costs do not double. Selling more of both products leads to lower unit costs. This phenomenon exemplifies economies of scope.

Economies of scope occur when a firm reduces costs through the production of multiple goods. The economies arise from an underutilized asset. For example, a manufacturer adds a new product to raise the utilization of its assembly line, or an insurance firm's expansion into investment products raises the productivity of its agents. Also, a firm's technology is applied to additional products. For instance, a state-of-the-art inventory management system is extended from retailing clothing to retailing food.

Economies of scope lead to firms that are larger according to measures of total employment, revenue, profit, and sales revenue from several products. Measures of market concentration are insufficient to estimate the buying or selling power of diversified firms. A highly diversified firm with a fractional share in one market is markedly stronger

---

### Exercise 5.7

(a) What distinguishes economies of scale, economies of experience, and economies of scope?

(b) Discuss the management implications of each.

(c) Provide examples of each from your place of work.

---

than an undiversified rival with an equal share in that market.

### The Very Long Run

The *very long run* is conceptually very important, though formal analysis is limited. In this economic time period firms have the opportunity to respond to technologies not previously known. The nature of the very long run is such that cost and output relationships cannot be calculated. How is an analyst to show the relationship between cost and output for a technology that does not currently exist? This limitation does not minimize the conceptual importance of this economic time period, however. It serves as a useful reminder that markets are dynamic in nature and that effective decision makers anticipate changes in their environment.

### Summary

This chapter examines the costs of production, helping decision makers to understand how costs are determined, how costs change over time, and how the structure of costs affects the structure of the competitive environment. The analysis of costs is often a critical component of a firm's strategic plan. In Chapter 6, the analysis of costs is coupled with the study of revenues and profit maximization.

### Review Terms

| | |
|---|---|
| Accounting and economic profits | Marginal cost |
| Capital budgeting | Market period |
| Concentration and justifiable concentration ratios | Minimum efficient scale |
| Economies and diseconomies of scale | Operating leverage |
| Economies of scope | Short run |
| Fixed and variable costs | Storage costs |
| Fixed and variable factors of production | Transfer prices |
| Learning curve economies | Transaction costs |
| Long run | X-inefficiency |

### Discussion Questions

1. Jane quit her job, at which she was earning $50,000 in total compensation, and used $75,000 of her savings, which had been earning 7 percent per year, to open a business. In the first year of operation, the business generated gross revenues of $170,000, and her operating costs were as follows: (a) materials = $18,000, (b) wages = $35,000, (c) rent = $30,000, and (d) utilities plus insurance = $15,000.

   (a) Calculate Jane's accounting profit.
   (b) Calculate Jane's economic profit.
   (c) If Jane continues to earn the same amount from this business in following years, should she stay or leave the business?

2. A manufacturing firm's study of its short-run input and output data is as follows:

*Table D5.1*

| Production Data | | | |
|---|---|---|---|
| Output | Units of Variable Factor | Average Product | Marginal Product |
| 0 | 0 | | |
| 20 | 1 | | |
| 35 | 2 | | |
| 45 | 3 | | |
| 54 | 4 | | |
| 61 | 5 | | |
| 65 | 6 | | |

(a) Calculate the average and marginal products.
(b) Identify the range of increasing and diminishing returns to the variable factor.
(c) If the wage is 7.3 units of output, how many units of the variable factor are employed?

3. Using the data from problem 2, make the following assumptions: (a) the firm's fixed cost is $100 and (b) a unit of the variable factor costs $20. Complete the short-run cost and output table (Table D5.2).

4. Assume this firm sells each unit of output for $5. In this short-run time period, how many units should it produce? Discuss the decision rule.
5. Comment upon the relative size of the firm's fixed and variable costs. Based upon this observation, what are the implications for the degree of operating leverage?
6. Complete the following table based upon the data from problem 3.

*Table D5.3*

| Output | Fixed Cost | Variable Cost | Profit |
|---|---|---|---|
| 0 | | | |
| 20 | | | |
| 35 | | | |
| 45 | | | |
| 54 | | | |
| 61 | | | |
| 65 | | | |

(a) Calculate the degree of operating leverage assuming the firm's sales rise from forty-five to fifty-four units.

*Table D5.2*

| Costs and Output | | | | | | | |
|---|---|---|---|---|---|---|---|
| Output | Units of Variable Factor | Variable Cost | Average Variable Cost | Fixed Cost | Total Cost | Average Total Cost | Marginal Cost |
| | | | | | | | |
| | | | | | | | |
| | | | | | | | |
| | | | | | | | |
| | | | | | | | |
| | | | | | | | |
| | | | | | | | |

(b) Discuss the managerial implications of the calculation of the degree of operating leverage.

7. Assume the four-firm concentration ratio is 35 percent and the justifiable four-firm concentration ratio is 50 percent.

(a) What are the cost pressures in this industry?

(b) What do you expect to happen in this industry?

(c) What should a small firm in this industry expect to occur?

(d) What are the competitive initiatives of a large firm in this industry?

8. Discuss the management implications for a firm that anticipates significant learning curve economies.

9. Distinguish between increasing marginal product, economies of scale, learning curve economies, and economies of scope.

# Case Study 5.1

# Charles Betz, Inc.

Charles Betz, Inc., produces gauges of different performance specifications for sale to manufacturers of automobiles, small aircraft, boats, construction equipment, and air conditioners. The gauges vary by their features, which include size, technical performance, and reliability. Price and customer service variables are also important aspects of interfirm rivalries.

## The Production Problem

Blake Christopher, product manager for the watercraft product, has assembled data showing that 6,500 gauges were sold in this segment in 2006. As seen in Table C5.1, the company sold 500 units in this segment, a 7.7 percent market share.

   Blake expects his sales to grow at 13 percent per year. This growth rate is about 1.5 percentage points faster than the market. The belief is that prior engineering investments reduce the time needed to

*Table C5.1*
**Watercraft Segment Data, 2006**

| Variable | Value |
| --- | --- |
| Betz's unit sales | 500 |
| Segment growth rate | 13% |
| Betz: first-shift capacity | 600 units |

introduce product upgrades, which yields a three-month first-mover advantage each year.

## The Choices

Blake sees three options for managing capacity and production: (1) hire more people and increase output of the current shift, (2) expand to a second shift, or (3) add productive capacity. Under each option, increases in materials and marketing costs are the same.

## Add Personnel

To expand production, the firm could add more personnel to the first shift. However, engineering estimates suggest that output can be increased only by a maximum of 10 percent by hiring more people because there are few additional opportunities for specialization and the division of labor.

## Overtime

A second shift of workers can be started. A second shift (1) allows additional production up to the first-shift capacity (600 units), (2) imposes a labor cost premium of 50 percent over the first shift's $10.50 unit labor cost, (3) necessitates an additional $250,000 per year in supervisory and administrative costs, and (4) can be stepped up annually to meet market demand.

## Add Capacity

Each additional unit of capacity costs $12,500. There is a one-year lag from the time of ordering and paying for the capacity increase until it is available for use. Capacity cannot be easily added in small increments. Capacity increases of less than 200 units of output carry a 30 percent premium. Additions of each 200 units of capacity yield economies of scale that lower the labor cost per unit output by 5 percent. Additional capacity has a useful life of fifteen years, and the firm's cost of capital is 12 percent.

## Questions and Problems

Assume the role of Blake Christopher. Prepare a memo that covers the following topics:

(a) The size and timing of the production capability problem
(b) The options for responding to the production capability problem
(c) The pros and cons of each of the options
(d) A recommendation based on the data

# Chapter 6

# Market Structures, Firm Behavior, and Pricing

This chapter introduces the microeconomic environments in which firms operate. The four market structures—monopoly, oligopoly, monopolistic competition, and perfect competition—are described to explain how these environments affect the way managers make decisions.

---

**Learning Objectives**

The successful reader understands:

- The different market structures, their key assumptions, and their implications for firm behavior
- The implications of market structure for pricing
- The nature of the strategic interaction between firms in different market structures

---

## Introduction to Market Structures

As has been discussed throughout this book, managers make decisions according to the prevailing economic environment. Consider the manager who must determine how many units of a particular product to produce and what price to set for the product. Clearly, the process the manager employs to make these decisions depends on the type of market the manager's firm is operating in. The firm may be a small player in a highly competitive market in which supply and demand forces determine a market price that the manager is forced to abide by. This manager is a *price-taker*. At the other end of the spectrum, the firm could be the sole provider of a product and have control over price. This manager is a *price-maker*. Certainly, there are varying degrees of control a manager has over price between these two extreme cases. This chapter examines four categories of market structure to demonstrate how the manager's decision process changes in different microeconomic environments.

In Chapter 4, the goods market is described as a group of households and firms that come together for the purpose of buying and selling a product or service. Economists find it useful to classify markets in four broad categories: monopoly, oligopoly, monopolistic competition, and perfect competition. Each market classification is characterized by the control sellers have over price, the number of sellers in the market, the level of product differentiation, the conditions for entry into the market, the use of advertising in the market, and the focus of the selling firms' managers.

In a *monopoly* there is only a single seller. There is no product differentiation, as the monopolist's product is the only one available of its kind for buyers. The monopolist's market position is pro-

**Application Box 6.1**

The Pfizer Corporation has a patent for impotence pills that work by inhibiting an enzyme called PDE-5. Pfizer held a monopoly on its famous little blue pill, Viagra, from 1997 to 2003, and it generated huge profits. In 2002 alone, Pfizer made $1.7 billion from sales of Viagra. These profits are justified by Pfizer because of the extremely high cost of drug development. Pfizer's monopoly on the product allowed Pfizer to charge a high price for the drug. Pfizer's claim on the oral PDE-5 inhibitor is valid until 2019. However, monopoly protection from patents is not always foolproof. Two other drug companies, GlaxoSmithKline and Eli Lilly, argued that they had PDE-5 inhibitors developed before Viagra; they just were not used for impotence. Both companies entered this profitable market in 2004 with their respective products, Levitra and Cialis.

*Source:* Matthew Herper, "Pfizer's Definition of 'Invention,'" Forbes.com, March 6, 2003, http://www.forbes.com/2003/03/06/cx_mh_0306pfe.html.

tected, so it is impossible for other sellers to enter the market. The protection could be the result of a patent granted by the government for a new innovation, or it could stem from the fact that the firm controls all of the resources necessary to produce the product.

Some monopolies, known as *natural monopolies,* build an expensive infrastructure over time that is prohibitively costly for other firms to duplicate. Often these firms are regulated by the government and are only permitted to set prices that yield a reasonable profit for the firm. Public utilities are good examples and are described in more detail later in the chapter.

Three additional characteristics of monopolies are important. First, a monopolist advertises only to increase public awareness of its product. For example, drug manufacturers advertise directly to consumers to encourage patients to ask doctors for treatments even though the drug has no competition. Second, the management of a monopoly is focused primarily on maximizing profit. As long as the monopolist understands its product's consumer demand and costs of production, the monopolist sets a price that generates the most profit possible. This problem is examined in greater detail later in the chapter. Third, a monopoly is often fleeting. Products sold in a monopoly environment are regularly superseded by new technologies or affected by expiring patents.

In an *oligopoly* there are a few firms selling a similar product or service. Because there is a small number of sellers, there is the possibility that the firms collude to share monopoly-sized profits. Although overt price fixing is illegal in the United States, firms easily watch movements in their competitors' prices and match them when appropriate. The temptation to undercut a competitor's prices is great, the lure being increased market share and profits. However, one of the principal teachings in economics is the *fallacy of composition*—what is good for one is not always good for all. Clearly, if all of the firms in the oligopoly lower their prices, then market share is unaffected and the firms share meager profits. The strategic nature of oligopolies is explained through a study of *game theory,* and both are examined later in the chapter.

Product differentiation in oligopolies depends on the nature of the industry. Steel and aluminum are examples of homogeneous products in oligopolies, and airline travel is becoming more of a standardized product as carriers focus on cutting costs. Video game consoles (GameCube, PlayStation, and Xbox), on the other hand, are quite differentiated, as are automobiles. The dif-

## Application Box 6.2

The costs of entry in an oligopoly can be quite high. The Federal Express Corporation was founded by Fred Smith in the early 1970s. Smith's original concept for Fed Ex was the topic of a term paper he wrote in a Yale economics course. He believed that a successful shipping company should actually own its planes. (At the time other shipping companies used cargo space on commercial airlines.) He also designed the hub-and-spoke distribution system. Smith used a $4 million inheritance and $91 million in venture capital to launch his firm. Not only was the cost of entry high, but it took a number of years for Fed Ex to turn a profit. In 1976, Fed Ex turned the corner and reported a profit of $3.6 million on an average daily volume of 19,000 packages.

*Source:* Robert Bruner, *Case Studies in Finance* (New York: McGraw-Hill, 2003), p. 59.

ference between the industries has to do with the way firms set themselves apart from their competition—via lower prices or via enhanced product characteristics. It should come as no surprise, then, that companies in an oligopoly that compete on product characteristics tend to conduct a lot of advertising. However, when there is little product differentiation in the industry, companies are less likely to advertise.

Entering an oligopoly is difficult but not impossible. Typically firms in an oligopoly experience significant economies of scale, so the cost of entry into these industries is high. The management of a firm entering an oligopoly is focused initially on the length of time it takes the firm to recover its fixed costs. Once a firm is profitable, management focuses on increasing market share, maximizing profit, and capitalizing on strategic opportunities.

In *monopolistic competition,* there are many sellers. Each firm in this type of market sells only a small share of the entire industry's output. The key component of this market structure is product differentiation. While there are many firms selling similar products, each firm distinguishes its own product by making it slightly different from other available substitutes. The market for these products is extremely competitive, and each firm attempts to capitalize on some monopoly power with its unique product offering. For example, many athletic apparel companies sell shirts and shorts that display their unique logo. Consumers become loyal to the brand, and they are willing to pay higher prices. In any sporting goods store today, apparel with the Nike Swoosh will have significantly higher prices than similar clothes with a generic brand.

Nike has some control over the price it sets on its apparel, and the company charges a premium over the market price for sportswear. However, Nike is still very dependent on the market price. Because there are numerous sellers of athletic apparel, Nike cannot charge too high a price. Brand loyalty only goes so far. This is what distinguishes monopolistic competition from pure monopoly. In monopolistic competition, consumers have other choices, while in a pure monopoly there is only one product option.

Monopolistic competition is different from an oligopoly in that there are many producers of a product. There is no possibility for strategic interaction among the firms in the determination of prices or output. The decisions of one firm do not affect the decisions of other firms because each firm is a small player in the industry. The decision Nike makes to raise or lower the prices of its apparel has little impact on the decisions of other firms in the industry.

Two additional characteristics of monopolistic competition are important to note. First, entry into

**Application Box 6.3**

In contrast to the oligopoly, the cost of entry in monopolistic competition is much less. In 1995, a University of Maryland football player named Kevin Plank became frustrated that he had to change his sweat-soaked cotton T-shirt numerous times during a football game. After his playing days ended, Plank spent time in New York City's garment district searching for a fabric that would be light, comfortable, and, most importantly, would not retain moisture. He developed a T-shirt that was designed to wick moisture away from the body and keep a player cool and dry. The shirts looked "shiny and tight," and he gave them to players at the University of Maryland to try. He started his business in the basement of his grandmother's house in Washington, D.C., on a small budget. Today, Plank's company, Under Armour, is a profitable sports apparel company. Under Armour is an example of a successful venture in a monopolistic competition market. Under Armour created a small monopoly position by creating a product with distinctive characteristics. Although Under Armour is successful, its monopoly is threatened by copycat products. The entry into this market is easy, so other companies—Nike, Adidas, Starter, and Reebok—have all created similar shirts.

*Source:* www.underarmour.com.

this market type is relatively easy. The costs associated with entry are not nearly as high as they are in an oligopoly. Second, marketing is the key to success for firms in these markets. Understanding the needs and preferences of consumers, developing unique product offerings, and communicating the firm's distinctiveness to consumers are essential.

Profits erode very quickly, and firms constantly upgrade their products. Firms in monopolistic competition rely heavily on advertising. Nike uses advertising quite effectively to associate its Swoosh trademark with athletic elitism and hip fashion. Consumers envision themselves as better athletes and in style with the Nike logo on their clothing. Managers in these industries focus on creating product distinction, marketing, gaining monopoly pricing power, and managing costs.

*Perfect competition* is the end of the market structure spectrum where there are many sellers offering identical products. Firms operating in perfect competition are price-takers. Because there are many buyers and sellers in the market, no one buyer or seller has an influence on the price, which is set by the combined forces of supply and demand. The traditional example of a product in a perfectly competitive market is an agricultural good (wheat, corn, milk, etc.). One farmer's wheat is exactly the same as another farmer's wheat. If one farmer attempts to sell wheat at a price higher than the market price, buyers simply go to other farmers for their wheat.

Because the competition is intense in a perfectly competitive market, only firms that produce at the lowest possible cost survive. Managers in perfectly competitive firms focus almost solely on reducing their costs of production. If any firms on the outside looking in see profit potential, they enter the market easily. As a result, consumers enjoy the benefits of low prices and society reaps the benefits of efficient production. That is, scarce resources are allocated by market forces to their most efficient use.

Individual firms in a perfectly competitive market typically do not advertise because the benefits of advertising are spread among all sellers. Because there is no product distinction, consumers do not care whether they get their wheat from one farm or another. Industry-wide advertising ("Got milk?" and "Beef, it's what's for dinner") is conducted and

*Table 6.1*
**Market Structures**

|  | Monopoly | Oligopoly | Monopolistic Competition | Perfect Competition |
|---|---|---|---|---|
| # of firms in market | One | Few | Many | Very many |
| Type of product | Unique | Standardized or differentiated | Differentiated | Standardized |
| Control over price | Complete | Some | Very narrow | None |
| Conditions of entry | Blocked | High obstacles | Relatively easy | Easy |
| Advertising | Mostly informational | Many ads for differentiated products | Highest level of advertising | Very little— some industry advertising |
| Management's primary focus | Profit maximization | Gaining market share, maximizing profits, strategic interaction with competitors | Product differentiation, managing costs | Cost-efficient production |

paid for by collective groups of sellers to promote the entire industry.

Profits for individual firms are meager, and firms prefer to operate in market structures where more monopoly power is available. Firms in perfectly competitive markets focus on efficient production and cost containment in the short run, and they attempt to differentiate their product from the rest of the market if possible in the long run. Monopolistic competition offers greater potential for profit through some ability to charge a premium over the market price.

Table 6.1 summarizes the four categories of market structures.

## Monopoly Pricing and Profit Maximization

Consider the manager who operates a firm that is a monopolist and sells a single product. As mentioned in the previous section, this monopolist is a price-maker. As the sole seller of the product, the manager of the firm must decide the price to set for the product and also how many units of the product

### Exercise 6.1

Consider a product or service that your company offers for sale. Describe the market conditions your company sells in with respect to number of competitors, type of product, control over price, conditions of entry, level of advertising, and your company management's focus. Which of the four market structures would you use to describe the market in which your company operates? Provide an example of a product or service not yet described in the chapter that best represents each of the four market structures.

to produce. The firm's objective is to maximize profit, which is simply the difference between the firm's revenue and its costs. Algebraically, the relationship is *Profit = R – C.*

The revenue component (*R*) of profit is generated by multiplying the quantity (*Q*) of product sales by the price (*P*) set by the firm: $R = P \times Q$. The relationship between the price set by the firm and the quantity sold follows one of the most basic principles of economics: the law of demand. The law of demand states that, everything else equal, the higher the price of a good, the fewer the units of the good that will be demanded by consumers and sold by firms.

A monopolist is constrained by the law of demand. If a monopolist sets too high a price, consumers elect to go without the product or buy a loose substitute. For example, an electric company may have a local monopoly, but households could use candles if the electric company charges too much for electricity.

Figure 6.1 graphically displays the relationship between price and quantity with an example of a linear downward-sloping demand curve. The horizontal axis shows the number of units of the product sold at any unit in time, while the vertical axis shows the price per unit. At a price of $40, zero units of the product are sold. As the firm lowers its price, consumers demand more units of the product. At $34, three units of the product are sold; at $10, fifteen units are sold. This particular demand function has a linear relationship between price and quantity: for every $2 drop in price, the firm sells an additional unit of the product.

Understanding how consumers respond to changes in price via the demand curve is the key to estimating revenue. A firm that estimates its demand function accurately is able to select a price to realize its greatest potential profit. Later in this chapter, the realities of estimating demand are discussed. For now, it is assumed that the firm has

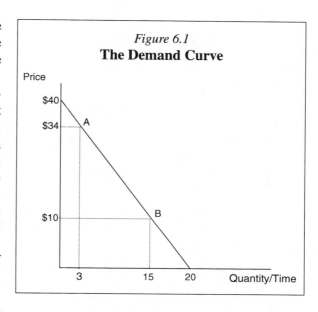

*Figure 6.1*
**The Demand Curve**

perfect information regarding its demand function. That is, the monopoly firm knows exactly how consumers respond to changes in its price.

Algebraically, the relationship between price and quantity for the demand function is shown in Table 6.2. The equation in Table 6.2 allows the firm to predict how many units of its product will be sold at any given price. The entire mapping of price to quantity is depicted by the demand line in Figure 6.1.

*Table 6.2*
**A Demand Function**

$$Q = 20 - 0.5P$$
*Q* is the quantity demanded, and
*P* is the price set by the firm.

Not only is the firm able to predict how many units of its product will be sold at any given price, but it will also be able to predict how much revenue it can expect at any given price. At point A in Figure 6.1, the firm sets a price of $34 and sells three units. The revenue the firm receives at this price is $102

*Table 6.3*
**Revenue Analysis**

| Q | P | R | MR |
|---|---|---|---|
| 0 | $40 | $0 | |
| 1 | 38 | 38 | $38 |
| 2 | 36 | 72 | 34 |
| 3 | 34 | 102 | 30 |
| 4 | 32 | 128 | 26 |
| 5 | 30 | 150 | 22 |
| 6 | 28 | 168 | 18 |
| 7 | 26 | 182 | 14 |
| 8 | 24 | 192 | 10 |
| 9 | 22 | 198 | 6 |
| 10 | 20 | 200 | 2 |
| 11 | 18 | 198 | −2 |
| 12 | 16 | 192 | −6 |
| 13 | 14 | 182 | −10 |
| 14 | 12 | 168 | −14 |
| 15 | 10 | 150 | −18 |
| 16 | 8 | 128 | −22 |
| 17 | 6 | 102 | −26 |
| 18 | 4 | 72 | −30 |
| 19 | 2 | 38 | −34 |
| 20 | 0 | 0 | −38 |

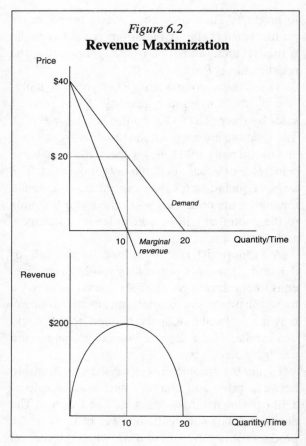

*Figure 6.2*
**Revenue Maximization**

(= 3 × $34). At point B in Figure 6.1, the firm sets a price of $10 and sells fifteen units. The revenue the firm receives at this price is $150 (= 15 × $10). Clearly, the firm makes a greater amount of revenue at point B. An obvious question at this point is: what price and quantity combination yields the greatest revenue for the firm?

Table 6.3 offers the answer by exhibiting the potential revenue for every quantity and price combination along the demand function. When the firm sets a price of $20 and sells ten units, it makes the maximum revenue possible at $200. Table 6.3 also displays *marginal revenue* (MR). Marginal revenue is the additional revenue the firm receives by lowering

*Exercise 6.2*

Consider a monopolist with a consumer demand function $Q = 100 − 5P$. Use Microsoft Excel (or another spreadsheet software package) and create a table that shows price (P), revenue (R), and marginal revenue (MR) for every possible quantity sold from 0 to 100. What combination of price and quantity maximizes revenue? Construct a graph of the demand function and marginal revenue. Show the revenue-maximizing price and quantity on the graph. Also construct a graph of the revenue curve.

its price and selling one additional unit. When the firm lowers its price from $40 to $38, it goes from selling zero units to one unit. Revenue increases from $0 to $38, and marginal revenue is $38. A further decrease in price to $36 allows the firm to sell two units. Revenue increases to $72, and marginal revenue is $34. As the firm lowers its price to $20, revenue continues to increase at a decreasing rate.

At a price of $20, the firm sells ten units and receives $200 in revenue. Marginal revenue is only $2 when price is reduced from $22 to $20. If the price is lowered below $20, marginal revenue is negative and revenue declines. At this point, the gain in quantity demanded is not enough to make up for the drop in price. For revenue maximization, the firm lowers its price, which increases quantity demanded, as long as marginal revenue is positive. Once marginal revenue becomes negative the firm stops lowering its price because the firm's total revenue starts to decline. The firm maximizes revenue when marginal revenue is zero. The firm's revenue-maximizing price ($20) and quantity (ten) are graphically displayed in Figure 6.2.

The firm's objective is to maximize profit, however, not revenue. There are cases where firms have zero costs and just maximize revenue. However, firms usually do have costs and maximize profit where the profit is simply $R - C$. To select a price and production quantity to maximize profit, a firm weighs both its demand function and its cost function.

A firm's cost of production is comprised of fixed and variable costs. As described in the previous chapter, fixed costs are those costs that the firm must pay in the short run even if production were to cease. Typically, fixed costs include facility costs, utilities, and equipment costs. Variable costs are those costs that depend directly on the production of each unit of the product, such as materials and labor.

*Table 6.4*
### A Cost Function

$$C = 26 + 12Q$$

$C$ represents the firm's total cost and $Q$ is the number of units produced.

Consider the previous example using the demand function in Table 6.2. The firm's costs of production are shown in Table 6.4. The firm's fixed costs are $26, and its variable costs are $12 per unit.

The analysis of profit in Table 6.5 includes a column for total cost ($C$), marginal cost ($MC$), profit, and marginal profit. The firm attains a maximum profit of $72 when it sets a price of $26 and sells seven units of its product. Notice that the situation here is analogous to the maximization of revenue example. As the firm lowers its price from $40, marginal profits are positive until the price drops to $26. The monopolist maximizes profit when marginal profit is zero.

Another interesting result is important to note here. The firm has a constant marginal cost of $12. That is, the firm's additional cost as each unit is produced is $12. As the firm lowers its price from $40 to generate demand and additional revenue, marginal revenue is greater than the $12 marginal cost. For example, dropping the price from $28 to $26 and moving from six to seven units yields an additional $14 of revenue. Because the cost associated with producing the seventh unit is $12, the firm makes an additional $2 in profit. Note that the marginal profit is $2 for the seventh unit. However, producing and selling the eighth unit offers only $10 of marginal revenue. This is $2 less than the marginal cost of $12. The monopolist maximizes profit when marginal revenue is equal to marginal cost ($MR = MC$). The firm's profit-maximizing price ($26) and quantity (seven) are graphically displayed in Figure 6.3.

### Exercise 6.3

Consider again the monopolist from Exercise 6.2 with a consumer demand function $Q = 100 - 5P$. The monopolist has a cost function $C = 31.2 + 4Q$. Use Microsoft Excel (or another spreadsheet software package) and complete the table created in Exercise 6.2. Specifically, add columns for total cost ($C$), marginal cost ($MC$), profit, and marginal profit. What combination of price and quantity maximizes profit? Construct a graph of the demand function, marginal revenue, and marginal cost. Show the profit-maximizing price and quantity on the graph. Also construct a graph of the revenue and profit curves.

Table 6.5
**Profit Analysis**

| Q | P | R | MR | C | MC | Profit | Marginal Profit |
|---|---|---|----|---|----|--------|-----------------|
| 0 | $40 | $0 | | $26 | | −$26 | |
| 1 | 38 | 38 | $38 | 38 | $12 | 0 | $26 |
| 2 | 36 | 72 | 34 | 50 | 12 | 22 | 22 |
| 3 | 34 | 102 | 30 | 62 | 12 | 40 | 18 |
| 4 | 32 | 128 | 26 | 74 | 12 | 54 | 14 |
| 5 | 30 | 150 | 22 | 86 | 12 | 64 | 10 |
| 6 | 28 | 168 | 18 | 98 | 12 | 70 | 6 |
| 7 | 26 | 182 | 14 | 110 | 12 | 72 | 2 |
| 8 | 24 | 192 | 10 | 122 | 12 | 70 | −2 |
| 9 | 22 | 198 | 6 | 134 | 12 | 64 | −6 |
| 10 | 20 | 200 | 2 | 146 | 12 | 54 | −10 |
| 11 | 18 | 198 | −2 | 158 | 12 | 40 | −14 |
| 12 | 16 | 192 | −6 | 170 | 12 | 22 | −18 |
| 13 | 14 | 182 | −10 | 182 | 12 | 0 | −22 |
| 14 | 12 | 168 | −14 | 194 | 12 | −26 | −26 |
| 15 | 10 | 150 | −18 | 206 | 12 | −56 | −30 |
| 16 | 8 | 128 | −22 | 218 | 12 | −90 | −34 |
| 17 | 6 | 102 | −26 | 230 | 12 | −128 | −38 |
| 18 | 4 | 72 | −30 | 242 | 12 | −170 | −42 |
| 19 | 2 | 38 | −34 | 254 | 12 | −216 | −46 |
| 20 | 0 | 0 | −38 | 266 | 12 | −266 | −50 |

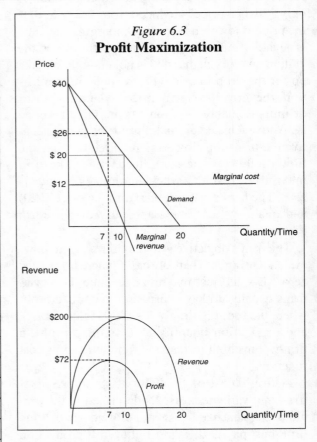

Figure 6.3
**Profit Maximization**

### Revenue-Sharing Contracts Versus Profit-Sharing Contracts

Managers must understand their objective. When firms enter into revenue or profit-sharing contracts, their profit objective depends on the contract. The *monopoly pricing model* described above helps managers determine how their decisions are affected by different contracts.

Consider a firm that enters into a joint selling relationship with another firm. One firm is responsible for all of the costs associated with the production of the product, and the other firm either provides information essential to the sale of the product or owns a retail outlet where the product is sold. Examples include an independently owned McDonald's franchise and the McDonald's Corporation, and the authors of a textbook and their publisher. How do the firms determine how much money each firm receives? Do they split profit or do they share revenue? Their decision has significant implications that are analyzed using the monopoly pricing model.

In economics circles, the problem is often described as the *author-publisher problem,* so that particular problem is used to illustrate the differences between profit-sharing and revenue-sharing contracts. Consider that a textbook is a monopoly product and that the publisher is responsible for all of the costs of printing and producing the book. Certainly, the authors have high opportunity costs of writing the textbook—lost time with family, lost opportunity to work on other projects, and so on. However, the value of their opportunity cost is ignored for this example.

Assume the demand function for the textbook displayed in Table 6.6. The publisher is responsible for setting the price of the book, and the publisher pays all of the costs to produce the book. The publisher's cost function is depicted in Table 6.7. Using this example, the differences between a profit-sharing contract and a revenue-sharing contract are examined.

For simplicity, assume that the publisher and the authors agree to a 50-50 revenue-sharing contract. The publisher gives half of the revenue from the

*Table 6.6*
### Demand Function for a Textbook

$$Q = 1,000 - 20P$$

$Q$ is the number of books demanded by consumers and consequently produced by the publisher, and $P$ is the price of the book.

*Table 6.7*
### Cost Function for a Textbook

$$C = 1,500 + 5Q$$

The publisher has a fixed setup charge of $1,500, and the publisher pays $5 in other costs per book produced.

sales of the book to the authors and pays all of the costs of production. When the publisher determines the price to set, the publisher's objective is not to maximize total profit. The publisher's objective is to maximize the profit it actually receives (= ½ $R - C$).

Under a 50-50 revenue-sharing contract, the publisher sets a price of $30 and sells 400 books. (The analysis is left for the reader to do in discussion question 2 at the end of the chapter.) The publisher receives $6,000 in revenue, pays $3,500 in costs, and nets $2,500 in profit. The authors receive the other half of the revenue, $6,000. Note that the total profit between both parties of the 50-50 revenue contract is $8,500.

One of the primary problems with a revenue-sharing contract is that the parties involved will not agree on the price that is to be set. The authors do not pay any of the costs of producing the book and have a different objective than the publisher. The authors' objective is to maximize their half of the revenue (= ½ $R$). Although it is the publisher's responsibility to set the price of the book, the authors offer their opinion. Because the authors do not have the costs to contend with, they would like to see

## Application Box 6.4

A rift between Miami-based Burger King Corporation and its national franchisee association became public in October 2005. The national association of independently owned Burger King franchises resisted efforts by the Burger King Corporation to offer a "value menu" and other competitive price initiatives. Because the franchisees paid the costs of production and shared a percentage of sales revenue with the Burger King Corporation, the franchisees wanted to set prices higher than what the Burger King Corporation preferred.

*Source:* "Burger King Breaks with Franchisee Group," Associated Press, October 20, 2005.

## Application Box 6.5

Hollywood movie studios have a history of using creative accounting to reduce their payments to partners in profit-sharing agreements. The Paramount Studios film *Coming to America* collected more than $350 million in revenue, and columnist Art Buchwald, who wrote the story the film was based on, expected to receive a share of the film's profit. Paramount then reported that the film not only had not made a profit but had incurred an $18 million loss! Buchwald took Paramount to court, and the judge in the case sided with Buchwald, calling Paramount's accounting practices "unconscionable." Paramount padded the costs of the film to make the film appear to be unprofitable. In the aftermath of this case, authors and actors negotiate for a share of a film's revenue or a predetermined and verifiable definition of a film's profit.

*Source:* Ross Engel and Bruce Ikawa, "Where's the Profit?" *Management Accounting,* January 1997.

a price of $25 set for the book to have 500 sold. (Again, the analysis is left for the reader.) Under this scenario, the authors receive $6,250. This is more than they receive when the publisher sets the price. The publisher receives $2,250. Note that the total profit for both parties is again $8,500.

The second problem with a revenue-sharing contract is exposed when a profit-sharing contract is considered. If the parties agree to share profits, their objectives are aligned such that they both want to set the same price for the book. They both want to maximize total profit and take their share. To maximize total profits, the publisher sets a price of $27.50 and sells 450 books. The author and publisher split a profit of $8,625. Note that this profit is greater than the total profit generated in the revenue-sharing contract. In fact, if the author and publisher share the profits 70 percent to the author and 30 percent to the publisher, they both earn more than in the revenue-sharing contract where the publisher sets the price. The profit-sharing contract dominates the revenue-sharing contract for both parties.

If profit-sharing contracts generate more money for both parties and align incentives so that both parties want the same price, why do revenue-sharing contracts even exist? The answer is that revenue-sharing contracts are easy to enforce and administer. It is much easier for firms to multiply the number of sales by the price than to have to deal with verifying and calculating costs. Many firms spread costs over numerous products. Determining the most appropriate allocation of those costs to each product is difficult. Unscrupulous firms pad costs in a profit-sharing agreement to make their income statements appear as though profits are lower than they actually are. Unless costs are verifiable in court, the other party has a hard time proving that profits on their product were higher. Because of this problem, revenue-sharing contracts tend to prevail in these types of arrangements even though profit-sharing arrangements are better economically.

## Demand Estimation

The demand functions described to this point in the chapter represent consumers' responses to changes in price at one snapshot in time. The world in which we live is constantly changing, and firms react to changes in the economic environment. As described in Chapter 4, the demand function does not merely depend on price. Demand also depends on numerous other variables that represent change in the firm's business climate.

Consider the demand function in Table 6.8 for product X. The income variable has a positive relationship with product X. That is, as the average income level increases in the firm's economic environment, more of product X is demanded. The coefficient for the variable $Y$, 0.0005, indicates the specific effect. As the average level of income increases by \$10,000, demand increases by five units.

*Table 6.8*
**Demand Function with Many Variables**

$$Q_x = 2 + 0.0005Y + 0.1P_s - 0.5P_x$$

$Q_x$ is the quantity demanded of product X,
$Y$ is the average income level of consumers,
$P_s$ is the price of a substitute good, and
$P_x$ is the price of product X.

The price of substitute goods also has a positive relationship with product X. As the price of the substitute good increases, consumers substitute product X for the other good. For every \$10 that the price of the substitute increases, the demand for product X increases by one unit.

Assume that during the current production period, the business climate is such that the average income level is \$35,000 and the price of the substitute good is \$15. By substituting these values for the variables in the Table 6.8 equation, the equation reduces to what is shown in Table 6.9. This is the same demand function found in Table 6.2 and displayed in Figure 6.1. The intercept, 20, in the reduced demand function includes within it an income level of \$35,000 and a substitute good's price of \$15. At this moment in time, the monopolist maximizes profit by selecting a price on the assumption that the economic environment remains unchanged. As the monopolist makes a change the price of product X, the resulting change in the quantity demanded is simply a movement along the demand curve.

*Table 6.9*
**Reduced Demand Function when
$Y$ Is \$35,000 and $P_s$ Is \$15**

$$Q_x = 2 + (0.0005 \times 35,000) + (0.1 \times 15) - 0.5P_x$$
$$= 20 - 0.5P_x$$

If the income level or the price of the substitute good changes, the result will be a shift in the demand function. Once the demand curve shifts, the monopolist would then have to go back and determine the price that maximizes profit under these new conditions. Consider that the price of the substitute good rises to \$25. The new demand function is displayed in Table 6.10.

*Table 6.10*
**Reduced Demand Function when
$Y$ Is \$35,000 and $P_s$ Is \$25**

$$Q_x = 2 + (0.0005 \times 35,000) + (0.1 \times 25) - 0.5P_x$$
$$= 22 - 0.5P_x$$

With the increase in demand, the monopolist will now receive more quantity demanded at every price. To maximize profit, the monopolist can now raise its price to $28, sell eight units, and make a profit of $102. With the increase in demand, the monopolist sets a higher price, sells more units, and makes an additional $30 in profit.

---

### Exercise 6.4

Consider a monopolist with a consumer demand function $Q_x = 2 + 0.001Y + 0.4P_s - 0.5P_x$, where $Q_x$ is the quantity demanded of product X, $Y$ is the average income level of consumers, $P_s$ is the price of a substitute good, and $P_x$ is the price of product X. The monopolist has a cost function $C = 31.2 + 4Q$. Currently the average income is $40,000 and the price of the substitute good is $25. Use Microsoft Excel (or another spreadsheet software package) to find the monopolist's profit-maximizing price and quantity. What should the monopolist do if the average level of income increases to $50,000? What if the average level of income is $40,000 and the price of the substitute good drops to $5?

---

It has been assumed to this point in the chapter that the monopolist knows its demand function and the exact algebraic relationship between quantity demanded and other economic variables. In the real world, the manager responsible for pricing is not handed an algebraic demand equation from the CEO. The manager estimates the demand relationship using gut instinct, past experience, consumer surveys, and/or data analysis. A manager who wishes to determine the profit-maximizing price and quantity to sell will still have to generate an expected algebraic relationship between quantity demanded and price using some method of estimation.

*Table 6.11*
### Data for Demand Estimation

| Region | Quantity | Price | Average Income | Price of Substitute Good |
|--------|----------|-------|----------------|--------------------------|
| 1 | 1,152 | $45 | $35,000 | $25 |
| 2 | 1,148 | $53 | $45,000 | $37 |
| 3 | 1,185 | $28 | $30,000 | $35 |
| 4 | 849 | $72 | $28,000 | $60 |
| 5 | 1,188 | $51 | $55,000 | $26 |
| 6 | 1,316 | $17 | $29,500 | $45 |
| 7 | 906 | $82 | $45,500 | $28 |
| 8 | 943 | $68 | $34,000 | $57 |
| 9 | 1,536 | $35 | $37,500 | $56 |
| 10 | 960 | $58 | $40,000 | $35 |
| 11 | 752 | $78 | $38,800 | $28 |
| 12 | 1,405 | $26 | $24,000 | $35 |
| 13 | 1,142 | $37 | $35,000 | $28 |
| 14 | 1,221 | $63 | $46,000 | $45 |
| 15 | 1,208 | $34 | $27,000 | $24 |
| 16 | 893 | $67 | $46,800 | $15 |

If the manager is fortunate to have data from consumer surveys or from previous sales of the product, regression analysis is used to estimate the demand equation. Regression analysis was explained in the appendix to Chapter 1. Table 6.11 shows historical sales data for a product offered in different regions of the country. The table also indicates each region's average income and the price of a substitute good. Assume that the firm charges different prices in each of these sixteen regions.

A regression equation is generated using Microsoft Excel and displayed in Table 6.12. (See the appendix to Chapter 1 for a specific explanation of how these coefficients are generated in Excel.) The regression analysis produces an estimate of the demand for this product.

If the manager wants to sell in a new region

### Table 6.12
### Demand Function Generated Using Regression Analysis

$$Q = 1129.39 + 0.01Y + 4.93P_s - 10.96P$$

$Q$ is the quantity demanded of the good,
$Y$ is the average income level of consumers,
$P_s$ is the price of a substitute good, and
$P$ is the price of the good.

where the income level is $45,000 and the price of the substitute good is $25, the demand function in Table 6.12 is used to determine the profit-maximizing price and quantity. The manager uses the economic data from the new region to reduce the estimated demand function.

### Table 6.13
### Reduced Demand Function when $Y$ Is $45,000 and $P_s$ Is $25

$$Q = 1129.39 + (0.01 \times \$45,000) +$$
$$(4.93 \times \$25) - 10.96P$$
$$= 1702.64 - 10.96P$$

Assume the firm has $2,000 in fixed costs and pays $5 for each unit of production. Using the estimated demand equation, the manager maximizes profits by setting a price of approximately $80 and selling 826 units. (The analysis is left to the reader.)

## The Natural Monopoly and Government Regulation

Suppose the monopolist described earlier in the chapter obtained its monopoly position by developing a network infrastructure that was too costly for another firm to duplicate. Gas, electric, telephone, cable television, and other public utilities are good examples. Once a monopoly network is established, it is virtually impossible for another firm to enter the incumbent's territory. The high fixed start-up costs would be difficult to pay off under competitive market pricing. The economies of scale in these industries are so high that they become a one-firm industry on their own or naturally. Such firms are described as natural monopolies.

Monopolies are scrutinized by the government for numerous reasons. They typically charge prices that are higher than many consumers willingly pay. Monopolies also operate inefficiently. Chapter 5 explains that firms operate efficiently when they produce the number of goods that yields their lowest possible average total cost. If all firms in society operate efficiently, then society's resources are allocated in the best possible way. Allowing a monopoly to persist undermines that possibility. The government allows some monopolies to occur for a limited time with the patent system. These firms are rewarded for a creating a new innovation and undertaking years of costly research and development.

The government regulates natural monopolies and forces these firms to charge a price that is fair both to the firm and to consumers. Using the monopoly from earlier in the chapter, the method the government uses for price regulation is easily explained. The monopolist described in Figure 6.1 had the demand function $Q = 20 - 0.5P$ and the cost function $C = 26 + 12Q$. Average cost is defined as the cost of production at any unit divided by the number of units produced. The average cost function is displayed in Table 6.14.

### Table 6.14
### An Average Cost Function

$$AC = (26 \div Q) + 12$$

Table 6.15
**Natural Monopoly**

| Q | P | R | MR | C | MC | Profit | AC |
|---|---|---|---|---|---|---|---|
| 0 | $40 | $0 | | $26 | | −$26 | |
| 1 | 38 | 38 | $38 | 38 | $12 | 0 | |
| 2 | 36 | 72 | 34 | 50 | 12 | 22 | 25.00 |
| 3 | 34 | 102 | 30 | 62 | 12 | 40 | 20.67 |
| 4 | 32 | 128 | 26 | 74 | 12 | 54 | 18.50 |
| 5 | 30 | 150 | 22 | 86 | 12 | 64 | 17.20 |
| 6 | 28 | 168 | 18 | 98 | 12 | 70 | 16.33 |
| 7 | 26 | 182 | 14 | 110 | 12 | 72 | 15.71 |
| 8 | 24 | 192 | 10 | 122 | 12 | 70 | 15.25 |
| 9 | 22 | 198 | 6 | 134 | 12 | 64 | 14.89 |
| 10 | 20 | 200 | 2 | 146 | 12 | 54 | 14.60 |
| 11 | 18 | 198 | −2 | 158 | 12 | 40 | 14.36 |
| 12 | 16 | 192 | −6 | 170 | 12 | 22 | 14.17 |
| 13 | 14 | 182 | −10 | 182 | 12 | 0 | 14.00 |
| 14 | 12 | 168 | −14 | 194 | 12 | −26 | 13.86 |
| 15 | 10 | 150 | −18 | 206 | 12 | −56 | 13.73 |
| 16 | 8 | 128 | −22 | 218 | 12 | −90 | 13.63 |
| 17 | 6 | 102 | −26 | 230 | 12 | −128 | 13.53 |
| 18 | 4 | 72 | −30 | 242 | 12 | −170 | 13.44 |
| 19 | 2 | 38 | −34 | 254 | 12 | −216 | 13.37 |
| 20 | 0 | 0 | −38 | 266 | 12 | −266 | 13.30 |

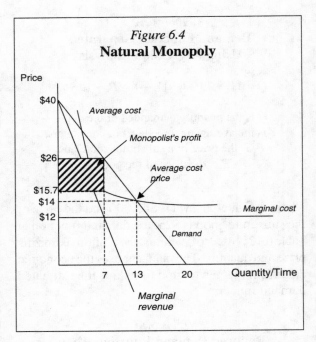

Figure 6.4
**Natural Monopoly**

Table 6.15 displays the data for these functions and includes a column for the average cost of production (*AC*). When this monopoly operates unregulated, it sets a price of $26 and sells seven units of the good. The firm generates revenue of $182 (= $26 × 7), and the monopolist's average cost at seven units of production is $15.71. Note that the firm's total cost is about $110 (= $15.71 × 7). The difference between the price the monopolist sets ($26) and the av-

erage cost ($15.71) is $10.29. The monopolist makes a profit of about $72 (= $10.29 × 7). The monopolist's profit is shown as the shaded region in Figure 6.4.

When the government regulates the monopoly, it forces the monopolist to charge its *average cost price*. The firm charges a price so that the resulting quantity produced yields an average cost equal to the price. When price equals average cost, the firm makes a profit of zero. The *average cost price* of the monopolist displayed in Table 6.15 is $14. At this price, the firm sells thirteen units and has an average cost of $14. Profits are zero for the firm. Certainly this is a better outcome for consumers, as the price is considerably lower and more consumers can afford to purchase the good.

However, is a zero profit fair for the monopolist? Remember that in Chapter 5 economic costs were defined to include opportunity costs. The profits described here are economic profits, not

## Application Box 6.6

On January 1, 1998, regional competitive markets for electricity generation services were put in place in a few states across the United States. Electricity consumers in these markets could select the company that would generate their electricity. The electricity provider physically connected to the consumer would be required to transmit the other company's electricity over its lines. Although the government had always regulated electricity company monopolies with average cost pricing, consumer groups argued that many of the fixed costs included in the average cost price had been paid off years before, and thus electric companies were making a profit greater than their fair return, even under average cost pricing. Forcing competition in the market by allowing consumers to choose the company that generates their electricity would drive the price down to a marginal cost price. The Electricity Forum, Inc., reports that prices have dropped 6–13 percent below the average cost price in regions offering electricity choice since 1998.

*Source:* The Electricity Forum, Inc. www.electricityforum.com.

accounting profits. Average cost pricing forces a firm to make zero economic profits. The opportunity cost for the monopolist is the return it would receive in another line of business. At zero economic profit, the firm is permitted to make a fair accounting profit. Natural monopolies are regulated by the government to provide a reasonable compromise between the firm's desires and consumers' wishes.

### *Exercise 6.5*

Consider again the monopolist from Exercise 6.3 with a consumer demand function $Q = 100 - 5P$. The monopolist has a cost function $C = 31.2 + 4Q$. Use Microsoft Excel (or another spreadsheet software package) and add to the table created in Exercise 6.3. Specifically, add a column for average total cost ($AC$) and determine the price the monopolist would be required to charge if it was regulated by the government.

## Oligopoly

In an oligopoly there are a few firms selling a similar product or service. These industries are typically characterized by high fixed costs and low marginal costs of production. It is difficult but not impossible for new firms to enter the market. Because of the small number of firms in this market structure, the economic analysis of an oligopoly centers on the strategic interaction between firms. Typically firms in an oligopoly produce similar products and intense competition exists between all the firms in the oligopoly. Any action that one firm makes is closely observed by the other firms. Consequently, firms regularly retaliate against other firms' actions by cutting prices or introducing product enhancements to increase market share. The actions of firms in an oligopoly are interdependent. Each firm is affected by the actions of other firms, and each firm's market power is dependent on the success or failure of every other firm.

Imagine that the monopoly in the previous section becomes a two-firm oligopoly (a duopoly). If the two firms agree to set a price of $26 for their product, they split the $72 profit evenly. We assume that each produces and sells 3.5 units (it is a divisible product). Each makes $91 (= 3.5 × $26) in revenue; they split the fixed cost of $26 evenly;

**Application Box 6.7.
The Airline Oligopoly, Part 1**

In the fall of 1997, Northwest made an across-the-board 5 percent fare increase on a Friday afternoon and then sat back and waited. Although price collusion is illegal in the United States, airlines typically set price increases to see if their rivals will follow. These signals are often sent on a Friday afternoon. Even with the Internet, the majority of travel reservations are still made during the workweek. Northwest figured that its signal could be rescinded on Monday morning without too much damage done if no other carrier raised its price. By Sunday afternoon, every major airline, except for Southwest, matched the fare increases. The process was meant to be kept quiet, as the airlines had signed an agreement with the Justice Department in 1992 to agree not to signal price changes via computer reservation databases. United Airlines, however, decided late Sunday evening to undo the increase on routes where it competed directly with Southwest. This request was misinterpreted, and the prices on all of United's routes were lowered back to their original levels. The result was chaos as US Airways, Delta, American, and Continental scrambled to decide what to do. Eventually, United corrected the mistake and the price "agreement" lasted for a short time.

*Source:* Susan Carey, "All in a Day's Flying," *Wall Street Journal,* September 9, 1997.

and each pays its own cost of production of $42 (= 3.5 × $12). Each firm receives $36 (= $91 − $13 − $42) in profit.

As shown in the last section, the $72 in total profit is the most the two firms make as a group.

However, each firm has an incentive to try to make more than its $36. Consider that one of the firms charges a price of $20. At $20 (see Table 6.15), consumers demand ten units of the good. Suppose the other firm sells its product for $26. Out of the ten units sold, suppose that two units are still being sold at $26. Perhaps these customers did not get the message that the other firm is selling them for $20, or, as is more likely the case, suppose the cheaper firm has an eight-unit production capacity. The $20 firm receives $51 in profits: $160 in revenue (= 8 × $20), $13 in fixed costs, and $96 in variable costs (= 8 × $12). The $26 firm will receive $15: $52 in revenue (= 2 × $26), $13 in fixed costs, and $24 in variable costs (= 2 × $12). The $51 in profit is a big incentive for the firm to lower its price. Although the price-cutter is better off, note that the total profit earned by both firms is now lower: $66 (= $51 + $15).

What is good for one firm, though, is not good for both. If both reduce their price to $20, they split a $54 profit (see Table 6.15). Each makes only $27. This is considerably less than the profit they shared at an agreed price of $26. What is troubling about this scenario is that each has a strong incentive to individually cut its price when the product is selling at $26. Unless some outside collusive agreement can be reached, these firms are expected to follow their personal incentive and charge $20. Unfortunately, this leads them to a suboptimal outcome, where each receives $27.

The price-cutting scenario is an example of an economic game. The outcome of the game depends on each firm's decision to set a price of $20 or $26. Each firm considers what the other player is likely to do before making a choice. This strategic interaction between the two firms is analyzed by economists using *game theory*.

The emergence of oligopoly markets in the early twentieth century motivated economists to begin studying how firms interrelate. Two notable econo-

## Application Box 6.8
## The Airline Oligopoly, Part 2

Since the September 11, 2001, terrorist attacks, the airline industry has undergone significant changes in the way in which rivals compete. Typically, firms in an oligopoly compete on price or on product characteristics. Before September 11, the airlines tried to keep customers loyal and distinguish themselves with frequent-flier rewards, private airport lounges, and other perks. The September 11 terrorist attacks coincided with a global macroeconomic slowdown and caused a major reduction in the demand for airline travel. As competition for travelers intensified, the airlines began cutting fares and eliminating the Saturday-night stay-over requirement for cheaper fares. Low-cost, smaller airlines began successfully competing with the major airlines on a few regional routes. These smaller airlines used to be short-lived, as they would be shut down with fierce price competition

from the major airlines; the big airline would take a short-term loss to put the new entrant out of business. However, short-term losses were not acceptable during these difficult economic times, and the low-cost airlines began to prevail. Low prices and efficiency are now the keys to success in today's market. Southwest Airlines only requires a flight to be 60 percent full to break even, while the major carriers require a flight to be 90 percent full. Travelers care only about price, and they can easily fare-shop with online reservation services such as Expedia.com. The airlines responded with limited perks, a less distinguished product, and increased price competition.

*Source:* Rose Rubin and Justin Joy, "Where are the Airlines Headed? Implications of Airline Industry Structure and Change for Consumers," *Journal of Consumer Affairs,* Summer 2005, pp. 215–29.

mists, John Von Neumann and Oskar Morgenstern, published *The Theory of Games and Economic Behavior,* in 1947. While a number of mathematicians had previously studied the way firms relate in oligopoly markets, Von Neumann and Morgenstern were the first to present a rigorous methodology for examining economic games. They showed that the *minimax* technique is used in a certain class of games to identify an equilibrium outcome.

The minimax technique suggests that a firm examines its choices and selects the "best of the worst" of the possibilities. Consider the game matrix displayed in Table 6.16. The matrix displays each firm's possible choices: set a price of $26 or $20. Each of the cells in the matrix shows the payoff both firms will receive in each of the four possibilities. In each cell firm A's payoff appears first, and firm B's payoff is second. If firm A se-

lects a price of $26, the worst payoff it receives is $15. If firm A selects a price of $20, the worst payoff it can receive is $27. Because the better of the two worst outcomes is $27, firm A's minimax selection is $20. The game is symmetric, so firm B's minimax selection is also $20. The minimax technique identifies the equilibrium outcome of

*Table 6.16*
**Price-Cutting Game**

|  |  | Firm B | |
|---|---|---|---|
|  |  | Set $26 Price | Set $20 Price |
| Firm A | Set $26 Price | 36, 36 | 15, 51 |
|  | Set $20 Price | 51, 15 | 27, 27 |

this game to be where both firms undercut each other and set a price of $20.

The price-cutting game in Table 6.16 is classified as a *prisoner's dilemma*. Players have an opportunity to cooperate with each other to achieve their best combined payoff. However, their own personal incentive leads the players to select a choice that turns out to be the lowest combined payoff. Games and puzzles with this structure were first examined by Merrill Flood and Melvin Dresher in 1950 as a part of the Rand Corporation's study of game theory to advise the government on global nuclear strategy. Albert Tucker then invented the prisoner's dilemma story to help explain the puzzle to a group of Stanford psychologists.[1]

Tucker described two partners in a crime who are brought into a police station for questioning. The suspects are placed in separate interrogation rooms. The suspects have the opportunity to cooperate with each other and not talk to the police. If they both do not confess, they are charged with a lesser crime and each suspect receives one year in prison. The payoffs are in Table 6.17. If both confess to the police, each receives five years in prison.

It appears that the prisoner's choice at this point is obvious. Not confessing yields the least amount of jail time for both suspects. However, if one of the suspects confesses while the other one does not confess, the confessor receives a deal from the police and does not receive any jail time. The other suspect is punished for not confessing and receives ten years in prison.

One of the primary lessons of game theory is to consider the choices of a rival player and to consider a best response to each of the rival player's choices. In the prisoner's dilemma game, consider suspect A's best response to each of suspect B's choices. If suspect B does not confess, suspect A should confess. When suspect B does not confess, suspect A receives no jail time by confessing and

one year of jail time by not confessing. No jail time is better than one year of jail time, so suspect A's best response when suspect B does not confess is to confess. When suspect B confesses, suspect A's best response is also to confess, as five years of jail time is better than ten.

When a player in a game has the same best response to every choice of the other player, the best response is called a *dominant strategy*. In the prisoner's dilemma game, suspect A has a dominant strategy to confess, as confessing is a best response to either of suspect B's choices. Because the game is symmetric, suspect B also has a dominant strategy to confess. The outcome {confess, confess}, in which both players receive five years of jail time, is called a *dominant strategy equilibrium*, as both players have a dominant strategy to confess.

*Table 6.17*
**The Prisoner's Dilemma**

|              |             | Suspect B   |         |
|--------------|-------------|-------------|---------|
|              |             | Not Confess | Confess |
| Suspect A    | Not Confess | 1, 1        | 10, 0   |
|              | Confess     | 0, 10       | 5, 5    |

The game is known as the prisoner's dilemma because there is another outcome in which *both* players are better off. If both players go against their dominant strategy and do not confess, each receives only one year of jail time. Not confessing requires a great deal of trust in the other player, as the incentive to follow the dominant strategy is strong.

The prisoner's dilemma describes a class of games that have the following two characteristics: both players in the game have a dominant strategy, and there is an outcome of the game in which neither player chooses the dominant strategy and yet both players receive a better payoff than the one provided by the dominant strategy equilibrium. Typically, the players in a prisoner's dilemma have the opportunity to cooperate with each other to receive the best social outcome. However, the incentive to defect on the cooperative agreement is compelling, so the best outcome is difficult to obtain.

There are numerous examples of the prisoner's dilemma in everyday life. Consider the construction of a new church hall. Typically, a church solicits funds from the congregation to raise money for this type of project. If everyone in the church pays a fair share of the costs, then a beautiful new hall is built. However, the incentive for an individual to be a free rider is very strong. Because the hall is available for everyone in the church to use, an individual who does not pay can still enjoy the benefits of the new hall. However, if too many individuals shirk on their share, the hall is not built or a smaller, less functional hall is built.

As another example, when students work together on a team project for an MBA class, they can share the work to create a high-quality product. However, the incentive is strong for a member with high opportunity costs (work and family demands) to take a free ride off the rest of the group. If everyone on the team receives the same grade, the free riding of one team member may not be too damaging. So the free rider gets a decent grade with little or no work. However, if all of the team members follow this logic, the results could be disastrous.

Clearly, church halls get built and MBA teammates produce high-quality projects. How does cooperation happen in light of the prisoner's dilemma? If the payoffs in the prisoner's dilemma are left unchecked, the results are rather negative (see Application Box 6.9). However, church congregations and MBA students enforce cooperation through various means, effectively changing the payoffs of the game. The church publishes the names of donors and uses guilt tactics to ensure that church members pay their fair share. MBA students assign group members tasks with the indirect threat of disdain if a member does not complete his or her assignment. In both examples, future relationships come into play. In most cases, if a prisoner's dilemma game is a one-time game in which the participants never see each other again, the defect strategy is typically played and the result is suboptimal. However, cooperation does occur in practice when the parties realize that a future relationship is at stake. MBA students have other classes together or become business associates. Church members intend to be a part of their congregation for life. A defection could mean the end of a relationship, so players cooperate and go against their individual incentive in order to extend their association.

The prisoner's dilemma offers insight into the way in which firms in an oligopoly operate. Pricing and joint venture decisions within an oligopoly are classic examples of a prisoner's dilemma. While the government stifles attempts to overtly collude on price, firms understand the need to set higher prices to generate close-to-monopoly profits. While monopoly profits are typically unattainable because of the incentive to lower prices to improve market share position, firms in an oligopoly rarely lower prices to the level of their marginal costs. Through an unspoken partnership, these firms find a way to maintain profitability.

The coordination of research projects between firms in an oligopoly is also difficult. During the development of high-definition television, firms developed very specific standards so that the technologies each firm developed could function together. For example, when Mitsubishi developed high-definition broadcasting equipment, it had to be compatible with Sony's high-definition television receivers. Neither company wanted to

## Application Box 6.9

In the 1970s airplane manufacturers positioned themselves to develop a wide-body commercial aircraft. McDonnell Douglas, Lockheed, and Boeing were all at the time involved in the manufacture of commercial and military aircraft. While the market for a wide-body airplane was predicted to be extremely lucrative, it was also understood that it would take a 60 percent market share just to break even. The need for these three companies to jointly produce a wide-body airplane was apparent. Together these companies could share the development costs and split an enormous profit. Unfortunately, each company feared being deceived by the others and having a plane developed outside of the joint venture. Without any coordination mechanism initiated by the government, the prisoner's dilemma reared its ugly head and the three companies chose to develop their own planes individually. McDonnell Douglas and Lockheed both lost huge sums of money and would have gone out of business were it not for their government contracts. The government finally stepped in and subsidized Boeing's development of the now famous Boeing 747.

*Source:* Laura Tyson, *Who's Bashing Whom: Trade Conflict in High Technology Industries* (Washington, D.C.: Institute for International Economics, 1994).

This type of coordination game is described using a puzzle called the battle of the sexes. Consider two friends, Kirk and Sandra, who enjoy spending time with each other. Both have very busy lives and try to coordinate a date every Friday evening. For this particular Friday evening they discussed meeting at either the opera house or a basketball game. Both Kirk and Sandra were away on separate business trips during the week, and they were planning on meeting each other outside the building at either event. However, they both forget on Friday afternoon where they had finally decided to go. Kirk does not carry a cellular telephone, so they have no way of communicating before the event. Each has to pick an event and hope the other picks the same event.

The payoffs of the game appear in Table 6.18. Both Kirk and Sandra receive payoffs of zero if they do not coordinate and end up at different events. Kirk is a big fan of the opera, so he receives an extra payoff for being at the opera with Sandra. Similarly, Sandra is a big basketball fan, so she receives the extra payoff while at the basketball game with Kirk.

The puzzle here is that neither player has a dominant strategy. There is no predictable outcome of the game, as there is when a dominant strategy equilibrium exists. The minimax technique does not work on this game, as Von Neumann and Morgenstern's method applies only to games where at least all but one player has a dominant strategy. It is clear that both Kirk and Sandra prefer to be

give away its secrets too early in the development phase of high-definition television, but compatible equipment had to be developed. Each company developed what it hoped would be a standard, and then the companies negotiated and made adjustments after the fact to connect with the other company's product.

*Table 6.18*

### The Battle of the Sexes Game

|      |       | Sandra |      |
|------|-------|--------|------|
|      |       | Opera  | Game |
| Kirk | Opera | 3, 1   | 0, 0 |
|      | Game  | 0, 0   | 1, 3 |

**Application Box 6.10**

Suppose two individuals are offered a choice between options A and B, and each must select without observing the other's choice. If both select A, then each receives $1. If both select B, then each receives $100. If they do not coordinate, then each receives $0. It seems apparent that they would both select B and receive the $100. However, choosing B is not a dominant strategy. If one player selects A, the other player's best response would also be to choose A. Both {A, A} and {B, B} are Nash equilibriums. How could one ever get caught in an outcome such as {A, A}? Consider the keyboard that is being used to type this book. It is known as the QWERTY keyboard, and it was designed to actually slow typists down to keep the old-fashioned typewriter hammers from getting stuck. Since the advent of computers, more efficient keyboard layouts have been designed, but given what everyone else is using, it is a best response for the new typist to learn the QWERTY keyboard. Thus, the QWERTY keyboard is an {A, A} Nash equilibrium.

together, but at the time of Von Neumann and Morgenstern, a characterization of equilibrium outcomes in these types of games had not been invented yet.

Enter John Forbes Nash Jr., a student of Von Neumann at Princeton in the late 1940s. In his twenty-seven-page dissertation written in 1950, Nash invented an equilibrium concept that changed the face of game theory forever and won him the Nobel prize in 1994. Nash's concept was not dependent on players having a dominant strategy. Nash focused on the outcome and why players would remain in a particular outcome. A *Nash equilibrium,* as it is now known, is an outcome in which every player is choosing the best response to what every other player is doing. No player has an incentive to change his or her choice given what everyone else selected.

In the battle of the sexes game in Table 6.18, both {opera, opera} and {game, game} are Nash equilibriums. Given that Kirk and Sandra coordinate and make the same choice, neither has an incentive to change his or her choice. Nash was the first to characterize equilibriums in games that have multiple equilibriums.

The dominant strategy equilibrium in the prisoner's dilemma game, {confess, confess} (see Table 6.17), is also a Nash equilibrium. Neither player has an incentive to switch to not confessing when the other player confesses. A dominant strategy equilibrium is always a Nash equilibrium. However, a Nash equilibrium is not necessarily a dominant strategy equilibrium.

The Nash equilibrium enlightens the possible equilibriums in a coordination game such as the battle of the sexes, but it does not help with the determination of an expected outcome. In the Kirk and Sandra example, additional information is required. Perhaps Kirk is in the doghouse and knows that it is best for him to show up at the basketball game, where Sandra will be happiest. Sandra knows that she is deserving of attending her favorite event, so she goes to the basketball game as well. In the high-definition television example, the firm that moves first is most likely to set the standard. In some cases, the dominant firm in the market is the firm that gets the standard it wants. Using game theory and the Nash equilibrium concept helps a manager to ascertain various outcome possibilities in a business situation, but the manager may need to understand other influences to determine a specific expectation.

Oligopolies require firms to consider the strategic implications of their actions. Whether firms are dealing with colluding to set high prices to collect monopoly profits or must consider the research standards required for joint product development, they must understand the lessons of game theory.

---

### Exercise 6.6

(a) Consider a scenario in your business or personal life that shares the same characteristics of a prisoner's dilemma game. Explain why the cooperation outcome is so difficult to obtain. Create a model of the game using a game matrix and payoffs. The payoffs can be expressed in dollars or utility (level of satisfaction).

(b) Consider a scenario in your business or personal life that shares the same characteristics of a coordination (battle of the sexes) game. Create a model of the game using a game matrix and payoffs. The payoffs can be expressed in dollars or utility (level of satisfaction). Identify the Nash equilibriums in the game. Which outcome is/was expected to occur? Why?

---

## Monopolistic Competition

In monopolistic competition, there are many sellers trying to differentiate products from the rest of the competition. The term *monopolistic competition* refers to the competitive nature of the industry blended with the capability of firms to gain a foothold via a brief yet profitable monopoly. Sellers in this market structure easily enter and exit. When one firm develops a profitable venture, it is not long before it is copied by other firms.

A manager in a firm with a product in this type of market structure focuses on product differentiation. Not only must the firm be innovative, but it must communicate its brand, its uniqueness, and its message through effective advertising. Not only must a firm's product be distinctive from the competition, but consumers must believe that the product is unique. The firms are not simply selling fast food, shirts, and a university education. They are selling McDonald's hamburgers, Nike shirts, and a Mount Saint Mary's University education. Only with this monopoly power is the firm in this market structure able to obtain some control over the price it sets to maximize profit.

The manager who successfully creates a distinctive product and achieves a monopoly position faces a downward-sloping demand curve similar to the pure monopolist. Without product distinction, the firm accepts the price set by a competitive market and the firm's demand curve is flat. There are two important differences from the pure monopolist. (1) In monopolistic competition, there are close substitutes for the firm's product. The substitutes may not have the same distinctive characteristics, but there will be a limit to the price consumers pay for the firm's product. (2) The demand curve is not forever commanded by the firm. If the firm's product is profitable, copycat products are created by competitors. The firm is forced to share the demand curve. It is important for managers to maintain market share through brand advertising and continued innovation.

While the firm holds a monopoly position with its distinctive product, it maximizes profits as the pure monopolist does, by setting a price such that marginal revenue equals marginal cost ($MR = MC$). Figure 6.5 displays a graph of the demand curve with the firm's profit-maximizing price. Note that in this graph, unlike the pure monopolist, marginal costs are increasing significantly. This cost curve represents the many firms in competitive industries that become inefficient when operating on a large scale. This firm is also making a profit, as the profit-maximizing price is greater than average cost.

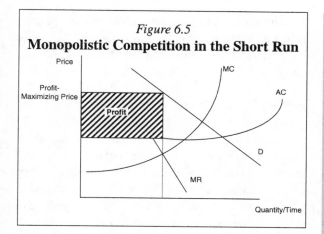

*Figure 6.5*

**Monopolistic Competition in the Short Run**

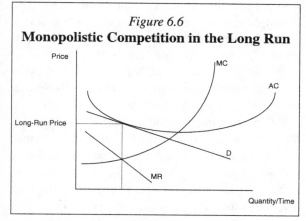

*Figure 6.6*

**Monopolistic Competition in the Long Run**

**Application Box 6.11**

While managers in monopolistic competitive markets should be focused on creating distinctive products, they should also be very aware of what their competition is producing. It is not uncommon for firms to copy the innovations of their competition. In his 1994 book *Managing Imitation Strategies,* Steven Schnaars describes twenty-eight cases in which imitators prevailed over the industry pioneers. He identifies three basic strategies that successful imitators used: (1) sell lower-priced, generic versions of the pioneer's product once it becomes popular, (2) sell an improved version of the pioneer's product, and (3) use capital, distribution, and marketing advantages and overpower the pioneer's market.

*Source:* Steven Schnaars, *Managing Imitation Strategies* (New York: Simon and Schuster, 1994).

Once competitors realize that the firm's distinctive product is profitable, they enter the market and erode the firm's profit. The firm's demand curve shifts to the left as competitors capture demand. The original firm has less control over price, so the demand curve will flatten out as well. Figure 6.6 depicts the eventual long-run outcome. The market will be attractive to competition until all of the profits are gone. In the long run, the firm sets a price equal to its average cost and makes a zero economic profit.

Monopolistic competition provides consumers with lower prices than what they would have with a pure monopoly, but as is shown in the next section, prices are higher in the long run than in a perfectly competitive market. Firms also are not forced to produce at their most efficient level, meaning that firms are operating with excess capacity. Note that in Figure 6.6, the firm in the long run does not produce at the minimum of the average total cost curve. From a cost perspective, society is better off allocating resources in a more efficient manner.

However, consumers are presented with a wide variety of product choices in monopolistic competition. The need for firms to make their products distinctive provides consumers with the opportunity to purchase a good that best meets their needs. A walk down the health and beauty aids aisle at the supermarket presents the consumer with shampoos for all types of hair: oily, dry, normal, heat-treated, permed, colored, curly, thick, and thinning.

Advertising is the vehicle firms use to educate

---

### Exercise 6.7

Describe a firm that produces in a monopolistic competition market.

(a) How does the firm distinguish its product?

(b) How do the firm's competitors distinguish their products?

(c) Describe the condition for entry into this market.

(d) Is the firm able to maintain monopoly power?

(e) Discuss the pricing strategies employed by the firms in the market.

(f) Describe the advertising strategies used by the firms.

---

consumers about their product options. Economists debate the value of advertising. On one hand, advertising is wasteful because it adds to the costs of production with no increase in the product's value. Successful advertising convinces consumers that there are no other alternatives, thereby increasing barriers to entry and reducing competition. Critics of consumerism point out that advertising creates perceived needs that are not truly necessary. On the other hand, advertising educates consumers and reduces their search time for particular products. Advertising lowers inventory carrying costs for firms by telling consumers where and when certain products are available for sale. The manager in a monopolistic competitive market determines whether the benefits of advertising outweigh the costs.

Managers in monopolistic competition protect their monopoly position for as long as possible. They do this by creating additional barriers to entry into their product's market. Managers patent their technologies, although it is not a foolproof strategy,

as competitors attempt to invent around the patent. Being a first mover can be vital, as the firm obtains buyer loyalty, maintains market share, and retains economic profit for a longer period.

### Perfect Competition

A manager operating in a perfectly competitive market has absolutely no control over the price the market sets on the product. There are many sellers in the market, and every seller offers an identical product. Because there are so many buyers and sellers in the market, no one buyer or seller has an influence on the price set by the combined forces of supply and demand. If a seller attempts to sell at a price higher than the market price, buyers simply go to other sellers for the same product.

Because firms in perfectly competitive markets are price-takers, their demand curve is a flat line at the market price of the product. The market price is also their marginal revenue. Suppose, for example, that the market price is $10. The firm is unable to sell any product at a price above $10, and it is foolish to sell lower than $10. The firm's demand curve is a flat line at $10. The firm's marginal revenue is the same as the demand line. For every product that the firm sells, it receives an additional $10 in revenue.

Figure 6.7 displays a perfectly competitive firm with increasing marginal costs. The firm sets its production output such that its marginal cost does not exceed marginal revenue. The manager of a perfectly competitive firm follows the $MR = MC$ rule to maximize profit. The example in Figure 6.7 shows a firm that is making an economic profit in the short run, as the market price is greater than average cost at the profit-maximizing output. A perfectly competitive firm does not make an economic profit in the long run, because it is easy for other firms to enter the market and take away the profit.

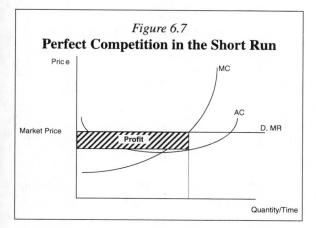

*Figure 6.7*
**Perfect Competition in the Short Run**

In the long run, additional firms enter this profitable market. The market supply curve shifts to the right with the increased number of sellers, and the market price of the product decreases. The price continues to drop until the perfectly competitive firm is no longer making a profit. Figure 6.8 shows the long-run outcome.

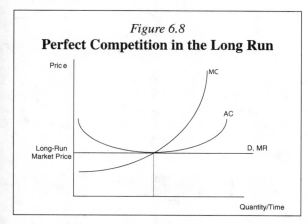

*Figure 6.8*
**Perfect Competition in the Long Run**

In the long run, the perfectly competitive firm produces where marginal revenue equals marginal cost and price equals average cost. The firm makes zero economic profit, but it does make an accounting profit. However, the firm does no better than its next best alternative in another market. Another notable result is that the firm is producing at the lowest point on its average cost curve. The firm has no excess capacity, and its resources are allocated efficiently. Perfect competition provides the best situation for society, as consumers pay the lowest possible price and firms do not waste resources in inefficient markets.

Managers of perfectly competitive firms focus on managing their businesses as cost-effectively as possible. Because competition is so intense in a perfectly competitive market, only firms that produce at the lowest possible cost survive. If more efficient firms outside the market see profit potential, they enter and drive inefficient firms out of business.

---

***Exercise 6.8***

Describe a product that is sold in a perfectly competitive market. Describe the conditions in this market with respect to distinctiveness of competitors' products, number of competitors, control over price, conditions of entry, and level of advertising.

---

**Summary**

This chapter described the microeconomic environments in which firms operate. The process by which managers make decisions—including how to determine price, calculate production needs, and implement a marketing plan—depends heavily on the microeconomic structure of the industry. Each of the four market structures—monopoly, oligopoly, monopolistic competition, and perfect competition—were described to help managers understand how dependent they are on these economic environments. To maximize profit, increase market share, and effectively compete, managers must understand their firm's strategic position in its industry.

## Review Terms

| | |
|---|---|
| Average cost pricing | Monopolistic competition |
| Best response | Monopoly |
| Coordination game | Nash equilibrium |
| Cost-efficient | Natural monopoly |
| Dominant strategy | Oligopoly |
| Game theory | Perfect competition |
| Marginal cost | Prisoner's dilemma |
| Marginal profit | Product differentiation |
| Marginal revenue | Revenue and profit sharing |
| Minimax technique | |

## Discussion Questions

1. A spreadsheet software package such as Microsoft Excel can be used to quickly determine a monopolist's profit-maximizing price and quantity. Figure 6.9 shows an Excel spreadsheet using the demand function in Table 6.2 and the cost function in Table 6.4. The spreadsheet calculates the quantity demanded, revenue, cost, and profit for any price that is entered into cell B2. A price of $34 is entered into cell B2 as an example. The functions used in each of the cells are displayed in Table 6.19.

*Figure 6.9*
**Excel Spreadsheet**

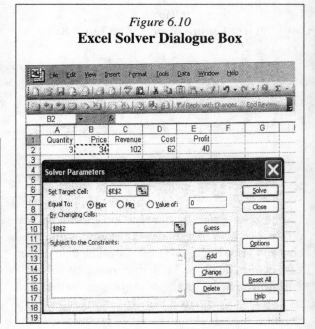

*Table 6.19*
**Excel Functions in Figure 6.9**

| Cell | Function |
|---|---|
| A2 | = 20 – 0.5*B2 |
| B2 | = 34 |
| C2 | = A2*B2 |
| D2 | = 26 + 12*A2 |
| E2 | = C2 – D2 |

Microsoft Excel has a Solver tool that searches for the price that maximizes the firm's profit. The Solver is under the "Tools" menu on the Excel menu. (If the Solver option does not immediately appear, select Tools/Add-ins and bring the Solver tool into the computer's memory.) The Solver dialogue box is displayed in Figure 6.10. The target cell, E2, is selected for maximization by changing cell B2. When the Solve button is selected,

*Figure 6.10*
**Excel Solver Dialogue Box**

*Figure 6.11*
**Excel Solver Solution**

Excel will find the price that maximizes the firm's profit. The results are shown in Figure 6.11.

Consider again the monopolist from Exercise 6.3 with a consumer demand function $Q = 100 - 5P$. The monopolist has a cost function $C = 31.2 + 4Q$. Use Microsoft Excel (or another spreadsheet software package) and the Solver tool to find the monopolist's profit-maximizing price and quantity.

2. Consider an author and a publisher who sign a contract to publish a book. The demand function for the book is $Q = 1,000 - 20P$. The publisher alone is responsible for the costs of the book: $C = 1,500 + 5Q$. Use Microsoft Excel (or another spreadsheet software package) and the Solver tool to find the following:

   (a) Under a 50-50 revenue-sharing arrangement, what price would the publisher set for the book? How many books are sold? How much would each party receive?
   (b) Under a 50-50 revenue-sharing arrangement, what would the authors like to set as the price of the book? How many books would be sold if they could set the price? How much would each party receive?
   (c) Under a 70-30 profit-sharing contract (70 percent for the author), what price would the publisher set for the book? How many books are sold? How much would each party receive?
   (d) Compare and contrast the contracts in questions (a) and (c).
   (e) Now consider the company that you work for. Describe a scenario in which your firm contracts with another party. How are the monies from the agreement shared? On profit or revenue? Why?

3. Consider a monopolist with the estimated consumer demand function in Table 6.12: $Q = 1129.39 + 0.01Y + 4.93P_s - 10.96P$. The monopolist has a cost function $C = 2,000 + 5Q$. Currently the average income is $45,000 and the price of the substitute good is $25. Use Microsoft Excel (or another spreadsheet software package) and the Solver tool to find the monopolist's profit-maximizing price and quantity. Examine Table 6.11 and determine what the monopolist should have charged in each of the sixteen regions if it wanted to maximize profits. How much profit was lost by not pricing optimally in all of the sixteen regions?

4. You are the ticket-pricing manager for the Pittsburgh Steelers. You recently entered into a contractual agreement with the National Football League (NFL) in which you will share the revenue for luxury box seats at the Steelers' new stadium. The Steelers will receive 60 percent of the revenue and the NFL receives 40 percent. The demand curve for luxury seats is estimated to be $Q = 5,000 - 0.5P$, where $P$

represents the price and $Q$ represents the number of seats sold. The Steelers pay the $200 marginal cost of providing the seats (to pay for food and attendants).

(a) Assuming that the Steelers maximize their profits, what price will the Steelers set for luxury box seats? How many luxury box seats will they sell? How much will the Steelers receive and how much will the NFL receive?

(b) If the NFL could set the price, what would the price be? How many seats will be sold?

(c) What type of problems will the revenue-sharing contract cause? Can you design a contract that will alleviate these problems (be specific)?

5. What is the difference between a dominant strategy equilibrium and a Nash equilibrium? Describe a business scenario in which all involved have a dominant strategy. Describe another business scenario in which no one has a dominant strategy, yet all involved are best responding to what everyone else has done.

6. Consider the following pie-sharing game. Sandy makes an apple pie and offers her two favorite clients, Charlie and John, some of the pie. Charlie and John make their demands simultaneously. Sandy is a little eccentric and her clients will get what they ask for as long as their demands do not exceed the entire pie. So if they both demand half of the pie, they both get it. If they both demand a quarter, then they each get one-quarter. However, if John demands three-quarters of the pie and Charlie demands a half, then they both get nothing. Consider the payoffs in Table 6.20.

*Table 6.20*
**Pie-Sharing Game**

|  |  |  | John |  |  |
|---|---|---|---|---|---|
|  |  | No Pie | ¼ Pie | ½ Pie | ¾ Pie | Whole Pie |
| Charlie | No Pie | 0 , 0 | 0 , ¼ | 0 , ½ | 0 , ¾ | 0 , 1 |
|  | ¼ Pie | ¼ , 0 | ¼ , ¼ | ¼ , ½ | ¼ , ¾ | 0 , 0 |
|  | ½ Pie | ½ , 0 | ½ , ¼ | ½ , ½ | 0 , 0 | 0 , 0 |
|  | ¾ Pie | ¾ , 0 | ¾ , ¼ | 0 , 0 | 0 , 0 | 0 , 0 |
|  | Whole Pie | 1 , 0 | 0 , 0 | 0 , 0 | 0 , 0 | 0 , 0 |

(a) Define the term *dominant strategy*. Are there any in this game?

(b) Define the term *Nash equilibrium*. Are there any in this game? If there are, find all of them, and explain why each is a Nash equilibrium.

(c) Why was John Nash's discovery of his equilibrium concept—later to be known as the Nash equilibrium—important to understand how managers behave in oligopoly industries?

(d) Consider the Nash equilibriums identified in part (b). If John and Charlie were managers of competing companies vying for market share instead of apple pie, how would you expect the game to be played? Consider any assumption you had to make to answer the question, and how your answer changes if you alter the assumptions.

7. Suppose Fred and Wilma are partners on the game show *Friend or Foe*. They just met thirty seconds before the game began. They earn $10,000 answering trivia questions and go to the trust box. In the trust box, they must each simultaneously choose Friend or Foe. If they both choose Friend, they split the $10,000 equally. If

one chooses Friend while the other chooses Foe, the Foe gets all $10,000 while the Friend gets nothing. If they both choose Foe, they each get a $100 parting gift.

(a) Model this game using a game matrix.
(b) Does either player have a dominant strategy?
(c) Use the minimax technique to find an equilibrium. Under what conditions will the minimax technique work?
(d) Where are the Nash equilibriums (if they exist)?
(e) Is this game a prisoner's dilemma?
(f) What would you expect the outcome of the game to be? Explain your expectation clearly. Other than changing the payoffs of the game, could any other influence or information get you to change your expectation of the outcome of this game?

8. The Meadows housing development has fifty-five homes. When the homes were built, a single security company took care of wiring the neighborhood and connecting each home's security system with its central office. The residents can choose to purchase a monthly security protection plan from the company. At first, the residents were glad to have the security company, but the service price was high, and they soon realized that no competitor wanted to rewire the neighborhood—the security company had evolved into a natural monopoly. As a result of the high price, many residents chose not to have the protection.

(a) Suppose the demand function for the security company services within the Meadows is $Q = 55 - 0.5P$, where $Q$ is the number of residents purchasing the security service and $P$ is the monthly price. The security company's cost function is $C = 800 + 10Q$. Assuming that the security company wants to maximize its profits, what price does it set? How many residents will use the service? What will be the security company's monthly profit?
(b) Suppose the local government steps in to regulate the security company and forces it to set a price. What price would be set for the monthly service? How many residents would purchase the service?

9. Suppose a business owner is a monopolist in the firm's market. The owner faces the following daily demand for the product: $P = 200 - 2Q$. The costs of production are $C = 750 + 40Q$.

(a) Find the monopolist's profit-maximizing price and output.
(b) When the monopolist is maximizing profit, how much profit does the firm make? Why would the government choose to regulate this monopolist?
(c) If the government decided to regulate this monopolist, what price would the monopolist be forced to charge? How does the government justify this regulation?
(d) Suppose the government loosens its regulation as three additional firms enter the market and provide some competition. (All of the companies have the same cost structure.) How would you classify this new market structure? Assuming that there will only be four firms in this market for many months, what will happen to the price in the market? Will there be an equilibrium price? How

does this price compare with the prices you found in parts (a) and (d)?

(e) Suppose after a year, many firms enter the market and the market becomes perfectly competitive. (Assume that all firms have the same cost structure.) What happens to the market price?

(f) Describe the market structure transition in the above problem from monopoly to perfect competition. Describe what has happened in terms of corporate profits, consumer surplus, and productive efficiency.

**Note**

1. William Poundstone, *Prisoner's Dilemma: John von Neumann, Game Theory, and the Puzzle of the Bomb* (New York: Bantam Doubleday Dell, 1992), pp. 117–19.

# Case Study 6.1

# Permalens

## Part A: 2009

### Introduction

Mary Verdolino, CEO of Beye-o-tronics Corporation, sits down at her desk and smiles. Although the beautiful trees outside her corner office this fall afternoon in the year 2009 are reason enough to be happy, she is holding in her hand a letter from the Food and Drug Administration that approves the Permalens for sale to the general public in the United States. With this approval she expects that the Permalens will be accepted internationally as well.

Ten years earlier, Mary Verdolino left her biomedical engineering laboratory and a full professorship at Harvard University to start Beye-o-tronics. Her dream was to engineer a biosynthetic lens that would affix to the cornea and permanently correct a patient's vision. She found numerous private investors and raised $150 million to fund the necessary research and development.

However, her progress was slow, and she ultimately exhausted almost all of her financial capital. Over the years, her investors became increasingly nervous that the Permalens would not come to fruition. Beye-o-tronics applied for and received the international patent rights to the Permalens in December 2008. No other company could produce a similar product until the year 2016. However, the clock was ticking on the monopoly rights to the Permalens, and Beye-o-tronics' investors were worried that FDA approval would come too late to take advantage of a market without competition. Mary is relieved to have the acceptance by the FDA, because now Beye-o-tronics can finally provide a return for its investors.

Mary has been preparing for this moment, and she is ready to begin selling the Permalens to the general public in the first quarter of 2010. A trained ophthalmologist is needed to implant the Permalens, and her staff has already partnered with and trained 1,000 ophthalmologists in the United

States and 500 in the United Kingdom to perform the procedure.

The Beye-o-tronics marketing machine is ready to move as well. Television, Internet, radio, and newspaper advertisements have been prepared. Brochures for doctors' offices are ready to be mailed. Most experts believe that the Permalens will replace both Lasik surgery and the need for contact lenses. Beye-o-tronics plans an extensive direct-mail campaign to contact lens wearers based on a consumer database purchased earlier in the year.

At this point, Mary is ready to pull the trigger. However, she is waiting for her chief economist to make a recommendation on a pricing strategy for the Permalens. Although she was a world-renowned scientist at Harvard, Mary realized before starting this venture that she needed to gain some business acumen. She completed an MBA at Harvard (finishing sixth in her class), so she certainly has some ideas on pricing strategy. However, she wants to hear from her chief economist before making a decision.

### Production of the Permalens

Beye-o-tronics decided to manufacture the Permalens in both the United States and the United Kingdom. Two production facilities were built using the monies from the initial $150 million investment—one near Boston and one outside of London. The facility in the United States costs $30 million to operate annually, while the facility in England costs $20 million annually. (All figures in the case are presented in U.S. dollars.)

Beye-o-tronics invented a process that melds a soft and pliable plastic (similar to a soft contact lens) to live corneal tissue. A patient visits an ophthalmologist for an initial consultation. At this appointment, the patient's eye is measured and a microscopic scraping of corneal tissue is extracted. Within a month, Beye-o-tronics' production facility uses the genetic coding from the patient's tissue to grow a Permalens. The Permalens is a biosynthetic lens that is unique to each patient and includes both reproduced cells from the patient's original tissue sample and a plastic corrective contact lens. The Permalens is shipped to the ophthalmologist in a climate-controlled and sterile environment. The ophthalmologist affixes the Permalens to the outside of the patient's existing cornea. Installing the new lenses takes less than ten minutes per eye, requires no invasive surgery, and provides permanent eye correction. The equipment an ophthalmologist requires to install the Permalens is very minimal. Even the most severe cases of myopia are correctable with the Permalens. Beye-o-tronics' complete cost of producing each Permalens is $200 (in both the United States and United Kingdom).

### Lasik History/Data

Maria DeBitetto, vice president of marketing for Beye-o-tronics, has spent much of the past year studying the market for Lasik surgeries in the United States and the United Kingdom. She collected data on the relationship between the number of Lasik surgeries and numerous economic variables. Maria is convinced that a higher prime interest rate discourages spending on Lasik surgeries. She believes that consumer confidence indexes and disposable income are good predictors of spending on Lasik surgeries. While she feels strongly that a reduction in the price of Lasik would lead to more surgeries, she is not convinced that her data contain enough variation in price to show this. Maria also feels that any increase in the net present value of wearing contact lenses leads to more Lasik surgeries.

Maria believes that these variables will affect Permalens sales in exactly the same way they affect Lasik surgeries. Maria told Mary that a statistically significant coefficient representing how a change

*Table C6.1*
## Lasik Eye Surgery Data, United States, 2000–2009

|                | Number of Lasik Surgeries | Average Price | Prime Interest Rate | Change in Disposable Income | Consumer Confidence Index | NPV Contact Lenses |
|----------------|---------------------------|---------------|---------------------|-----------------------------|---------------------------|--------------------|
| Jan.–Jun. 2000 | 188,447 | 2,500 | 8.75% | 1.13%  | 86  | 5,700 |
| Jul.–Dec. 2000 | 218,296 | 2,505 | 9.50% | 1.92%  | 84  | 5,720 |
| Jan.–Jun. 2001 | 178,836 | 2,505 | 8.50% | −1.23% | 74  | 5,750 |
| Jul.–Dec. 2001 | 176,165 | 2,510 | 6.50% | −2.45% | 70  | 5,870 |
| Jan.–Jun. 2002 | 267,274 | 2,515 | 4.75% | −2.68% | 85  | 6,000 |
| Jul.–Dec. 2002 | 289,823 | 2,520 | 4.70% | 0.34%  | 88  | 6,125 |
| Jan.–Jun. 2003 | 310,110 | 2,520 | 4.25% | 0.12%  | 100 | 6,134 |
| Jul.–Dec. 2003 | 342,397 | 2,525 | 4.00% | 0.49%  | 105 | 6,200 |
| Jan.–Jun. 2004 | 392,322 | 2,525 | 4.00% | 3.78%  | 106 | 6,250 |
| Jul.–Dec. 2004 | 357,360 | 2,520 | 4.50% | 4.21%  | 107 | 6,300 |
| Jan.–Jun. 2005 | 327,180 | 2,505 | 5.50% | 3.45%  | 105 | 6,350 |
| Jul.–Dec. 2005 | 244,270 | 2,505 | 6.75% | 2.11%  | 84  | 6,225 |
| Jan.–Jun. 2006 | 245,813 | 2,500 | 7.00% | 0.23%  | 80  | 6,140 |
| Jul.–Dec. 2006 | 208,396 | 2,495 | 7.50% | 0.78%  | 76  | 6,240 |
| Jan.–Jun. 2007 | 252,599 | 2,494 | 8.00% | 1.45%  | 89  | 6,300 |
| Jul.–Dec. 2007 | 294,551 | 2,490 | 8.00% | 4.45%  | 93  | 6,440 |
| Jan.–Jun. 2008 | 263,813 | 2,490 | 8.50% | 5.67%  | 90  | 6,500 |
| Jul.–Dec. 2008 | 252,727 | 2,490 | 8.50% | 2.34%  | 106 | 6,540 |
| Jan.–Jun. 2009 | 230,519 | 2,485 | 9.00% | 1.23%  | 105 | 6,550 |
| Jul.–Dec. 2009 | 253,567 | 2,483 | 9.50% | 3.60%  | 107 | 6,650 |

*Notes*

# of Lasik surgeries: counted on a per-eye basis

Average price: on a per-eye basis and adjusted for inflation in U.S. dollars

Prime interest rate: interest rate charged to most creditworthy customers

Percentage change in national disposable income: change from previous six-month period

Consumer Confidence Index: U.S. (University of Michigan) and UK (GfK Martin Hamblin)

NPV contact lenses: net present value of the average lifetime expense of wearing a pair of contact lenses

*Table C6.2*
## Lasik Eye Surgery Data, United Kingdom, 2000–2009

| | # of Lasik Surgeries | Average Price | Prime Interest Rate | Change in Disposable Income | Consumer Confidence Index | NPV Contact Lenses |
|---|---|---|---|---|---|---|
| Jan.–Jun. 2000 | 117,365 | 2,200 | 8.90% | 3.45% | 4 | 4,275 |
| Jul.–Dec. 2000 | 106,976 | 2,224 | 8.80% | 2.34% | 2 | 4,290 |
| Jan.–Jun. 2001 | 97,965 | 2,226 | 6.50% | −2.45% | 1 | 4,313 |
| Jul.–Dec. 2001 | 100,666 | 2,230 | 4.60% | −4.13% | −1 | 4,403 |
| Jan.–Jun. 2002 | 87,651 | 2,218 | 4.70% | −2.12% | −3 | 4,500 |
| Jul.–Dec. 2002 | 83,800 | 2,217 | 3.75% | −1.98% | −5 | 4,594 |
| Jan.–Jun. 2003 | 110,378 | 2,220 | 3.30% | 1.23% | 2 | 4,601 |
| Jul.–Dec. 2003 | 113,613 | 2,224 | 3.40% | 4.30% | 2 | 4,650 |
| Jan.–Jun. 2004 | 110,660 | 2,225 | 3.80% | 5.60% | 3 | 4,688 |
| Jul.–Dec. 2004 | 120,612 | 2,218 | 4.50% | 2.33% | 4 | 4,725 |
| Jan.–Jun. 2005 | 124,217 | 2,215 | 5.75% | 1.77% | 5 | 4,763 |
| Jul.–Dec. 2005 | 116,251 | 2,215 | 6.25% | 0.11% | 4 | 4,669 |
| Jan.–Jun. 2006 | 92,217 | 2,212 | 7.00% | −0.78% | −2 | 4,605 |
| Jul.–Dec. 2006 | 75,588 | 2,212 | 7.43% | −5.23% | −4 | 4,680 |
| Jan.–Jun. 2007 | 77,495 | 2,210 | 7.70% | 1.45% | −7 | 4,725 |
| Jul.–Dec. 2007 | 112,520 | 2,210 | 8.60% | 5.76% | 2 | 4,830 |
| Jan.–Jun. 2008 | 102,459 | 2,206 | 9.50% | 2.45% | 3 | 4,875 |
| Jul.–Dec. 2008 | 117,317 | 2,205 | 10.25% | 0.45% | 6 | 4,905 |
| Jan.–Jun. 2009 | 87,168 | 2,204 | 11.00% | −1.30% | −1 | 4,913 |
| Jul.–Dec. 2009 | 75,202 | 2,200 | 11.50% | −2.56% | −4 | 4,988 |

*Notes:*

# of Lasik surgeries: counted on a per-eye basis

Average price: on a per-eye basis and adjusted for inflation in U.S. dollars

Prime interest rate: interest rate charged to most creditworthy customers

Percentage change in national disposable income: change from previous six-month period

Consumer Confidence Index: U.S. (University of Michigan) and UK (GfK Martin Hamblin)

NPV contact lenses: net present value of the average lifetime expense of wearing a pair of contact lenses in the prime rate affects Lasik surgeries would be a good predictor of how a similar change in the prime rate would affect Permalens sales. Both Maria and Mary want to hear what the chief economist thinks about this.

### Consumer Survey Results

Throughout the development and testing of the Permalens, the marketing department, headed by Maria DeBitetto, conducted numerous consumer surveys. The surveys helped Beye-o-tronics obtain valuable information, including how consumers would eventually perceive the Permalens when it hit the market. Beye-o-tronics also wanted to know how consumers would respond to different prices. Using the consumer surveys, Maria put together an estimate of six months of sales over a progression of prices.

Maria believed that combining the analysis of the Lasik data and the consumer survey could create an estimation of a demand equation. A regression equation generated from the consumer pricing data would estimate the Permalens demand function, while the coefficients from the Lasik data could help Beye-o-tronics predict how this demand function might shift with changes in the economic variables.

### Contract with Doctors

As previously noted, Beye-o-tronics has identified 1,000 ophthalmologists in the United States and 500 in the United Kingdom to begin selling and implanting the Permalens in patients in January of 2010. Beye-o-tronics intends to dictate the price of the Permalens. All of the doctors will be required to set the same price for the Permalens, as Beye-o-tronics does not want doctors discounting the lens. However, Beye-o-tronics plans to charge different prices in the United States and the United Kingdom. The doctors will be required to sign a contract stating that they

*Table C6.3*

**Pricing Survey of Potential Permalens Consumers**

|  | Potential Sales of Individual Lenses (Six Months) | |
| --- | --- | --- |
| Price (U.S.$) | U.S. | U.K. |
| $250 | 171,697 | 85,880 |
| 300 | 162,067 | 84,870 |
| 350 | 154,995 | 82,049 |
| 400 | 145,554 | 80,907 |
| 450 | 140,902 | 71,690 |
| 500 | 130,624 | 70,637 |
| 550 | 122,140 | 69,206 |
| 600 | 118,418 | 64,441 |
| 650 | 107,471 | 54,580 |
| 700 | 95,946 | 53,139 |
| 750 | 93,301 | 51,442 |
| 800 | 83,458 | 51,318 |
| 850 | 77,487 | 39,808 |
| 900 | 65,729 | 35,480 |
| 950 | 59,958 | 34,935 |
| 1,000 | 57,270 | 30,827 |
| 1,050 | 47,025 | 25,148 |
| 1,100 | 38,995 | 22,257 |
| 1,150 | 36,229 | 22,021 |
| 1,200 | 20,107 | 11,059 |
| 1,250 | 20,097 | 10,946 |
| 1,300 | 13,891 | 10,931 |
| 1,350 | 10,235 | 10,110 |
| 1,400 | 7,891 | 10,003 |
| 1,450 | 5,322 | 6,513 |
| 1,500 | 2,568 | 1,298 |

will charge Beye-o-tronics' price; in turn, the doctors will keep 20 percent of the revenue collected. Beye-o-tronics will set an initial price, and based on economic conditions, Beye-o-tronics intends to change the price of the Permalens every six months.

## Economic Forecast

Beye-o-tronics' economics team provided the forecast in Table C6.4 of the expected economic conditions over the upcoming six years.

*Table C6.4*
### Economic Forecast

| United States | Prime Interest Rate | Change in Disposable Income | Consumer Confidence Index |
|---|---|---|---|
| Jan.–Jun. 2010 | 10.00% | 1.00% | 100 |
| Jul.–Dec. 2010 | 10.50% | 0.50% | 95 |
| Jan.–Jun. 2011 | 11.00% | –0.50% | 90 |
| Jul.–Dec. 2011 | 10.00% | –1.00% | 88 |
| Jan.–Jun. 2012 | 9.00% | –2.00% | 85 |
| Jul.–Dec. 2012 | 8.00% | –2.50% | 80 |
| Jan.–Jun. 2013 | 7.50% | 0.50% | 81 |
| Jul.–Dec. 2013 | 7.00% | 1.00% | 82 |
| Jan.–Jun. 2014 | 6.50% | 1.50% | 84 |
| Jul.–Dec. 2014 | 6.50% | 2.00% | 85 |
| Jan.–Jun. 2015 | 6.00% | 2.50% | 88 |
| Jul.–Dec. 2015 | 5.50% | 3.00% | 90 |

| United Kingdom | Prime Interest Rate | Change in Disposable Income | Consumer Confidence Index |
|---|---|---|---|
| Jan.–Jun. 2010 | 12.00% | –3.12% | –2 |
| Jul.–Dec. 2010 | 12.00% | –1.28% | 1 |
| Jan.–Jun. 2011 | 11.00% | –0.50% | 1 |
| Jul.–Dec. 2011 | 10.50% | 0.22% | 1 |
| Jan.–Jun. 2012 | 10.00% | 0.50% | 2 |
| Jul.–Dec. 2012 | 9.50% | 1.00% | 2 |
| Jan.–Jun. 2013 | 9.00% | 1.40% | 4 |
| Jul.–Dec. 2013 | 9.00% | 0.56% | 5 |
| Jan.–Jun. 2014 | 8.50% | 1.22% | 6 |
| Jul.–Dec. 2014 | 8.50% | –0.34% | 2 |
| Jan.–Jun. 2015 | 9.00% | –0.55% | –1 |
| Jul.–Dec. 2015 | 9.50% | –0.75% | –2 |

## Part A Assignment

Mary Verdolino wants you, her chief economist, to make a recommendation for the initial price of the Permalens in both the United States and the United Kingdom. Mary also wants the following economic forecast analyses of Beye-o-tronics' monopoly position over the next six years: a break-even analysis, a profitability analysis, and a sensitivity analysis.

## Part B: 2019

### Introduction

Mary Verdolino, chairman and CEO of the Beye-o-tronics Corporation, frowns as she looks over the latest market share reports for the Permalens. Beye-o-tronics' patent on the Permalens expired at the end of 2015, and since then three other companies have begun to sell similar products. Beye-o-tronics has been forced to reduce the price of the Permalens to match its competition's price, and yet Beye-o-tronics' market share continues to decline.

Mary believes that her competitors found ways to produce the Permalens product more cheaply than Beye-o-tronics can. Mary is the first to admit that even though the loss of patent rights was expected, Beye-o-tronics was not prepared to deal with increased competition. The Permalens is still marketed as the "original permanent contact lens made with quality that cannot be duplicated." However, Mary is not convinced.

Beye-o-tronics' market share eroded in the United States fairly quickly as competitors developed production facilities that are smaller and much cheaper to maintain. To further save on costs, the other companies are using their U.S. production facilities to produce lenses that are

*Table C6.5*
**Beye-o-tronics Market Share and Profit, 2016–2019**

| United States | Total Market Sales (Units) | Beye-o-tronics Market Share | Market Price | Beye-o-tronics Fixed Costs | Beye-o-tronics Variable Costs | Beye-o-tronics Gross Profit (Loss) |
|---|---|---|---|---|---|---|
| Jan.–Jun. 2016 | 120,000 | 94% | $900 | $18,000,000 | $200 | $40,656,000 |
| Jul.–Dec. 2016 | 145,000 | 86% | $765 | $18,000,000 | $200 | $33,376,400 |
| Jan.–Jun. 2017 | 156,000 | 72% | $578 | $19,000,000 | $210 | $9,349,568 |
| Jul.–Dec. 2017 | 180,000 | 64% | $499 | $19,000,000 | $210 | $2,795,840 |
| Jan.–Jun. 2018 | 200,000 | 45% | $430 | $19,000,000 | $210 | ($3,070,000) |
| Jul.–Dec. 2018 | 250,000 | 35% | $395 | $20,000,000 | $220 | ($8,143,750) |
| Jan.–Jun. 2019 | 280,000 | 32% | $340 | $20,000,000 | $220 | ($12,294,400) |
| Jul.–Dec. 2019 | 305,000 | 30% | $299 | $20,000,000 | $220 | ($15,507,350) |

| United Kingdom | Total Market Sales (Units) | Beye-o-tronics Market Share | Market Price | Beye-o-tronics Fixed Costs | Beye-o-tronics Variable Costs | Beye-o-tronics Gross Profit (Loss) |
|---|---|---|---|---|---|---|
| Jan.–Jun. 2016 | 65,000 | 94% | $900 | $11,000,000 | $200 | $20,772,000 |
| Jul.–Dec. 2016 | 70,000 | 86% | $865 | $11,000,000 | $200 | $18,618,400 |
| Jan.–Jun. 2017 | 80,000 | 80% | $755 | $11,000,000 | $210 | $14,216,000 |
| Jul.–Dec. 2017 | 100,000 | 77% | $650 | $12,000,000 | $210 | $11,870,000 |
| Jan.–Jun. 2018 | 120,000 | 65% | $599 | $12,500,000 | $210 | $13,169,800 |
| Jul.–Dec. 2018 | 140,000 | 62% | $550 | $12,500,000 | $220 | $11,370,000 |
| Jan.–Jun. 2019 | 155,000 | 58% | $499 | $13,000,000 | $220 | $7,596,090 |
| Jul.–Dec. 2019 | 175,000 | 57% | $459 | $13,000,000 | $220 | $6,261,725 |

being sold in the United Kingdom. The only real competitive advantage Beye-o-tronics has against competition in the United Kingdom is the ability to service its customers much faster. However, Mary is considering closing the facilities in the United Kingdom.

Mary used to believe that Beye-o-tronics' long relationship with ophthalmologists would help the company maintain market leadership. However, the competition was very savvy in marketing directly to consumers to get them to demand the competitor's lenses from their doctors. The competition even managed to negotiate a 95-5 sharing arrangement with the doctors. Beye-o-tronics thought that its 80-20 arrangement would give doctors an incentive to push the Permalens. However, this did not seem to make a difference. In the face of declining profits, Mary reduced the doctors' share to 10 percent in January 2018.

Mary has heard rumblings that her competitors' profits, while still in the black, have begun to decline as the price of the Permalens dropped below $300 in late 2019. A very reliable source indicates that one of her competitors is planning to raise its price in both the United States and the United Kingdom to $599 in January 2020. It is, of course, illegal for Mary to make agreements with her CEO counterparts on the issue of setting prices. However, it is common practice for competitors to leak information about their intentions on price. This is how Mary has been able to keep up with the drastic decline in prices over the last four years.

When a competitor announces a change in its price, the change is typically made public very quickly. However, Beye-o-tronics needs at least two weeks to match these prices in order to coordinate with doctors and insurance companies. The marketing blitz from the competitor is usually enough to negatively impact Beye-o-tronics' sales even after the competitor's price has been met.

### Part B Assignment

Mary Verdolino wants you, her chief economist, to make a recommendation for the price of the Permalens in both the United States and in the United Kingdom for January 2020. Mary also wants you to recommend a future strategy for the Permalens and Beye-o-tronics given the recent decline in market share and profitability.

To assist with your analysis, construct a two-player game theory model in which Beye-o-tronics, as one player, and all other competitors, considered collectively as another player, can set a price of either $299 or $599 in the United States. Consider carefully the payoffs in each cell of the game model. You will have to make assumptions regarding the payoffs, as not all of the data are available to Beye-o-tronics. Explain the assumptions you make, and explain how dependent your results are on these

assumptions. Is your game model a prisoner's dilemma? What does the game theory model imply about this pricing decision and the future of Beye-o-tronics?

## Part C: 2029

### Introduction

In the fall of 2029, there are around one hundred boutique producers of permanent contact lenses in the United States. Technological innovations in biosynthetic lenses have advanced to the point that it is fairly inexpensive to produce a Permalens-type product. The price of a permanent contact lens is now only $99. While some producers tried to set higher prices with various innovative colored lenses, it was not long before the innovation was duplicated by another company and prices declined again.

Mary Verdolino's Beye-o-tronics Corporation is one of these boutiques. Mary is well into retirement, and she runs the boutique at a local university to have access to a laboratory to conduct other research. She is able to live off her retirement savings. The university charges her $5,000 rent each year since she is producing a commercial product. She has hired a permanent graduate assistant for $15,000 a year to help, and she is able to hire short-term help on a part-time basis when necessary.

The materials to produce each lens cost only $5. Mary is continuously astounded at how much cheaper the product is to make compared to twenty years earlier. Mary and her graduate assistant can handle, by themselves, the production of 1,000 lenses during a year's time. However, if the production schedule requires her to produce more than 1,000, she is forced to hire more graduate students. Unfortunately for Mary, reliable graduate assistants are hard to find, so she has had to raise her graduate student stipends as she

*Table C6.6*
**Beye-o-tronics Costs of Production**

| Fixed Costs: |
| --- |
| $5,000 for university fee and $15,000 for permanent graduate assistantship |

| Variable Costs: |
| --- |
| $5 per lens production cost |
| Production of 1,001–2,000 lenses: $25,000 for additional graduate assistant funding |
| Production of 2,001–3,000 lenses: $30,000 for additional graduate assistant funding |
| Production of 3,001–4,000 lenses: $35,000 for additional graduate assistant funding |
| Production of 4,001–5,000 lenses: $40,000 for additional graduate assistant funding |
| Production of 5,001–6,000 lenses: $45,000 for additional graduate assistant funding |

increases production. Her costs of production are detailed in Table C6.6.

### Case C Assignment

Mary is planning for 2030, and she believes she can find enough buyers if her laboratory produces 6,000 lenses in the upcoming year. However, she asks you, her graduate assistant, to make a recommendation on the number of lenses Beye-o-tronics should produce, as Mary needs to submit a request for temporary workers for the upcoming year.

# 7

# The Economics of Business Strategy

A well-defined and articulated competitive strategy is fundamental to an organization's success. A firm's competitive strategy expresses how it seeks to differentiate its products from those of rivals, creates value for its buyers, and guides operational decision making across an organization. An effectively designed and executed competitive strategy leads a firm to sustained superior financial performance relative to its rivals.

This chapter approaches the analysis of competitive strategy from an economics perspective. The emphasis is placed on the *positioning* of the firm relative to its macro- and microeconomic environments, thereby allowing the firm to take advantage of its strengths and opportunities and insulating it from threats and weaknesses.

## Learning Objectives

The successful reader understands

- Strategic analysis and planning and the role of economics
- The concept of positioning of the firm
- SWOT analysis and its application in strategy design
- How to define a firm's line-of-business strategy
- How to define a firm's corporate-level strategy
- How to monitor the effectiveness of a firm's competitive strategy

## Strategic Analysis and Planning

In many undergraduate and MBA degree programs, business strategy (or business policy) is a capstone course, integrating functional area studies in management, marketing, finance, operations, information management, and accounting into a holistic view of the firm. The course also develops a strategy-based approach to managerial decision making, seeking to help managers execute the firm's strategy effectively.[1] This chapter introduces rudimentary concepts of strategic analysis and emphasizes three important themes. First, the firm's micro- and macroeconomic environments affect its range of strategic options. Second, the economic, political, social, technological, and regulatory environments constitute conditions within which a firm operates and which affect its financial performance. Third, economic analysis bridges the study of the functional area of business.

### Levels of Strategy

The design of a firm's competitive strategy occurs at two levels. Multiproduct firms engage in a *corporate-level strategy,* which defines the intended relationships between a firm's multiple products or divisions. Three generic corporate-level strategies are presented in terms of expanding the vertical and horizontal reaches of the firm's production cost chain. The concept of the *line-of-business strategy* is applied to a single product or narrow group of products and refers to the means through which a seller seeks to distinguish its products from those of rivals.

### The Corporate-Level Strategy

The concept of corporate-level strategy applies to firms that produce multiple products or services. The diversification is examined through the production cost chain (see Figure 7.1).

Figure 7.1 shows the flow of resource inputs from raw materials through intermediate-stage processing to the final product and the end user. In Figure 7.1 the firm is identified at an arbitrary stage along the production cost chain. The question of corporate-level strategy arises when the firm diversifies into new markets and the diversification extends either *horizontally* or *vertically*. Horizontal diversifications extend the firm into other production cost chains and differ by the degree to which the new products are related to existing ones. For example, a beef slaughterhouse extends horizontally into poultry and pork products. More distant horizontal diversification extends its range of products to processed meats, microwavable meals,

and non-food products. Similarly, diversification extends vertically forward or backward along the production cost chain. The beef slaughterhouse vertically integrates backward by developing or purchasing feedlots and ranches. It vertically integrates forward by developing or purchasing a restaurant chain or butcher shops.

These diversification options lead to the discussion of a firm's corporate-level strategy. Conglomerate, hygiene, and leverage corporate-level strategies are discussed below.

### Conglomerate Strategy

A firm pursuing a *conglomerate* corporate-level strategy extends its product offerings to entirely unrelated products and markets. For example, a very successful family-owned restaurant generates cash in excess of the reinvestment needs of the

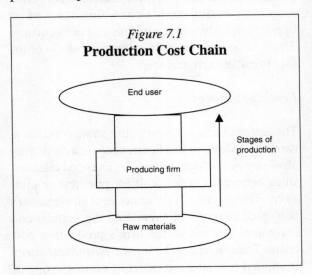

*Figure 7.1*
**Production Cost Chain**

End user

Stages of production

Producing firm

Raw materials

**Application Box 7.1**

Cendant is an $18 billion company that comprises dozens of the nation's most prominent businesses, including Century 21, Avis, Days Inn, and Orbitz. Cendant is planning a dramatic restructuring that reverses its conglomerate roots. The company will be divided into four groups (real estate, travel distribution, hospitality, and vehicle rental) and spun off into separately traded companies.

Henry Silverman, Cendant's chairman, told the *New York Times* that the announcement is a vivid acknowledgement that the era of conglomerates built through mergers and acquisitions may be over.

*Source:* Andrew Ross Sorkin, "Conglomerate Reverses Field; Plans Break-up," *New York Times,* October 24, 2005.

business and the family's need for income. The decision maker enjoys many investment options, including stocks, bonds, bank deposits, or the start-up or purchase of other businesses.

The nature of a conglomerate strategy is that a start-up or newly purchased business is unrelated to the existing business. For example, the family-owned restaurant purchases a self-service gasoline station. To emphasize the unrelated nature of the business, the gasoline station is located in another community, so restaurant patrons are not also gasoline patrons. Employees are not shared between the businesses, and the administrative functions are not merged. In the extreme, the financial success of the conglomerate is the sum of the distinct businesses.

*Hygiene Strategy*

Under a *hygiene* corporate-level strategy, the multiple lines of business generate efficiencies unavailable to single-product firms. As a result, the diversified firm is more profitable than the sum of its separate parts. Consider the following examples. (1) A firm expands horizontally by introducing a new product that is manufactured with currently owned assets. The new product raises the firm's asset utilization rate and generates economies of scope. The efficiencies allow the firm to price aggressively and to enhance its profitability at the same time. (2) A predominantly residential college develops evening and weekend academic programs and summer athletic camp activities. These programs use existing buildings and playing fields, and the incremental revenues from the new programs in excess of the incremental costs enhance the college's financial condition. (3) A beef slaughterhouse business extends horizontally into pork, poultry, and fish products. The firm gains efficiencies by marketing all of the products with one sales force. (4) The same slaughterhouse expands down

the production cost chain by developing feedlots to circumvent seller power. (5) The slaughterhouse integrates upward along the production chain by completing more of the intermediate-stage processing. Rather than ship large pieces of beef, it ships freezer-shelf-ready grocery products. Lower-priced slaughterhouse labor replaces higher-priced butchers, thereby lowering the cost of the beef on the shelf for the grocery.

*Leverage Strategy*

A *leverage* corporate-level strategy relies upon an organizational competence that extends over multiple products and enhances the market attractiveness and profitability of each. Three examples are offered. (1) A hotel chain holds an advantage over rivals through its human resources practices. Its hiring, training, and motivation techniques for low-wage service workers lead to a competitive advantage in the lodging industry. A leveraged corporate strategy extends these human resources practices and exceptional cleanliness and personal service into new lines of business, including restaurants, institutional food service, retirement communities, and managed-care facilities. (2) A manufacturer adept at building durable and inexpensive small engines extends its abilities, brand recognition, and distribution channels from lawn mowers to motorcycles, snow blowers, generators, and off-road vehicles. (3) A firm adept at more rapidly introducing product upgrades leverages that competence by bringing all its products to market more quickly than its rivals.

*Measuring and Sustaining a Corporate Strategy*

This section emphasizes two points: (1) corporate-level strategies require careful management, and (2) the effectiveness of the implementation of the strategy is continuously assessed. Conglomer-

## Application Box 7.2

A measuring system to monitor the execution of the corporate strategy helps guide decisions and provides an early diagnosis of problems.

Under a hygiene corporate strategy, the measurement of asset use rates provides evidence of the success of the strategy's execution.

For a leverage strategy, the number of buyers who purchase multiple products is a useful measurement for a company leveraging buyer trust and confidence. For a firm leveraging its ability to rapidly introduce new products, an appropriate measure is the date of release of new products or the span from product conception to release.

ate diversification is analogous to an investment portfolio, and the diversification is assessed in a similar way: in terms of industries, buyer groups, business cycle sensitivity, capital requirements, vulnerability to technological change, and the stages of the products' life cycle. In a conglomerate corporate-level strategy, decision makers apply a risk-adjusted required rate of return as the hurdle rate for financing new activities. This process allocates finite organizational resources through a market-like mechanism.

Increases in asset utilization rates reflect the successful implementation of a hygiene corporate strategy. To manage a hygiene corporate strategy, decision makers seek the flexible use of assets and resist the temptation to add assets. Consider an accounting firm with a large number of high-income personal tax clients. The firm diversifies into financial services and retirement planning. This diversification has aspects of a hygiene corporate strategy because the new line of business increases the utilization rate of the professional

staff over a year. To effectively implement the strategy, the accounting firm resists the temptation to add professional staff, and it selects and trains its personnel to deliver both tax and financial planning services.

The accounting firm's diversification into financial services also has aspects of a leverage corporate strategy. Clients who purchase tax services learn to trust the firm's technically proficient professionals, their confidentiality, and the timeliness of their work. The accounting firm leverages these skills and relationships into new financial management services, and the number of services its clients utilize is a measure of the effectiveness of the implementation of the leveraged strategy.

### Exercise 7.1

For your employer or a familiar firm, describe the corporate-level strategy. What variables would help the firm measure the effectiveness of the execution of its corporate-level strategy?

*Hygiene and Leverage Strategies and Equity Values*

The decision to diversify a business with the goal of conducting a hygiene or leverage corporate strategy includes choosing to develop a new product or acquire an existing producer. For example, a publicly traded life insurance company seeks to diversify into a broader range of financial services. It examines the share price of an existing brokerage company and considers the purchase of a controlling share of the company.

Referring to the equity value equation in Table 7.1, it is assumed that earnings and dividends are equal. The price of a share of stock is the present

### Table 7.1
### Equity Valuation Equation

$$P = \frac{D_1 + D_2 + D_3 + D_n}{(1 + r) + (1 + r)^2 + (1 + r)^3 + (1 + r)^n}$$

value of the expected stream of earnings. The interest rate used to discount the projected earnings into present value terms is the investors' required rate of return.

The life insurance firm knows the market price of a share of the brokerage firm's stock and offers a premium price to gain a controlling interest. The logic of the premium price is based upon the corporate-level strategy. From a hygiene strategy perspective, the life insurance company anticipates consolidating sales forces and investment analysts, realizing lower costs. The life insurance company also sees opportunities to leverage clients' trust in the brokerage firm to facilitate the sale of life insurance products. The same logic applies to insurance clients purchasing other investment products through the acquired brokerage firm. The expected benefits from the execution of a leverage strategy increase the value of the combined insurance and brokerage firm over the sum of the separate entities.

### Line-of-Business Strategy

To examine a line-of-business strategy, consider a consulting firm that submits a proposal to a prospective buyer, offering to provide specific services for $1,000. The buyer accepts the proposal, believing the consulting advice is worth $1,500 to it. This purchase improves the buyer's economic well-being. The buyer receives a benefit personally valued at $1,500 for $1,000. The $500 differential is known as *consumer surplus*.

The buyer's perceived benefit from the service depends upon its attributes, service, price, and transaction costs. Two simple truths emerge: buyers purchase a good or service only if the consumer surplus is greater than zero, and given a choice between two or more competing products, a buyer chooses the one with the larger consumer surplus.

One way to approach the analysis of the creation of consumer surplus is the *weighted value proposition*. The weighted value proposition is a tool to define a line-of-business strategy, which is the specific combination of product features, price, and customer services a firm delivers to gain a relative advantage over rivals.

### Weighted Value Proposition

The value proposition is a useful way for firms to define their line-of-business strategy (see Table 7.2).

### Table 7.2
### The Value Proposition

$$\text{Value Proposition} = \frac{\text{Results} + \text{Process Quality}}{\text{Price} + \text{Cost of Acquisition}}$$

The value proposition has four weighted components: results, process quality, price, and the cost of acquisition.[2] These variables, defined below, offer opportunities for a firm to distinguish its product from those of rivals. The weights are expressed as percentages and reflect the firm's relative emphasis on the components of value.

Table 7.3 is the weighted value proposition for a hypothetical automobile maker.

The *results* component of the value proposition describes the tangible features of a good or service. For the automobile manufacturer in Table 7.3, the tangible features of the product include seating capacity, acceleration, gas mileage, handling, style, and safety. The results component of the firm's intended delivery of value accounts for only 25 percent of the

*Table 7.3*
**Value Proposition for a Hypothetical Auto Manufacturer**

| Elements of Value | % Weight |
|---|---|
| Results | 25% |
| Seating capacity | 15% |
| Safety | 15% |
| Fuel efficiency | 30% |
| Comfort | 15% |
| Handling and acceleration | 15% |
| Options | 10% |
| Process quality | 40% |
| Dealership location | 15% |
| Sales force's knowledge of products | 15% |
| Cleanliness of dealership | 15% |
| No-haggle pricing | 30% |
| Courtesy of personnel | 25% |
| Price | 30% |
| Sticker price | 35% |
| Financing rate | 25% |
| Operating expenses | 25% |
| Trade-in value | 15% |
| Cost of acquisition | 5% |
| Hours of operation | 100% |

manufacturer, no-haggle pricing and the courtesy of the sales personnel are the two most important ways this seller seeks to build process quality.

The *price* variable in the value proposition includes the sticker price, financing rates, trade-in values, and the costs of operations and maintenance. Price is relatively less important than process quality, evidenced by the 30 percent weight assigned to price. Price is more important than results, which are the tangible features of the product. This firm seeks to attract and retain buyers through service variables rather than through product features. This statement does not mean that the automobile maker offers an inferior vehicle. Rather, the tangible features of the product meet buyer requirements, but the product's features are not superior to those of rivals. The source of competitive advantage relative to rivals is superior process quality.

*Cost-of-acquisition variables* are the inverse of process quality and involve the negative aspects of the transaction process. The cost-of-acquisition variables are not purposely put in place to hinder buyers; rather, they result from other decisions. For example, the firm in Table 7.3 recognizes that closing at five o'clock on Saturday afternoon is a deterrent to some buyers.

total. Within the results component, fuel efficiency provides 30 percent of the relative weight.

The *process quality* component of the value proposition includes variables that make the transaction process more comfortable and convenient for the buyer. The hypothetical automobile manufacturer emphasizes process quality over tangible features of the product, evidenced by the 40 percent weight assigned to process quality versus 25 percent for results. For the automobile manufacturer, process quality variables include speed of service, knowledgeable front-line personnel, and cleanliness of the dealership. For the hypothetical auto

---

**Exercise 7.2**

Ask several members of your firm to prepare their thoughts about the company's value proposition.

(a) Assess the extent to which the weighted value propositions are consistent.
(b) Use the results to explain your perception of morale in the organization and the level of confidence in senior management within your organization.

## Line-of-Business Strategies and Trade-offs

The concept of opportunity costs requires decision makers to consider alternative uses of scarce resources. Trade-offs extend this concept and involve one action precluding others. For example, a company adopts a policy to promote from within and surrenders the opportunity to recruit from the widest possible talent pool. With regard to the weighted value proposition, some elements of value impose trade-offs. A firm that heavily weights the technical qualities of its products incurs heavy research and development costs and high materials costs. To achieve technical precision, the firm trades off not being the low-cost producer or the low-price seller.

Importantly, existing technologies create trade-offs. In automobiles, for example, given known materials and engine technologies, greater passenger safety requires greater weight and imposes a trade-off of lower gas mileage. An automaker that prioritizes fuel efficiency sacrifices safety by making strategy-specific decisions in product design and procurement. Recognizing trade-offs is an important managerial function. It allows managers to send messages to buyers and employees that do not confuse priorities. Further, those who understand trade-offs are prompted to innovate. The automaker that chooses to surrender safety for fuel efficiency is driven to search for new technologies to improve materials and engine technologies to increase safety and fuel efficiency at the same time.

## Price and Product Differentiation Strategies

In determining a line-of-business strategy, two generic choices exist. Firms gain a competitive advantage by achieving lower costs and offering a satisfactory (but not superior) product at a lower price, or firms gain a competitive advantage by

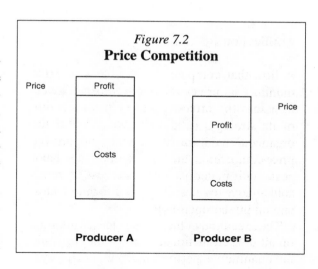

*Figure 7.2*
**Price Competition**

accepting higher cost to achieve a valued product difference that warrants a premium price.

Figure 7.2 displays the dictates of a price strategy. Producer B is a successful price competitor, achieving a larger profit while charging a lower price. The key to producer B's successful implementation of a low-price strategy is its relatively lower costs.

In markets characterized by commodity-like products, buyers are unable to distinguish between the physical characteristics of competing products. In such markets it is possible to compete successfully on process quality variables. For example, a family-practice physician with standard diagnostic and treatment skills enjoys a relatively more successful practice than rivals. The competitive advantage is achieved through process quality advantages, including minimizing waiting times and the prompt return of phone calls. If a process quality advantage is not achieved, competition is based on price. In markets in which firms seek advantages based on product features or service advantages, competing on price remains a viable option if some group of buyers highly values low price. For example, warehouse grocery stores eschew product selections and service in favor of lower prices to shoppers.

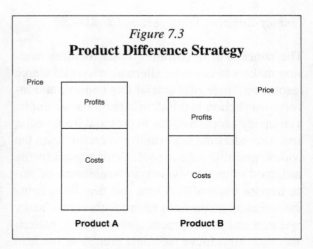

*Figure 7.3*
**Product Difference Strategy**

Competing on the basis of price is an attractive option under several market circumstances. In an industry characterized by untapped economies of scale, a low price allows a firm to increase its market share. The greater rate of production yields lower costs and a competitive advantage. Similarly, where learning curve economies are available, a relatively low price helps a firm capture more current sales, leading to learning economies and lower costs.

The execution of a price strategy requires complete and consistent decision making across the firm and over time. Consistent decisions align the functional area operations (product design, procurement, human resources, and marketing) with the goal of minimizing costs, which allows the firm to gain a price advantage without sacrifice of profit. Complete decisions enhance the firm's competitive advantage by ensuring that no opportunity to lower costs is overlooked. By understanding and acting on all activities that lower costs, the firm makes complete decisions and effectively implements its competitive strategy.

Figure 7.3 highlights the nature of competing on the basis of a product difference. A product differentiation strategy often necessitates incurring additional costs to gain an advantage based on product features or services. Figure 7.3 indicates that producer A incurs higher cost, charges a premium price, and earns superior profit.

Product difference strategies are successfully implemented if the firm offers a mix of product features and service that increases consumer surplus and warrants a premium price. A successful product difference strategy makes other products less attractive substitutes, lowering the cross-price

elasticity of demand. A successful product difference strategy allows a small-market-share niche
producer to overcome cost disadvantages in a market characterized by extensive economies of scale
or learning curve economies (see pages 148–152).

## Introduction to Strategic Planning

Strategic planning is a multistep process culminat-
ing in the execution and assessment of the firm's
competitive strategy. Figure 7.4 identifies the key
elements of the strategic planning process.

Figure 7.4 suggests that the strategic planning
process begins with an organizational mission
statement. The figure is deceptive because the
adoption of a mission statement is a complex and
iterative process that requires careful consideration
of the firm's internal and external environments.

Before taking costly and difficult-to-reverse actions to implement the firm's mission, two critical
tests are applied: Is the firm's resource base capable
of executing the mission and gaining an advantage
over rivals? Is the environment external to the firm
conducive to success?

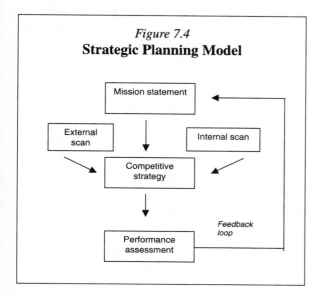

*Figure 7.4*
**Strategic Planning Model**

### The Mission Statement

A firm's mission statement establishes several
critical points: it defines the market within which
the firm seeks to compete, it identifies the manner
in which it intends to distinguish itself from rivals,
and it indicates the philosophy and values of the
organization. Effective mission statements have
three characteristics: they are buyer-focused, they
are expressed in relative terms, and they are unambiguous because they acknowledge trade-offs.

Table 7.4 is the mission statement for Rynk and
Associates, a hypothetical management consulting firm.

The mission statement in Table 7.4 sounds
pleasing but is ineffective for the following reasons.
(1) Rynk's mission statement refers to skilled professionals who are employed in a collegial setting. It
looks inward and not toward the delivery of benefits to
the clients. It is not buyer-focused. (2) The statement
suggests the firm does good work. However, the concept of competitive advantage is inherently relative in
nature, and the statement fails to establish a source of
advantage over rivals. It is not expressed in relative
terms. (3) Mission statements must be unambiguous
to potential clients and to employees. To accomplish
this, mission statements acknowledge trade-offs in the
creation of value. Rynk and Associates is concerned
with the quality of its service and the price. However,
frequently the delivery of a technically advanced

*Table 7.4*
**Mission Statement: Rynk and Associates**

Rynk and Associates is dedicated to providing high-
quality and affordable management consulting services
in the Washington, D.C., metropolitan area. With a
commitment to ethical business practices, Rynk and
Associates employs skilled professionals within a collegial environment. Rynk and Associates is dedicated
to responsible citizenship while providing owners and
employees with sound economic returns.

*Table 7.5*
**Angela's Catering Services**

Angela's Catering Services provides food services for large special functions, including weddings, birthdays, family reunions, office parties, and other special events. Angela's Catering Services is committed to relieving the stresses of hosting large numbers of guests by providing the fullest customized service.

---

service imposes additional costs. The trade-off does not allow the firm to be the low-price seller and the technical quality leader at the same time. The mission statement is ambiguous.

The same evaluative criteria can be used to look at the mission statement for Angela's Catering Services (see Table 7.5).

The Angela's Catering mission statement is more effective on several counts. (1) The statement is buyer-focused. The firm intends to provide buyers with customized catering for large and special events. (2) The mission is also expressed in relative terms. Angela's Catering provides the fullest customized services to relieve the stresses of planning and hosting events. (3) The statement is also unambiguous. The commitment to the fullest customized service establishes priorities. Angela's does not confuse priorities by including reference to price, breadth of menu selections, or gourmet foods.

---

*Exercise 7.3*

For your employer, review the mission statement. Make appropriate evaluations and recommendations.

---

## Mission Statements and Reality

Before an organization commits resources and assumes business risks, the mission is subject to two reality tests: Does the mission make sense given the realities of the marketplace? Does the firm command the resources needed to execute its mission effectively? The study defines *SWOT analysis,* which looks at strength, weakness, opportunity, and threat and is used to test the viability of a firm's mission.

### External Scanning, Threats, and Opportunities

External scanning examines marketplace conditions to determine their compatibility with the intended mission of the firm. The external environments are outside the control of the firm's management and define conditions within which the firm operates and which affect financial performance. These external conditions include demographic, political, social, and technological trends and the five forces of competition. The operative strategic planning questions are straightforward: What conditions external to the firm create *opportunities* and which pose *threats*? What are the options available to the firm to take advantage of these opportunities and be protected from the threats?

Table 7.6 identifies variables that constitute threats and opportunities. External environmental conditions are threats and opportunities at the same time, depending upon the firm. For example, the aging of the population is a threat to producers of

*Table 7.6*
**Threats and Opportunities**

| | |
|---|---|
| Size | Exposure to technology change |
| Market growth rate | Entry barriers |
| Market demographics | Seller and buyer power |
| Strength of rivals | Risk |
| Entry threats | Attractiveness of substitutes |
| Compatibility with social trends | Compatibility with tax policy |

baby food and baby products and an opportunity for firms engaged in travel, leisure, retirement planning, and medical care. Similarly, a rapidly growing market is an attractive opportunity for a firm with enough productive capacity and financial strength to grow. For a rival with the inability to finance rapid growth, a rapidly expanding market exposes its vulnerability and is a threat.

By scanning external environmental conditions, firms anticipate change and plan a response. For example, a retailer who scans applications for building permits, rezoning requests, and road construction projects translates population shifts into a first-mover advantage by buying or leasing property ahead of potential competitors. Similarly, monitoring changes in tax policy allows a financial services firm to develop new investment instruments to help clients take advantage of the changing regulatory environment.

External conditions affect a firm's financial performance. For example, a rapidly growing market creates favorable selling conditions. However, managers must avoid being deluded by financial success that is based upon favorable markets. Managers must examine the competitive strengths of their products. Strong products or services sustain a firm's financial performance when markets turn less favorable.

### Internal Scanning, Strengths, and Weaknesses

Internal scanning involves a rigorous assessment of the firm's resources and capabilities. At issue is whether the firm has the tools, finances, suppliers, distribution channels, and personnel to carry out its competitive strategy. The assessment identifies *strengths*, which are factors favorable for the firm and its ability to implement its mission, and *weaknesses*, which inhibit a firm's ability to implement its mission.

Table 7.7 provides a sample of variables that constitute strengths and weaknesses.

*Table 7.7*
**Strengths and Weaknesses**

| | |
|---|---|
| Age of plant | Distribution channels |
| Products in the pipeline | Supply chain management |
| Competitive strength of products | Labor skills |
| Cost structures | Location of facilities |
| Brand identity | Financial strength |

The assessment of a firm's strengths and weaknesses is interpreted relative to its competitive strategy, market conditions, and rivals' abilities. Offering a good product at a reasonable price is not sufficient. Winning in the marketplace occurs by offering a product that has a relative advantage over rivals. Also, an overall assessment of the firm's strengths and weaknesses is not sufficient. Often, a firm's success is constrained by a single weakness. Consider a firm in a technologically dynamic environment. Its current product is state-of-the-art, but the market is preparing for the next-generation product. The firm has the intellectual and physical capability to develop a new product, but its lack of cash and lack of access to external funds inhibit its ability to do so. Finally, a rigorous internal scan is very difficult to complete. For many managers it is hard to acknowledge harsh realities, share negative assessments with co-workers, shape employee expectations, and guide the firm's competitive strategy based on realities.

### SWOT Analysis

SWOT (strength, weakness, opportunity, and threat) analysis is a systematic process that leads to the best match between a firm's ability to compete and the markets within which it operates. The effective application of SWOT analysis (see Figure 7.5) leads to strategic decisions and the

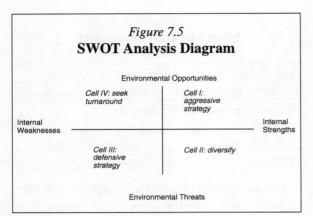

*Figure 7.5*
**SWOT Analysis Diagram**

Environmental Opportunities

Cell IV: seek turnaround

Cell I: aggressive strategy

Internal Weaknesses

Internal Strengths

Cell III: defensive strategy

Cell II: diversify

Environmental Threats

effective allocation of a firm's resources among competing uses.

Figure 7.5 classifies products on the basis of internal strengths and weaknesses and environmental opportunities and threats. The classifications yield a four-quadrant matrix. The classification system subjectively distinguishes between strengths and weaknesses and between opportunities and threats. However, the absolute values assigned to the classifications are less important than the relative positioning of products in the matrix.

Multiproduct firms allocate resources among the products or lines of business, and Figure 7.5 provides guidance. In cell I the firm enjoys both competitive strengths and favorable opportunities. These products or lines of business have a priority claim on an organization's assets. In cell II, a firm or line of business with internal strengths operates in an unattractive market. While it is inappropriate to direct vast resources to products in cell II, preserving the strengths of the business and reaping the proceeds to support diversification are wise moves. Cell III lines of business are the most troublesome. The combination of an internally weak firm operating in an unfavorable market setting does not warrant the use of scarce resources, and these products or business are destined to be

eliminated. Cell IV lines of business operate in a favorable market, but the firm has weaknesses. These conditions raise questions: Can a realistic turnaround plan be developed and implemented? Can the weaknesses be overcome, allowing the line of business to migrate from cell IV to cell I? In the absence of a convincing plan, cell IV business units are appropriately eliminated, with resources redeployed to more favorable situations.

### *Adoption of Mission Statement*

If the firm decides that internal and external environmental conditions are favorable, it implements the mission. In time, the firm assesses the effectiveness of the execution of its strategy and its financial outcomes to determine the appropriateness of its mission and strategy. The feedback ensures that the firm continuously monitors its mission, environments, and effectiveness.

### *Assessment of the Execution of the Mission*

Following the adoption and execution of a firm's mission and strategy, periodic assessments are necessary to diagnose the conditions of the firm and plan for the future. The assessments are done in stages. *Performance measures* monitor the execution of the value proposition. For example, a price competitor monitors its price relative to rivals to determine if the intended competitive advantage has been achieved. For a firm emphasizing technical product features, appropriate comparisons are made to the firm's intentions and to rivals.

Because strategic planning seeks sustained superior performance, firms monitor their ability to continue to execute their competitive strategy. For the price competitor, monitoring costs of production is essential, and these costs relative to those of rivals indicate its ability to sustain a price advantage. For a firm competing on the technical qualities of its products, investments in research and development and products in development are similarly important indicators of future success.

The assessment of the financial performance of the firm is based on the examination of market share, profit, and stock price relative to the firm's goals. Importantly, financial performance is misleading. A firm challenged by a highly competitive market and strong rivals realizes modest financial success. In contrast, firms operating in markets characterized by rapid growth in demand, insufficient industry-wide production, or ineffective rivals enjoy conditions that mask operating problems. Within highly favorable markets even ineffective firms prosper. However, slower market growth or improvement by rivals leaves these firms vulnerable.

Following Figure 7.4, the assessment of the execution of the firm's strategy creates a feedback loop to a new examination of the mission. On an ongoing basis firms monitor their performance, mission, external environments, and internal abilities to determine the appropriateness of continuing on their competitive path and where corrections need to be made. Firms and markets are dynamic, and the continuous assessment of the internal and external environments is an essential ingredient of sustained success.

## Summary

This chapter examines the strategic planning process from the perspective of economists. The chapter has three principal themes: (1) Environments external to the firm define the conditions within which the firm executes its competitive strategy and which affect its financial success. (2) A firm's internal capabilities determine the extent to which the firm is able to take advantage of market opportunities or be protected from threats.

(3) Continuous monitoring of the key internal and external variables gives the firm the best chance of sustaining superior performance over time.

## Review Terms

| | |
|---|---|
| Competitive advantage | Price strategy |
| Competitive strengths | Product difference strategy |
| Corporate-level strategy | Strategy-specific decision making |
| Line-of-business strategy | SWOT analysis |
| Market attractiveness | Value proposition |
| Mission statement | |

## Discussion Questions

1. Using the Internet, gather mission statements for three firms. Evaluate the mission statements. What advice do you offer management in these firms?
2. Examine your employer's mission statement. Evaluate it in terms of the criteria established in this chapter.
3. Evaluate the environmental conditions external to your firm. Specify threats and opportunities. Rate the significance of individual threats and opportunities. Is the external environment compatible with the mission?
4. Discuss the five forces of competition for your employer in terms of threats and opportunities.
5. Evaluate your employer's internal strengths. Be specific, looking at personnel, equipment, distribution channels, financing, and brand recognition. Is the firm able to execute its mission and gain a competitive advantage?
6. Using your replies to questions 2, 3, and

4, complete a SWOT analysis. Place your firm or business unit in one of the four cells in the SWOT analysis map. Make appropriate recommendations to senior management.

7. How does your firm's line-of-business strategy affect your daily tasks and the manner in which you complete them?

8. How are your work responsibilities affected by your firm's competitive strategy? Is your compensation based on performance related to the execution of the strategy?

9. Describe the ways in which markets and the

firm's external environments are dynamic. Similarly, describe the ways in which a firm's internal strengths and weaknesses are dynamic. How does the constancy of change challenge management decision making? What is required to sustain success?

## Notes

1. William G. Forgang, *Strategy-Specific Decision Making* (Armonk, N.Y.: M.E. Sharpe, 2004).

2. James L. Heskett, W. Earl Sasser, and Leonard Schlesinger, *The Service Profit Chain* (New York: Free Press, 1997), pp. 12–15.

# Case Study 7.1
# Bayview Electronic Components

## The Firm

Bayview Electronic Components is a manufacturer of electronic components with a single plant on the Eastern Shore of Maryland. Annual revenues are approximately $12 million. Their components are primarily used in the manufacture of the electrical systems needed to operate heavy transportation vehicles. The primary quality characteristic that separates one producer's components from another producer's is the ability to withstand operational stress and the demands of high temperature, moisture, and dirt. Bayview has the engineering and production process expertise as well as a parts supplier base to fulfill the very demanding product performance requirements.

## The Growth Period

Jake Holzman, company president and the largest single shareholder (45 percent), is faced

with a significant challenge. Bayview enjoyed a three-year revenue and profit growth period, but the growth ended nine months ago. Over this growth period revenue increases were 25 percent annually and profit increases were 30 percent annually. The growth was due primarily to servicing the needs of its largest customer, a heavy industry transportation vehicle manufacturer. That single customer accounted for more than 80 percent of the sales and approximately 70 percent of the profits.

Jake knows that such reliance on a single customer has its drawbacks, but he is fearful of giving the customer the impression that he is less than 100 percent committed to its success. Bayview's sales force, which doubles as the customer service department, is almost fully consumed by servicing the needs of the major customer. Sales are also made to six other firms that deal with heavy transportation and military vehicle applications.

Bayview's production processes are very labor-intensive, and labor costs generally account for 70 percent of total direct production costs. Historically, the cost of this local semiskilled labor tended to be below the state's average, since labor in the area was underutilized. Worker benefits were modest at best. Jake always thought of this dependence upon manual labor as a plus in the event of a business slowdown. He once commented that his "labor force can be turned on and off like a water faucet." He would say: "Where else are these people going to work?" "Why risk the fixed-cost commitment of a significantly computerized production facility?"

While Bayview's major customer was extremely demanding, it provided profitable revenue growth while Bayview focused on the timely design, manufacture, and delivery of a very reliable product. For this major customer, the price of the product needed to be in a reasonable range, since competitors did exist. However, price was a less significant buying criterion than rapid delivery, high reliability, and Bayview's willingness and ability to make last-minute product modifications. The customer did not want the late delivery of a part to cause delay in the delivery of a vehicle costing several hundred thousand dollars. Bayview viewed the customer as high-maintenance since last-minute technical and quantity changes were frequent, but the compensation for this was historically dependable sales and profit growth.

## The Most Recent Nine Months

For the past nine months revenue growth has slowed by approximately an annualized rate of 20 percent. Critically, the major customer, facing a significant fall-off in the demand for heavy construction equipment, has placed strong pressure on product pricing. While all of the customer hand-holding and performance expectations remain in place, pricing has become a key buying criterion. Bayview has been warned by its major customer that virtually all vendor products and services will be bid competitively. Bayview is now required to reduce prices to preserve orders.

As these changes were taking place, several large retail distribution warehouses were built in the region, and the labor market has begun to tighten. Labor is getting scarce and costs are rising.

Jake now feels that he waited too long to diversify the customer base. Revenue provided by the major customer is dropping. The decline in revenue is attributable not to fewer orders but to smaller quantities per order. The up-front engineering and production process design is needed with each new product order, and this is not being reduced. The shorter production runs squeeze margins.

## The Organization

Bayview's organizational structure consists of the president's office and six key functional areas organized as departments.

- The human resources department holds responsibilities for hiring and training. Low- and modestly skilled production laborers are hired and trained for very specific, limited tasks. The turnover is high. Historically it was easier and more cost-effective to hire and train new personnel than to reduce turnover.
- The accounting and finance department handles financial record keeping and payroll. The work in this department is clerical. No job costing is done. Jake believes he has a "good feel" for which jobs are profitable and which are not.
- The sales and customer service staff attracts and retains customers, prices products, serves as a technical liaison with customers, and

prioritizes production. Virtually no resources are committed to advertising or marketing.

- The engineering department designs new products and production processes, sets standard costs of products (although the standards are not used for variance analysis on a postproduction basis), and provides production support. Engineering is the personal interest area of the owner.
- Production manages production, shipping, purchasing, and receiving. This department reports to sales, engineering, and the president's office.
- Quality control personnel inspect materials and work on solving each immediate need as it arises. This department often speaks directly with customers. The warehouse is full of undiagnosed customer returns.

Jake understands that the historical organization structure, division of duties, and performance measures (as minimal as they were) may no longer be appropriate.

**The Assignment**

Using information from the case study, help Jake Holzman and Bayview's leadership perform a SWOT analysis and report to the board of directors. Answers to the following questions will help you develop your analysis and prepare your report.

(a) Describe the external business climate that up to this point has influenced the operating performance of Bayview.

(b) Describe the internal organizational climate and operational practices that produced a growing and profitable firm. At this stage try not to make value judgments of good versus bad practices. The fact is that the firm was growing and profitable. In summary, please identify what you believe to be the historical strengths of Bayview.

(c) Identify and describe historical weaknesses that you believe contributed to Bayview's more recent problems.

(d) Describe notable changes that appear to be taking place in the external business climate.

(e) Given the changing business climate, identify and describe historical strengths that may cease to be virtues within the new business climate and weaknesses that may become even more exaggerated.

(f) Identify weaknesses that you believe may emerge within the new business climate that were hidden in the previous climate.

(g) Does the new climate offer opportunities that Bayview had previously not taken advantage of? Be sure to discuss opportunities from the perspectives of internal practices and processes and external revenue and value creation (noting that there is often overlap between the internal and external factors)

(h) What impediments exist to fully taking advantage of the opportunities that you have identified? Provide some degree of ranking in describing the significance of the impediment.

(i) Does the new climate create threats that need to be assessed and managed in the near term (next one to two years) and the longer term (next three to five years)? Identify those that you believe to be most significant and provide some description of the level of resource attention needed to address the threat. Be sure to address whether the threat can be eliminated (for all practical purposes), effectively minimized, identified and somewhat contained, or identified with the recognition that it will only become more significant as time moves on.

# Appendix
# Present Value Tables

# Present Value Interest Factor Table (PVIF Table)

| Periods/Interest Rate | 1% | 2% | 3% | 4% | 5% | 6% | 7% | 8% | 9% | 10% | 11% | 12% | 13% | 14% | 15% | 16% | 17% | 18% | 19% | 20% |
|---|---|---|---|---|---|---|---|---|---|---|---|---|---|---|---|---|---|---|---|---|
| 1 | 0.9900 | 0.9803 | 0.9708 | 0.9615 | 0.9523 | 0.9433 | 0.9345 | 0.9259 | 0.9174 | 0.9090 | 0.9009 | 0.8928 | 0.8849 | 0.8771 | 0.8695 | 0.8620 | 0.8547 | 0.8474 | 0.8403 | 0.8333 |
| 2 | 0.9802 | 0.9611 | 0.9425 | 0.9245 | 0.9070 | 0.8899 | 0.8734 | 0.8573 | 0.8416 | 0.8264 | 0.8116 | 0.7971 | 0.7831 | 0.7694 | 0.7561 | 0.7431 | 0.7305 | 0.7181 | 0.7061 | 0.6944 |
| 3 | 0.9705 | 0.9423 | 0.9151 | 0.8889 | 0.8638 | 0.8396 | 0.8162 | 0.7938 | 0.7721 | 0.7513 | 0.7311 | 0.7117 | 0.6930 | 0.6749 | 0.6575 | 0.6406 | 0.6243 | 0.6086 | 0.5934 | 0.5787 |
| 4 | 0.9609 | 0.9238 | 0.8884 | 0.8548 | 0.8227 | 0.7920 | 0.7628 | 0.7350 | 0.7084 | 0.6830 | 0.6587 | 0.6355 | 0.6133 | 0.5920 | 0.5717 | 0.5522 | 0.5336 | 0.5157 | 0.4986 | 0.4822 |
| 5 | 0.9514 | 0.9057 | 0.8626 | 0.8219 | 0.7835 | 0.7472 | 0.7129 | 0.6805 | 0.6499 | 0.6209 | 0.5934 | 0.5674 | 0.5427 | 0.5193 | 0.4971 | 0.4761 | 0.4561 | 0.4371 | 0.4190 | 0.4018 |
| 6 | 0.9420 | 0.8879 | 0.8374 | 0.7903 | 0.7462 | 0.7049 | 0.6663 | 0.6301 | 0.5962 | 0.5644 | 0.5346 | 0.5066 | 0.4803 | 0.4555 | 0.4323 | 0.4104 | 0.3898 | 0.3704 | 0.3521 | 0.3348 |
| 7 | 0.9327 | 0.8705 | 0.8130 | 0.7599 | 0.7106 | 0.6650 | 0.6227 | 0.5834 | 0.5470 | 0.5131 | 0.4816 | 0.4523 | 0.4250 | 0.3996 | 0.3759 | 0.3538 | 0.3331 | 0.3139 | 0.2959 | 0.2790 |
| 8 | 0.9234 | 0.8534 | 0.7894 | 0.7306 | 0.6768 | 0.6274 | 0.5820 | 0.5402 | 0.5018 | 0.4665 | 0.4339 | 0.4038 | 0.3761 | 0.3505 | 0.3269 | 0.3050 | 0.2847 | 0.2660 | 0.2486 | 0.2325 |
| 9 | 0.9143 | 0.8367 | 0.7664 | 0.7025 | 0.6446 | 0.5918 | 0.5439 | 0.5002 | 0.4604 | 0.4240 | 0.3909 | 0.3606 | 0.3328 | 0.3075 | 0.2842 | 0.2629 | 0.2434 | 0.2254 | 0.2089 | 0.1938 |
| 10 | 0.9052 | 0.8203 | 0.7440 | 0.6755 | 0.6139 | 0.5583 | 0.5083 | 0.4631 | 0.4224 | 0.3855 | 0.3521 | 0.3219 | 0.2945 | 0.2697 | 0.2471 | 0.2266 | 0.2080 | 0.1910 | 0.1756 | 0.1615 |
| 11 | 0.8963 | 0.8042 | 0.7224 | 0.6495 | 0.5846 | 0.5267 | 0.4750 | 0.4288 | 0.3875 | 0.3504 | 0.3172 | 0.2874 | 0.2606 | 0.2366 | 0.2149 | 0.1954 | 0.1778 | 0.1619 | 0.1475 | 0.1345 |
| 12 | 0.8874 | 0.7884 | 0.7013 | 0.6245 | 0.5568 | 0.4969 | 0.4440 | 0.3971 | 0.3555 | 0.3186 | 0.2858 | 0.2566 | 0.2307 | 0.2075 | 0.1869 | 0.1684 | 0.1519 | 0.1372 | 0.1240 | 0.1121 |
| 13 | 0.8786 | 0.7730 | 0.6809 | 0.6005 | 0.5303 | 0.4688 | 0.4149 | 0.3676 | 0.3261 | 0.2896 | 0.2575 | 0.2291 | 0.2041 | 0.1820 | 0.1625 | 0.1452 | 0.1298 | 0.1162 | 0.1042 | 0.0934 |
| 14 | 0.8699 | 0.7578 | 0.6611 | 0.5774 | 0.5050 | 0.4423 | 0.3878 | 0.3404 | 0.2992 | 0.2633 | 0.2319 | 0.2046 | 0.1806 | 0.1597 | 0.1413 | 0.1251 | 0.1110 | 0.0985 | 0.0875 | 0.0778 |
| 15 | 0.8613 | 0.7430 | 0.6418 | 0.5552 | 0.4810 | 0.4172 | 0.3624 | 0.3152 | 0.2745 | 0.2393 | 0.2090 | 0.1826 | 0.1598 | 0.1400 | 0.1228 | 0.1079 | 0.0948 | 0.0835 | 0.0735 | 0.0649 |
| 16 | 0.8528 | 0.7284 | 0.6231 | 0.5339 | 0.4581 | 0.3936 | 0.3387 | 0.2918 | 0.2518 | 0.2176 | 0.1882 | 0.1631 | 0.1414 | 0.1228 | 0.1068 | 0.0930 | 0.0811 | 0.0707 | 0.0618 | 0.0540 |
| 17 | 0.8443 | 0.7141 | 0.6050 | 0.5133 | 0.4362 | 0.3713 | 0.3165 | 0.2702 | 0.2310 | 0.1978 | 0.1696 | 0.1456 | 0.1252 | 0.1077 | 0.0929 | 0.0802 | 0.0693 | 0.0599 | 0.0519 | 0.0450 |
| 18 | 0.8360 | 0.7001 | 0.5873 | 0.4936 | 0.4155 | 0.3503 | 0.2958 | 0.2502 | 0.2119 | 0.1798 | 0.1528 | 0.1300 | 0.1108 | 0.0945 | 0.0808 | 0.0691 | 0.0592 | 0.0508 | 0.0436 | 0.0375 |
| 19 | 0.8277 | 0.6864 | 0.5702 | 0.4746 | 0.3957 | 0.3305 | 0.2765 | 0.2317 | 0.1944 | 0.1635 | 0.1376 | 0.1161 | 0.0980 | 0.0829 | 0.0702 | 0.0596 | 0.0506 | 0.0430 | 0.0366 | 0.0313 |
| 20 | 0.8195 | 0.6729 | 0.5536 | 0.4563 | 0.3768 | 0.3118 | 0.2584 | 0.2145 | 0.1784 | 0.1486 | 0.1240 | 0.1036 | 0.0867 | 0.0727 | 0.0611 | 0.0513 | 0.0432 | 0.0365 | 0.0308 | 0.0260 |
| 21 | 0.8114 | 0.6597 | 0.5375 | 0.4388 | 0.3589 | 0.2941 | 0.2415 | 0.1986 | 0.1636 | 0.1351 | 0.1117 | 0.0925 | 0.0767 | 0.0638 | 0.0531 | 0.0442 | 0.0369 | 0.0309 | 0.0259 | 0.0217 |
| 22 | 0.8033 | 0.6468 | 0.5218 | 0.4219 | 0.3418 | 0.2775 | 0.2257 | 0.1839 | 0.1501 | 0.1228 | 0.1006 | 0.0826 | 0.0679 | 0.0559 | 0.0462 | 0.0381 | 0.0316 | 0.0262 | 0.0217 | 0.0181 |
| 23 | 0.7954 | 0.6341 | 0.5066 | 0.4057 | 0.3255 | 0.2617 | 0.2109 | 0.1703 | 0.1377 | 0.1116 | 0.0906 | 0.0737 | 0.0601 | 0.0491 | 0.0401 | 0.0329 | 0.0270 | 0.0222 | 0.0182 | 0.0150 |
| 24 | 0.7875 | 0.6217 | 0.4919 | 0.3901 | 0.3100 | 0.2469 | 0.1971 | 0.1576 | 0.1264 | 0.1015 | 0.0817 | 0.0658 | 0.0532 | 0.0430 | 0.0349 | 0.0283 | 0.0230 | 0.0188 | 0.0153 | 0.0125 |
| 25 | 0.7797 | 0.6095 | 0.4776 | 0.3751 | 0.2953 | 0.2329 | 0.1842 | 0.1460 | 0.1159 | 0.0922 | 0.0736 | 0.0588 | 0.0471 | 0.0377 | 0.0303 | 0.0244 | 0.0197 | 0.0159 | 0.0129 | 0.0104 |
| 26 | 0.7720 | 0.5975 | 0.4636 | 0.3606 | 0.2812 | 0.2198 | 0.1721 | 0.1352 | 0.1063 | 0.0839 | 0.0663 | 0.0525 | 0.0416 | 0.0331 | 0.0264 | 0.0210 | 0.0168 | 0.0135 | 0.0108 | 0.0087 |
| 27 | 0.7644 | 0.5858 | 0.4501 | 0.3468 | 0.2678 | 0.2073 | 0.1609 | 0.1251 | 0.0976 | 0.0762 | 0.0597 | 0.0468 | 0.0368 | 0.0290 | 0.0229 | 0.0181 | 0.0144 | 0.0114 | 0.0091 | 0.0072 |
| 28 | 0.7568 | 0.5743 | 0.4370 | 0.3334 | 0.2550 | 0.1956 | 0.1504 | 0.1159 | 0.0895 | 0.0693 | 0.0538 | 0.0418 | 0.0326 | 0.0255 | 0.0199 | 0.0156 | 0.0123 | 0.0097 | 0.0076 | 0.0060 |
| 29 | 0.7493 | 0.5631 | 0.4243 | 0.3206 | 0.2429 | 0.1845 | 0.1405 | 0.1073 | 0.0821 | 0.0630 | 0.0484 | 0.0373 | 0.0288 | 0.0223 | 0.0173 | 0.0135 | 0.0105 | 0.0082 | 0.0064 | 0.0050 |
| 30 | 0.7419 | 0.5520 | 0.4119 | 0.3083 | 0.2313 | 0.1741 | 0.1313 | 0.0993 | 0.0753 | 0.0573 | 0.0436 | 0.0333 | 0.0255 | 0.0196 | 0.0151 | 0.0116 | 0.0090 | 0.0069 | 0.0054 | 0.0042 |

# Present Value Interest Factor of Annuity Table (PVIFA Table)

| Periods/Interest Rate | 1% | 2% | 3% | 4% | 5% | 6% | 7% | 8% | 9% | 10% | 11% | 12% | 13% | 14% | 15% | 16% | 17% | 18% | 19% | 20% |
|---|---|---|---|---|---|---|---|---|---|---|---|---|---|---|---|---|---|---|---|---|
| 1 | 0.9900 | 0.9803 | 0.9708 | 0.9615 | 0.9523 | 0.9433 | 0.9345 | 0.9259 | 0.9174 | 0.9090 | 0.9009 | 0.8928 | 0.8849 | 0.8771 | 0.8695 | 0.8620 | 0.8547 | 0.8474 | 0.8403 | 0.8333 |
| 2 | 1.9703 | 1.9415 | 1.9134 | 1.8860 | 1.8594 | 1.8333 | 1.8080 | 1.7832 | 1.7591 | 1.7355 | 1.7125 | 1.6900 | 1.6681 | 1.6466 | 1.6257 | 1.6052 | 1.5852 | 1.5656 | 1.5465 | 1.5277 |
| 3 | 2.9409 | 2.8838 | 2.8286 | 2.7750 | 2.7232 | 2.6730 | 2.6243 | 2.5770 | 2.5312 | 2.4868 | 2.4437 | 2.4018 | 2.3611 | 2.3216 | 2.2832 | 2.2458 | 2.2095 | 2.1742 | 2.1399 | 2.1064 |
| 4 | 3.9019 | 3.8077 | 3.7170 | 3.6298 | 3.5459 | 3.4651 | 3.3872 | 3.3121 | 3.2397 | 3.1698 | 3.1024 | 3.0373 | 2.9744 | 2.9137 | 2.8549 | 2.7981 | 2.7432 | 2.6900 | 2.6385 | 2.5887 |
| 5 | 4.8534 | 4.7134 | 4.5797 | 4.4518 | 4.3294 | 4.2123 | 4.1001 | 3.9927 | 3.8896 | 3.7907 | 3.6958 | 3.6047 | 3.5172 | 3.4330 | 3.3521 | 3.2742 | 3.1993 | 3.1271 | 3.0576 | 2.9906 |
| 6 | 5.7954 | 5.6014 | 5.4171 | 5.2421 | 5.0756 | 4.9173 | 4.7665 | 4.6228 | 4.4859 | 4.3552 | 4.2305 | 4.1114 | 3.9975 | 3.8886 | 3.7844 | 3.6847 | 3.5891 | 3.4976 | 3.4097 | 3.3255 |
| 7 | 6.7281 | 6.4719 | 6.2302 | 6.0020 | 5.7863 | 5.5823 | 5.3892 | 5.2063 | 5.0329 | 4.8684 | 4.7121 | 4.5637 | 4.4226 | 4.2883 | 4.1604 | 4.0385 | 3.9223 | 3.8115 | 3.7056 | 3.6045 |
| 8 | 7.6516 | 7.3254 | 7.0196 | 6.7327 | 6.4632 | 6.2097 | 5.9712 | 5.7466 | 5.5348 | 5.3349 | 5.1461 | 4.9676 | 4.7987 | 4.6388 | 4.4873 | 4.3435 | 4.2071 | 4.0775 | 3.9543 | 3.8371 |
| 9 | 8.5660 | 8.1622 | 7.7861 | 7.4353 | 7.1078 | 6.8016 | 6.5152 | 6.2468 | 5.9952 | 5.7590 | 5.5370 | 5.3282 | 5.1316 | 4.9463 | 4.7715 | 4.6065 | 4.4505 | 4.3030 | 4.1633 | 4.0309 |
| 10 | 9.4713 | 8.9825 | 8.5302 | 8.1108 | 7.7217 | 7.3600 | 7.0235 | 6.7100 | 6.4176 | 6.1445 | 5.8892 | 5.6502 | 5.4262 | 5.2161 | 5.0187 | 4.8332 | 4.6586 | 4.4940 | 4.3389 | 4.1924 |
| 11 | 10.367 | 9.7868 | 9.2526 | 8.7604 | 8.3064 | 7.8868 | 7.4986 | 7.1389 | 6.8051 | 6.4950 | 6.2065 | 5.9376 | 5.6869 | 5.4527 | 5.2337 | 5.0286 | 4.8364 | 4.6560 | 4.4864 | 4.3270 |
| 12 | 11.255 | 10.575 | 9.9540 | 9.3850 | 8.8632 | 8.3838 | 7.9426 | 7.5360 | 7.1607 | 6.8136 | 6.4923 | 6.1943 | 5.9176 | 5.6602 | 5.4206 | 5.1971 | 4.9883 | 4.7932 | 4.6105 | 4.4392 |
| 13 | 12.133 | 11.348 | 10.634 | 9.9856 | 9.3935 | 8.8526 | 8.3576 | 7.9037 | 7.4869 | 7.1033 | 6.7498 | 6.4235 | 6.1218 | 5.8423 | 5.5831 | 5.3423 | 5.1182 | 4.9095 | 4.7147 | 4.5326 |
| 14 | 13.003 | 12.106 | 11.296 | 10.563 | 9.8986 | 9.2949 | 8.7454 | 8.2442 | 7.7861 | 7.3666 | 6.9818 | 6.6281 | 6.3024 | 6.0020 | 5.7244 | 5.4675 | 5.2292 | 5.0080 | 4.8022 | 4.6105 |
| 15 | 13.865 | 12.849 | 11.937 | 11.118 | 10.379 | 9.7122 | 9.1079 | 8.5594 | 8.0606 | 7.6060 | 7.1908 | 6.8108 | 6.4623 | 6.1421 | 5.8473 | 5.5754 | 5.3241 | 5.0915 | 4.8758 | 4.6754 |
| 16 | 14.717 | 13.577 | 12.561 | 11.652 | 10.837 | 10.105 | 9.4466 | 8.8513 | 8.3125 | 7.8237 | 7.3791 | 6.9739 | 6.6038 | 6.2650 | 5.9542 | 5.6684 | 5.4052 | 5.1623 | 4.9376 | 4.7295 |
| 17 | 15.562 | 14.291 | 13.166 | 12.165 | 11.274 | 10.477 | 9.7632 | 9.1216 | 8.5436 | 8.0215 | 7.5487 | 7.1196 | 6.7290 | 6.3728 | 6.0471 | 5.7487 | 5.4746 | 5.2223 | 4.9896 | 4.7746 |
| 18 | 16.398 | 14.992 | 13.753 | 12.659 | 11.689 | 10.827 | 10.059 | 9.3718 | 8.7556 | 8.2014 | 7.7016 | 7.2496 | 6.8399 | 6.4674 | 6.1279 | 5.8178 | 5.5338 | 5.2731 | 5.0333 | 4.8121 |
| 19 | 17.226 | 15.678 | 14.323 | 13.133 | 12.085 | 11.158 | 10.335 | 9.6035 | 8.9501 | 8.3649 | 7.8392 | 7.3657 | 6.9379 | 6.5503 | 6.1982 | 5.8774 | 5.5844 | 5.3162 | 5.0700 | 4.8434 |
| 20 | 18.045 | 16.351 | 14.877 | 13.590 | 12.462 | 11.469 | 10.594 | 9.8181 | 9.1285 | 8.5135 | 7.9633 | 7.4694 | 7.0247 | 6.6231 | 6.2593 | 5.9288 | 5.6277 | 5.3527 | 5.1008 | 4.8695 |
| 21 | 18.856 | 17.011 | 15.415 | 14.029 | 12.821 | 11.764 | 10.835 | 10.016 | 9.2922 | 8.6486 | 8.0750 | 7.5620 | 7.1015 | 6.6869 | 6.3124 | 5.9731 | 5.6647 | 5.3836 | 5.1267 | 4.8913 |
| 22 | 19.660 | 17.658 | 15.936 | 14.451 | 13.163 | 12.041 | 11.061 | 10.200 | 9.4424 | 8.7715 | 8.1757 | 7.6446 | 7.1695 | 6.7429 | 6.3586 | 6.0113 | 5.6963 | 5.4099 | 5.1485 | 4.9094 |
| 23 | 20.455 | 18.292 | 16.443 | 14.856 | 13.488 | 12.303 | 11.272 | 10.371 | 9.5802 | 8.8832 | 8.2664 | 7.7184 | 7.2296 | 6.7920 | 6.3988 | 6.0442 | 5.7233 | 5.4321 | 5.1668 | 4.9245 |
| 24 | 21.243 | 18.913 | 16.935 | 15.246 | 13.798 | 12.550 | 11.469 | 10.528 | 9.7066 | 8.9847 | 8.3481 | 7.7843 | 7.2828 | 6.8351 | 6.4337 | 6.0726 | 5.7464 | 5.4509 | 5.1822 | 4.9371 |
| 25 | 22.023 | 19.523 | 17.413 | 15.622 | 14.093 | 12.783 | 11.653 | 10.674 | 9.8225 | 9.0770 | 8.4217 | 7.8431 | 7.3299 | 6.8729 | 6.4641 | 6.0970 | 5.7662 | 5.4669 | 5.1951 | 4.9475 |
| 26 | 22.795 | 20.121 | 17.876 | 15.982 | 14.375 | 13.003 | 11.825 | 10.809 | 9.9289 | 9.1609 | 8.4880 | 7.8956 | 7.3716 | 6.9060 | 6.4905 | 6.1181 | 5.7831 | 5.4804 | 5.2060 | 4.9563 |
| 27 | 23.559 | 20.706 | 18.327 | 16.329 | 14.643 | 13.210 | 11.986 | 10.935 | 10.026 | 9.2372 | 8.5478 | 7.9425 | 7.4085 | 6.9351 | 6.5135 | 6.1363 | 5.7975 | 5.4918 | 5.2151 | 4.9636 |
| 28 | 24.316 | 21.281 | 18.764 | 16.663 | 14.898 | 13.406 | 12.137 | 11.051 | 10.116 | 9.3065 | 8.6016 | 7.9844 | 7.4411 | 6.9606 | 6.5335 | 6.1520 | 5.8098 | 5.5016 | 5.2227 | 4.9696 |
| 29 | 25.065 | 21.844 | 19.188 | 16.983 | 15.141 | 13.590 | 12.277 | 11.158 | 10.198 | 9.3696 | 8.6501 | 8.0218 | 7.4700 | 6.9830 | 6.5508 | 6.1655 | 5.8203 | 5.5098 | 5.2292 | 4.9747 |
| 30 | 27.794 | 25.807 | 24.015 | 22.396 | 20.930 | 19.600 | 18.392 | 17.292 | 16.288 | 15.372 | 14.533 | 13.764 | 13.058 | 12.409 | 11.810 | 11.257 | 10.746 | 10.273 | 9.8347 | 9.4269 |

# Index